A Nation of Behavers

Martin E.
Marty

A Nation of
Behavers

 The
University of Chicago
Press

Chicago and London

MARTIN E. MARTY is professor of the history
of modern Christianity at the University of
Chicago and associate editor of the *Christian
Century*. The author of eighteen books, he was
awarded the National Book Award in 1972 for
*Righteous Empire: The Protestant Experience in
America*. Professor Marty is the recipient of
nine honorary degrees and is a Fellow of the
American Academy of Arts and Sciences.

The University of Chicago Press, Chicago 60637
The University of Chicago Press, Ltd., London
© 1976 by The University of Chicago
All rights reserved. Published 1976
Printed in the United States of America

80   98765432

Library of Congress Cataloging in Publication Data
Marty, Martin E   1928–
    A nation of behavers.

    Includes bibliographical references and index.
    1. United States—Religion—1945–   2. Sociology,
Christian—United States. I. Title.
BR515.M32   200′.973   76-7997
ISBN 0-226-50891-9 (cloth)
ISBN 0-226-50892-7 (paper)

To

Joseph M. Kitagawa
from whom
I borrowed the basic
idea for this book
and the time to
write it

We live in the description
of a place and not in the
place itself.

—*Wallace Stevens*

Contents

Acknowledgments   ix

1. Mapping Group Identity and Social Location   1

2. History and Religious Social Behavior   18

3. Mainline Religion   52

4. Evangelicalism and Fundamentalism   80

5. Pentecostal-Charismatic Religion   106

6. The New Religions   126

7. Ethnic Religion   158

8. Civil Religion   180

9. Epilogue: Mapping the American Future   204

Notes   207

Index   229

Acknowledgments

The social behavior of academic scholars calls them rubrically to thank the institutions, foundations, and fellowships that provided them leisure for writing a book. This book was written not in leisure but rather during five years in which administrative tasks were added to regular teaching assignments. So I shall thank fellow administrators, colleagues, and students who provided stimulus and help.

The historian of religion and my Dean, Joseph M. Kitagawa, unwittingly provided the basic ideas that gave coherence to my theme and wittingly provided some time for me to steal some mornings away from my office next to his. Two offices down the hall, Dean of Students Larry Greenfield took on special burdens when I was hard to find and contributed critical thoughts when I was easy to find. Assistant to the Dean Delores Smith has been patient and thoughtful with the many kinds of aid she has made available, particularly on the level of staff and resources. Julia Bloxom typed early drafts of the chapters and Cheryl Paymaster went far beyond the call of duty as she deciphered, retyped, and rearranged materials through a number of drafts. Diane McLaughlin, who might have thought she was an innocent bystander in the same office, also found herself caught up in a number of manuscript-improving steps.

Colleagues in the History Department, the Committee on the History of Culture, and the history of Christianity field constantly provide stimulus for inquiries like these. For their discussions of American history in this period I am most indebted to Arthur Mann, Neil Harris, Donald Scott, John Hope Franklin, and Jerald C. Brauer.

Many of the earlier doctoral graduates or candidates acknowledged in *Righteous Empire* (New York: Dial, 1970) made their contributions to themes in this volume as well. Now I would like to thank the additional scholars who in classes, seminars, conversations, and dissertation-writing taught me more than they knew they were teaching about the writing of religious history: Catherine Albanese, Richard Anderson, James Ash, James Bundy, Jonathan Butler, Paul Carnahan, Robert Choquette, James Connelley, Paul Dekar, Kent Druyvesteyn, C. Thompson Faulkner, Laurence Foster, Raymond Gadke, Everett Hunt, Peter Kountz, Robert Krivoshey, Keith Markell, Daniel Pals, Arthur Puotinen, Stephen Snyder, and Timothy Weber. James Wind edited and indexed this book.

Some themes that occur in these chapters were anticipated in a number of essays published during these years, and the current work draws on research that was used in other ways in those essays. Let me cite them: "Religious Behavior: Its Social Dimension in American History," *Social Research* 41, no. 2 (summer 1974): 241ff.; "The Occult Establishment," *Social Research* 37, no. 2 (summer 1970): 212ff.; a chapter in Vinson Synan, ed., *Aspects of Pentecostal and Charismatic Origins* (Plainfield, N.J.: Logos, 1975); and one in David Wells and John Woodbridge, eds., *The Evangelicals* (Nashville: Abingdon, 1975); "Ethnicity: The Skeleton of Religion in America," *Church History* 41, no. 1 (March 1972): 5ff., which had been the presidential address of the American Society of Church History in 1971; a popular article in *World View* 17, no. 5 (May 1974): 9ff., anticipated the theme of the chapter "Civil Religion." I acknowledge the cooperation of the appropriate editors and publishers.

In twenty previous books I find that only a half line was ever devoted to thanking my wife, Elsa, and only an oblique line referred to the contribution made by our five sons. This neglect was neither studied nor unstudied, but perhaps the highest kind of tribute, based on a reality that future historians might have difficulty discovering if I do not at least this time make my debt explicit. Jacob Burckhardt: "Everywhere in the past we encounter things which remain unexplained only because they were completely self-understood in their time and, like all daily matters, were not thought necessary to write down." This time it is necessary to write this down, given their understanding, cooperation, and contributions during these five years.

1 Mapping Group Identity and Social Location

This essay in contemporary history provides a new map of religious America based on the visible loyalties of people as evidenced in their beliefs and social behavior and expressed in their public quests for group identity and social location.

An essay in contemporary history must face the question posed by H. Stuart Hughes: "Is contemporary history real history?" He answered in the affirmative, after having faced several issues. To the charge that we "do not yet have 'the documents,' " he properly replies that while many archives of the living or recently dead remain closed, it is possible to overestimate the value of some of the documents in them. If anything, there is an overabundance of documentation. "Let us agree . . . —cheerfully rather than in despair—that for the mid-twentieth century there will never come a time when 'the documents' are available. Yet this history must be written; the public demands it and has a right to demand it. If we do not do the job, others less qualified will undertake it for us."

The second criticism has to do with perspective and is posed as a "charge that we do not as yet have sufficient perspective." In one sense, we never shall; in another, we have begun to gain perspective from the moment we have become aware of an event or trend, at which time some sorting and evaluating instantly begins. "The question of objectivity—of detachment—of moral judgment—proves to be no different whether it be the remote past or the recent present with which the historian is concerned." I hope that these pages are factually accurate and fair, and have taken considerable pains to make them so. Still, some passion may show through; if so, it is probably not as intense as the kind that can be evoked by certain issues in first- or sixteenth-century Christianity.

Concludes Hughes:

> *Somebody* must interpret our era to our contemporaries. Somebody must stake out the broad lines of social change and cultural restatement, and he must not be afraid to make predictions or chagrined at being occasionally caught out on a limb. . . . Today, the sociologists, like the historians, have grown cautious. . . . [Now] the historian who sees no incompatibility between his different roles—who is at least as much an artist as he is a social scientist—is uniquely equipped to lead others toward the imaginative fusion of these attributes, and thereby to illuminate the era in which we live.[1]

The credentials and performance of each such historian will be judged by others, but more of them have begun to "stake out the broad lines of social change and cultural restatement . . . [and] to illuminate the era in which we live," and this book aspires at least modestly to make a contribution.

A new map of religious America, one which locates six general zones in which most if not all "socially religious" citizens establish their loyalties, does not follow the boundaries of three earlier maps. If one did, it would be unnecessary. A map is needed in order for people to find their way, to avoid being lost; even a map of familiar territory is necessary if one is looking for something in particular. Maps are also used to encourage further exploration. The present one is written or drawn on such a scale that it both depends upon and calls for others using more close-up perspectives. As with space, so with time: if this is a study in contemporary or recent history, I believe the method and the map can be used with at least as promising an outcome on earlier periods of our history.

Maps include names, and naming is itself an act that contributes to the finding of group identity and social location. "Who am I?" is a question that is answered in part by addressing questions such as "Where am I? Who or what is near or far from me?" Mapping is part of what today is called "a social construction of reality."[2] To borrow the quotation of Wallace Stevens that is both the epigraph of this book and a citation in its last chapter, "We live in the description of a place and not in the place itself." At least, we live in the description *and* in the place. I should add that maps also give esthetic delights to many. Just as musicians can enjoy reading a score without hearing music or architects can delight in studying a floor-plan without visiting the building, it is possible that people can enjoy the mapped description of a place without coming to the place. It would please me to think that the present mapping offers enjoyment as well as social utility of sorts.

I have spoken of three earlier maps. It is quite natural for me, as a historian, to add: "Don't throw the earlier ones away." Each of them describes relationships, events, and situations that have left a sediment, have permanently altered the landscape. The present effort can be compared to the old parchment palimpsests, on which scholars superimposed new layers of writing on only half-erased old ones. Or to the glassine overlays provided in some atlases so that viewers can study complications in topography or changes effected through history. There are more than only four ways of mapping American religion, of course. Thus alphabetical classifications or other logical principles serve to organize books with titles like these: *Handbook of Denominations in the United States, These Also Believe, The Small Sects in America, The Religious Bodies of America, Yearbook of American Churches.*[3] (In 1973 the title of the latter was changed to *Yearbook of American and Canadian Churches*, a reminder of the close association and interplay of religious forces in the adjacent nations. Careful attention to the past and present of Canada will convince observers that that nation's emergent map of religion is similar to its southern neighbor's—as described here—in most respects. Our descriptions of "Mainline Religion," "Evangelicalism and Fundamentalism," "Pentecostal-Charismatic Religion," "The New Religions," and "Ethnic Religions" apply in both nations equally. Nor is Canada a passive or merely responsive partner. It has lived more closely with certain ethnic issues—for example, "Anglophonic versus Francophonic" religious cultures—than has the United States. Canada's cities have been especially hospitable to the New Religions, and Canada was the scene of central battles in the Fundamentalist controversy of the 1920s. Only in the case of "Civil Religion" is Canada so drastically different from the United States that this book's account will be of little help for understanding.)

Books describing American and Canadian church life on alphabetical or logical lines are useful, especially for reference, but their principle of ordering does not necessarily reflect historical events and developments in any direct way. The first of the three historical map designs reflects both the territorial and the theological situations of colonial America. In that period the primary and secondary associations of people's lives both served to support the individuals' identities. In nine of the thirteen colonies religion was established by law. This meant that in most cases one church had a near monopoly in a territory. Sects were more confined to the middle colonies or were segregated in the more tolerant of the nine that had established churches. In a sense the people who shared a place tended to share a world view and a set of religious opinions. Of course, not everyone practiced religion. But the cultural norms in most territories or areas were determined by the theological intentions and convictions of their elites. Mapping based on this situation reflects the world of 1492 to, say, 1776.

The second map grew out of and depicted the denominational reality and focused on institutional enterprises. The rise of religious freedom when the civil and religious realms became legally separate occasioned new forms of religious organization. Sidney E. Mead has shown that denomination-alism became the shape of American Protestantism—as it did of all American religion.[4] Denominations, organized on competitive principles, now were less focused on theology or belief than on intention and purpose. "Who am I?" No longer would one answer, "I am a citizen of Plymouth" (and thus a Puritan Separatist) or "A landowner from Virginia" (and consequently an Anglican vestryman). Now he or she could say much about what provided identity and location by answering, "I am a Presbyterian," or even, "I am a Cumberland Presbyterian." This suggested a different world than if one had said, "I am a Methodist." "I am a Quaker."

While neither of those maps would be fully reflective of today's realities, they both inform it. That together they still have descriptive potential is clear from efforts as recent as one in 1962 (based on data from 1950) and another published in 1974 (with material from 1971). These show how regionalized and denominationalized America remains, since in almost all counties one faith dominates, having either more than 50 percent or, in many cases, more than 25 percent of the church-goers' loyalties. Without such maps the observer, traveler, or explorer would certainly be lost. It is necessary to know about a Baptist "solid South," Mormon Utah, Lutheran power in the upper Midwest, and Roman Catholic concentrations in most cities.[5]

Overlaying these two maps is a third that suggests changes that had occurred in the United States by the middle of the twentieth century. These maps—which are now only metaphorical and can no longer be rendered cartographically—reflected life in pluralist America and had what might be called a political principle of organization. They usually had few lines and few clusterings of people, since they were designed to bring coherence in the midst of overwhelming pluralism. By that time, if one said "I am a Methodist," the hearer

would know very little, for there was far more difference between two kinds of Methodist than between one kind of
Methodist and another kind of Baptist. The styles of attachments and loyalties varied too greatly to permit the denominational answer to satisfy any more than the regional one did,
given the increased mobility that went with urban America.

The best-known of the third kind of maps was provided
by sociologist Will Herberg in *Protestant-Catholic-Jew*, a book
that argued that these three very broad religious elements
provided identification and social location whether people
"practiced" the faiths or were passive and casual. These can
be termed political because many of their norms came from
the one "American Way of Life" that Herberg said they all
celebrated. Concern for the *polis*, for the American element
in American religion, was the new preoccupation.[6]

Sociologists in this period have by no means all agreed with
Herberg's way of mapping. Some have pointed to the persistence of denominationalism in the midst of American-Way-
of-Life religions.[7] Others have concentrated on refining the
famous church-sect typologies as they have emerged in America.[8] Still others have made theoretical contributions, by dis-
tinguishing, for example, between "the sacred cosmos" and
"individual religiosity."[9] Because sociologists tend to study
specific religious institutions, more of them are content to
examine the denominational organization of life.

With historians it is different; it is hard to think of an integrative work in American religious history in the past third
of a century that does not use some political means of com-
prehending the pluralist experience. Historians, as people
who love the concrete and graspable, cannot let go of denominations. But denominations do not show enough about
identity and location. Thus Sidney Mead, who considered
denominationalism to be the shape of American religion, devoted his career to "the religion of the Republic" and seemed
bored by or even opposed to most elements of denominational life in *The Lively Experiment* or *The Nation with the*

Soul of a Church. Sydney E. Ahlstrom, in the mammoth *A Religious History of the American People*, gave dutiful attention to denominations, but he came alive as he traced the transformations of the Puritan legacy in the pluralistic American *polis*, the human city in the United States.[10]

In many cases, the title itself is a clue that the historian authors are working with the third style of mapping: *Protestantism in America: A Narrative History*, by Jerald C. Brauer; *From Sacred to Profane America: The Role of Religion in American History*, by William A. Clebsch; *Dissent in American Religion*, by Edwin Scott Gaustad; *Religion in America*, by Winthrop S. Hudson; *Righteous Empire: The Protestant Experience in America*, by Martin E. Marty; *A Christian America: Protestant Hopes and Historical Realities*, by Robert T. Handy; *From State Church to Pluralism*, by Franklin H. Littell; *God's New Israel: Religious Interpretations of American Destiny*, by Conrad Cherry; *The Religion of the Republic*, edited by Elwyn A. Smith; and *Redeemer Nation: The Idea of America's Millennial Role*, by Ernest Lee Tuveson.[11]

The current generation of historians will continue to work with this model and set of questions; it is hard to picture a "religious America"—or a post-religious America—that would not be curious about and informed by the question of religion in the *polis*. Historians will continue to tell their stories around the ideas of "left" and "right," "public" and "private," "sacred" and "profane" dialectics in national history. But unless I am sorely mistaken, all or almost all of them have begun to move beyond this approach and to begin sketching outlines of a map which this book tries to draw—as a guide for further exploration, revision, and improvement in the midst of the flux of history and of historians.

Political boundaries, "church and state issues," and theological reflections on the religion of the Republic do not tell us enough about the peoples' religiosity. More and more it becomes evident, and not only to anthropologists, sociologists, theologians, and historians of religion, that the question in recent decades is turning to the ways in which belief and social behavior are linked in citizens' expressions of loyalty to various religious clusters or movements. No more attention need be paid to this theme at present, since it demands a whole chapter (chapter 2).

If the relation of beliefs and social behavior has come to the fore, this is in no small measure the result of a manifest expression of quests for group identity and social location. So strong is this motif in the documents I have studied that at times I was tempted to call this book "The Identity Incident." A narrative history of this period would have to do justice to the myriad preoccupations with identity. The historian tends to back off a bit from treating a preoccupation or a trend as an event or an episode. But, as they say, "something happened," and happenings merit stories.

The identity incident occurred in the field of therapy, where the work of Erik Erikson has dominated through this period. As such, it also belongs to intellectual history, for Erikson through his acts of naming and defining contributed to the history of ideas. People might have had fashionable (or agonizing) "identity crises" even had Erikson not provided a term. Others have come up with equivalents of his diagnoses of "identity diffusion" for the sprawling personality type and "identity foreclosure" for the more constrictive ones. He is not alone in his attempt to define identity, but his view has become widely accepted as he speaks of "the accrued confidence that one's ability to maintain inner sameness and continuity . . . is *matched* by the sameness and continuity of one's meaning for others." Or "The term identity . . . connotes a persistent sameness within oneself (selfsameness) and a persistent sharing of some kind of essential character with others," or "the mutual complementation of ethos and ego, of group identity and ego identity."[12]

This is not an Eriksonian essay on psychohistory; Erikson's accounting of stages in the search for identity is a congenial one, but we are here not attempting to explain all manifestations of religious social behavior so much as to locate them. It is true that young people at a certain stage of development are making decisions that force the redrawing of the religious map—as when they desert mainline religion for Hare Krishna or Pentecostalism.[13] But we leave informed comment on such topics to others, seeing Erikson chiefly as the eponym or name-giver for many in this period.

One could continue both the therapeutic and intellectual historical lines of inquiry by reference to other thinkers, including Kurt Lewin, who spoke of "the uncertainty of belongingness."[14] Similarly, Erich Fromm could serve when he watches the individual's "growing isolation, insecurity, and . . . growing doubt concerning one's own role in the universe, the meaning of one's life, and with all that a growing feeling of one's own powerlessness and insignificance as an individual." His primary ties—and religions are implied here—give him a location: "This identity with nature, clan, religion, gives the individual security. He belongs to, he is rooted in, a structuralized whole in which he has an unquestionable place."[15]

For some the identity question is seen in its acute form. Thus Helen Harris Perlman observes:

> There is epidemic today a common malaise, a sickness of spirit, a disease that has been recognized, named, delineated by both psychoanalysts and social scientists. It has been the theme of a rising tide of literature, played out in the theatre of the absurd and in the novel of the lost soul: the seeking-but-never-finding personality. It has its graphic expression in art works that have neither form nor structure. . . . It has been called by many names, but its characteristic syndrome is a sense of lost or never achieved affirmative selfhood. The searching insights of Erikson first identified and illuminated this phenomenon

and traced out its roots and foliations. He has named
it "identity diffusion" and, at points of its acuteness,
"identity crisis."[16]

On its now chronic and public side, Harold R. Isaacs notes
its presence:

> We are experiencing on a massively universal scale a
> convulsing ingathering of people in their numberless
> grouping of kinds—tribal, racial, linguistic, religious,
> national. It is a great clustering into separatenesses that
> will, it is thought, improve, assure, or extend each group's
> power or place, or keep it safe or safer from the power,
> threat, or hostility of others. This is obviously no new
> condition, only the latest and by far the most inclusive
> chapter of the old story in which after failing again to find
> how they can co-exist in sight of each other without
> tearing each other limb from limb, Isaac and Ishmael clash
> and part in panic and retreat once more into their caves.[17]

The American religious version of such separatenesses and
retreats is, on the world scale, quite genteel. But whoever
reads the literature of mid-century aspiration finds a world
that did not expect the occurrence. Then the integrative and
universalizing language of the United Nations or, in religion,
the World Council of Churches spoke to the situation as now,
evidently, it does not.

For some this retribalization is largely a cognitive matter.
People share certain ideologies. But the observer of both the
world scene and the domestic religious situation will find that
most of the address to the question of basic group identity is
marked by social behavioral nuances and prescriptions. If
Congregationalism does not locate me, the Unification Church
of the Reverend Sun Myung Moon will, as it reinforces its
myth with precise injunctions and rituals. If I do not know
who I am in the new and generally boundaryless Catholicism,
I can become a Catholic Pentecostal and know to whom I

belong and exactly what is expected of me and of those around me.

The American religious versions of grouping and tribalism have not issued in armed conflict as have the inherited and reaffirmed alternatives in much of the world. Satirists and cartoonists can have a field day with adolescents faddishly going through their identity crises and middle-aged suburbanites suddenly finding themselves by speaking in tongues. Helen Harris Perlman presumes that in the past people also had such problems and crises. "Who and what were they, . . . where did they belong?" That the issue is "central in our concerns today is one of those recurring ironic evidences of how many other kinds of security we have achieved, that we can afford the luxury of striving for inner well-being!"[18] During the past decade most of the new religious allegiances have not resulted from the dispossessed peoples' strivings so much as from the exercise of options by the relatively leisured and affluent.

Harold R. Isaacs tries to account for the American story by reference to what he calls "postillusionary" times—as the late 1960s certainly turned out to be:

> In the United States, the breakdown of the worldwide white supremacy system after 1945 brought down like pricked balloons a whole cluster of illusions about the nature of the American society and raised in new ways and on a new scale the question of the character of the "American" identity. It opened up a time of wrenching change in all group relations within the society and within each group the beginning of an equally wrenching re-examination of itself.

Among these were "the crisis of 'black' and 'American' identity," the attacks on the white Protestants who had dominated, the people now "commonly lumped together under the pejorative label 'Wasp.' " (Before this period no one needed a name to give this former majority its place.) The opening Catholic

Church "became part of the great heaving and changing landscape" for its members. Old illusions about the "melting pot" were shattered. Disaffected youth rebelled in an effort to find a place for belonging other than in those characterized by the American establishment. In the period of refragmentation and retribalization, it was "difficult to picture a superbalkanized world," so there were efforts to imagine "new larger coherences." Religion in America had long been "balkanized" in territories and denominations; to change the metaphor, its "melting pot" did not work; what we are calling the fourth map has begun to be drawn in the quest for other coherences.

Isaacs correctly notes that "there is one thing we can say with certainty as we scan the group identity conflicts that crowd our contemporary scene: in one degree or another, religion figures in them all." Why should religion not be turned to so regularly since it provides, and here I quote his fine summary at length,

—a powerful personal-individual-emotional-subjective experience
—a powerful institutional-social-historical-objective actuality
—a way of dealing with the awesome forces of nature . . .
—a provider of a set of explanations for the inexplicable . . . a source of meaning [Weber]
—a way of ordering the vagaries of misfortune and good fortune . . .
—a supplier of significance for the insignificant . . .
—a source of solace . . .
—a source of authority, of commanding law to be obeyed . . .
—"a dramatization on a cosmic plane of the emotions, fears, and longings" stemming from each person's own relations with his/her father and mother . . . ([Freud,] Ernest Jones)
—as sanction and upholder of temporal authority, providing the halo of divine origin for earthly rulers,

defining and defending norms, public morality and
obligations, a bulwark against anarchy/evil, the
indispensable bonding cement in the social order, God as
'symbol of society' (Durkheim)
—as tool of power, blesser of the banners of
conquerors . . .
—or, contrastingly, religion as source of challenge to
authority as . . . in the many millenarian revolutionary
movements . . .[19]

In an industrial and democratic world, Thomas Luckmann
insists, "Personal identity becomes, essentially, a private phenomenon. This is, perhaps, the most revolutionary trait of
modern society."[20] It has meant that Americans are each
free to escape religion or change their loyalties. The years of
the identity incident—and they may continue for some time—
allow for much shifting of this sort. Hence the need for a new
map.

While in rather brief compass this book covers a large
landscape, it cannot attempt to do everything, either in con-
ception or in detail. It may be necessary to point to the most
obvious omissions by choice. Conceptually, no attempt will
here be made to suggest that the changes during this period
result only from the identity question and are expressed only
behaviorally. Such reductionism would not be fair to the
scope of motivations and styles of attachments evident in
contemporary America. Thus we are not saying that people
join a Pentecostal group only to find out who they are and
how to act, to find boundaries and behavioral demarcations.
It is always possible (and, I should like to think, probable)
that they also may truly believe the tenets of Pentecostal
faith. In old-fashioned language, this means that "at the hour
of death" (when group belonging is not too important) in
the midst of ontological shock, they commit their destinies to
the God or gods in whom they have believed. To suggest that
behavior is not integrally linked to belief and thought would
express an anti-intellectualism or a kind of behavioralism

that has never been very convincing to me. Here as often before I resort to a line of Rousseau who said in *The Social Contract* (V: II), "All my ideas are consistent, but I cannot expound them all at once." My thoughts are at least more or less consistent.

All this means that in many respects this is a book of narrative pointings and not behavioral explanations. The historian's thirst "for explanation in terms of group psychology and group behavior" is not yet satisfied. "The stern and demanding challenge of group psychology and its relation to history still confronts us, unsmilingly."[21]

So far as subject is concerned, I have not here mapped "secular religion" or "invisible religion." Simple or mere secularity[22] may characterize basic American life and modes, but it does not belong here since it serenely or steadfastly resists religious definition. (I know that some theologians sneak up on atheists and baptize them terminologically, insisting that the atheist is the truly religious person; to do so as a historian could only issue in confusion.) While according to the polls only a small percentage of the American people say that they do not believe in God, three out of five have little interest in worship or religious institutional life. In practical decision, most of the time most of them act the same way whether or not God exists.

Secular religion, on the other hand, is a kind of "religiocification"—to use a term that comes from the black movement—of secular humanism. One side of Unitarianism-Universalism or Ethical Culture Societies embodies this secular clarification, this godly way of being godless. But either such institutionalizations are statistically so small as to be insignificant or they merge into the public's understanding of Mainline Religion, Civil Religion, and the like. Beyond this, secular religion tends to be a private affair, unrelated to social and organizational life; it exists in the loneliness of a library carrel, a study, a mind apart. It should also be said that from one side all the religions are secular religions; even distanced from the hostile world, they all embrace it some-how or other.

Alongside secular religion is what Thomas Luckmann calls "invisible religion," a product of postindustrial society where religion is a private affair and may be experienced in-dividualistically and expressed in isolation. I suppose one could "get off the hook" by saying that if it is invisible, re-ligion does not belong on a map. Yet because it belongs to people who are visible it must also be visible. In that case it still need not be represented because this is a study of group identity and social behavior and not a biography of each private citizen.

Thomas Luckmann relegates the slightly social side of "invisible religion"—which may be America's majority faith! —to secondary institutions

which expressly cater to the "private" needs of "autono-mous" consumers. These institutions attempt to articulate the themes arising in the "private sphere" and retransmit the packaged results to potential consumers. Syndicated advice columns, "inspirational" literature ranging from tracts on positive thinking to *Playboy* magazine, *Reader's Digest* versions of popular psychology, the lyrics of popular hits, and so forth, articulate what are, in effect, elements of models of "ultimate" significance. . . .

The continuous dependency of the secondary institu-tions on consumer preference and, thus, on the "private sphere" makes it very unlikely that the social objectivation of themes originating in the "private sphere" and catering to it will eventually lead to the articulation of a consistent and closed sacred cosmos and the specialization, once again, of religious institutions. . . . We are observing the emergence of a new social form of religion characterized neither by diffusion of the sacred cosmos through the social structure nor by institutional specialization of religion.[23]

This invisible religion, then, is a social form of religion, and an extremely important one, but it is beyond the range of maps of social religion. Let it also be said that most "invisible religion" is marginal to or relates to one or another of the six general clusters we have isolated and named. The occultist who joins the Rosicrucians or a Spiritualist church may nurture and disseminate the symbols held by the do-it-yourself mail-order occultists who are not cultists. Mainline Religion has a huge half-believing and nonpracticing "Alumni Association" or set of inquirers who are all too invisible, according to religious leaders.

In summary, for the most part secularity and invisible religion are "ways" more than "places." And if they can qualify or suffuse one's belonging to some sphere or other of American religiosity, it should also be said that there is much room for "plural belonging." Many Mainline church members are also, say, Ethnic Religionists as Chicanos or Italians and Civil Religionists in their observance of national rites. The first and the sixth cluster here, Mainline Religion and Civil Religion, are most open to what Erikson calls "identity diffusion"; in recent years they have suffered for their inability to attract people of more constrictive interests who express "identity foreclosure." These are more likely to be Evangelicals and Fundamentalists, Pentecostals and Charismatics, or members of the New Religions, groups that have grown during this period.

In the following six chapters the names of the various zones or clusters will be capitalized. There is always a danger of reification and a consequent loss of the people about whom one is speaking. So I have chosen to use the most common, regularly applied, and sometimes even banal designations, attempting to stay with the words adherents regularly employ. In order to eliminate confusion, however, they will appear capitalized in order to suggest some specificity. The alternative would have been to apply or invent scientifically and historically more appropriate names. Thus we shall see that the New Religions are not new, simply because they are called that; nor are all others happy to yield the name "Evangelical" to "Neo-Evangelicals," or to think of Civil Religion as the most appropriate term for its category. But these are the names that have persisted and been most widely accepted and it is not likely that attempts by a single historian to be perfectly accurate (or a bit cute) conceptually would change the naming. If there are spaces between these clusters, spheres of belonging that are not species of these genera, voids or unmapped areas, they have escaped me entirely.

2　History and Religious Social Behavior

Observers of American religion regularly need to map the terrain. Its bewildering pluralism, they soon learn, resists a single or permanent outline. Participants, who make up the national majority, have a similar need. They may express it less formally, but it is more personal and urgent. To take one not wholly random illustration of their problem: psychologist and historian Robert Jay Lifton has spoken of a *"historical,* or *psychohistorical* dislocation, the break in the sense of connection men have long felt with vital and nourishing symbols of their cultural traditions—symbols revolving around family, idea systems, religions, and the life cycle in general." People regard these as irrelevant, burdensome, or even inactivating. Yet one cannot avoid carrying them within, or being affected by them.

Similarly, "the *flooding of imagery* produced by the extraordinary flow of post-modern cultural influences over mass communication networks" also alters peoples' religious sensibilities. The images media convey "cross over all boundaries" until the individual "can maintain no clear boundaries." The result may be a style of self-process "characterized by an interminable series of experiments and explorations, some shallow, some profound, each of which can readily be abandoned in favor of still new, psychological quests." The well-known "identity diffusion" or "identity confusion" isolated by Erik Erikson may result.[1]

The act of describing the landscape and its landmarks will not save souls or make all sad hearts glad. But it can contribute to a sorting-out process that will be helpful to both

18

participants and observers. Most mapping today is done by journalists, feature writers, television commentators, friends and neighbors, pollsters, anthropologists, and sociologists. Historical pointings and explanations seem to be less regularly available than they once were. In the academic community other disciplines have often tended to displace them. In the larger society historical interpretations are not often regarded as accessible or profitable. Historical inquiry needs all the help it can get if it is to regain its place. No single form of "new history," no isolated fresh interpretation, and no gifted historian by himself or herself will accomplish all that is needed. But efforts from many vantages are valid.

Societies do not have memories, as individuals do, but they need them. The person who lacks recall of the past will be bemused by the need to make choices and decisions without benefit of precedent. Memories of previous experiences need not always be conscious. They may have been stored in the mind in such a way that they have become part of habit and routine. They must be available at appropriate moments, particularly when a person "stops to think."[2]

Lacking a natural corporate memory but finding a need for its equivalent, members of societies turn to storytellers to help meet that need. In primitive societies these stories may have become embodied in folklore, folk songs, and ritual. In the past an aged sage might serve a leader by keeping both oral and written records of battles and treaties. In more literate cultures diarists, annalists, chroniclers, and the like could help impart a sense of worth to the daily lives of people or could provide a range of choices for those who had to make them.

The more formal historian has often tried to discern larger frameworks for the bare narratives. New circumstances force a need for changed ways of discussing such contexts. Yet new generations of storytellers and historians have to be aware of those who have already named and shaped past events or trends. We may not go so far as Hitler's propaganda minister Josef Goebbels, who said that "whoever says the first word to the world is always right."[3] But the first reporters of or reflectors on a set of events often have much to do with the vision of those who follow them. They initiate a tradition whose main outlines at least influence subsequent historians.

The Social Uses of Religious History

Leaving aside for the present account the versions of the past left by apologists at the time of Spanish exploration and settlement—though some of them, like Bartolomé de Las Casas, both merit and are receiving renewed attention—we can point to a tradition that began in New England. There William Bradford, Cotton Mather, and Jonathan Edwards in vastly differing ways set terms for inquiry that still influence those who want to tell stories of religion in the 1960s.[4] Their landscape and vision were shaped by their experience of an established religion in a culture whose leaders at least shared a largely common metaphysical outlook.

Today's historian of American religion has been no less influenced by mid-nineteenth–century writers who gave names to forces in the earlier national period. It was their genius to discover meanings in a nation that was devoted to religious freedom, voluntaryism, and the denominational pattern. Robert Baird and Philip Schaff, Protestant pioneers, or the great Catholic founder John Gilmary Shea may not be read widely today. But their outlines and namings provided guidance for people who are.[5] The development of subsequent professional and academic history "in the age of science" and in the midst of new styles of secularization also changed the settings and concepts of today's historians.

How one looks at movements or groups as varied as the Black Muslims, the Catholic Charismatics, Protestant "Jesus people," exponents of Eastern religions in America, and the mutations of old faiths is determined in part by what one

knows of signposts and landmarks left on the earlier landscape. Only a minority of the people, of course, regularly and
formally consult historical records or accountings in order to
help them discern directions for society. Lawyers and judges
do, for they argue on the basis of precedent. Economists and
legislators do, so that they can project trends or determine
policies. So might literate diplomats. Some thoughtful citizens
provide a market for historians' writings.

The larger public receives its tales through the tricklings-
down from scholarly historians or by seepage from populari-
zations. George Washington's cherry-tree encounter is known
to people who have never heard of Mason Locke Weems,
who told about it. People who have never heard of Frederick
Jackson Turner or Charles Beard have often been influenced
at fourth or fifth hand by chains of people who found their
theories of the impact of the frontier or of economic determinism to be congenial. William Bradford's *Of Plymouth
Plantation, 1620–1647*, was wholly lost from view for many
decades. But before it had been lost, many historians and
mythmakers had already copied from it and used its outlines.
During the period after its disappearance, the book still ex-
erted influences.[6]

Various media transmit the selective tricklings and seep-
ages. Mass media of communications certainly play their
part: witness the projection of images that had to do with the
American Bicentennial on television. Textbooks serve as
imparters to millions of children at the most decisive stages of
their development. Ruth Miller Elson's remarkable collation,
Guardians of Tradition, illustrates how this transmission also
transforms.[7] The public rituals and ceremonies of a culture
usually include many elements of myth and story.

The process of "shaping by story" applies to the parts as
well as to the whole of society. The records of batting aver-
ages inform devotees of athletics; the history of various stocks
helps investors decide on the merit of corporations in changing economies. The members of a society live in a number of

worlds, segmentations of life that find parallel in the sections of their newsmagazines. They inhabit partly separate worlds of the arts, of politics, of science, of entertainment—and of religion. Each of these worlds is marked by its own set of names and shapes, landmarks and signposts. Some histories of these worlds inform chiefly those who are responsible for life in them. Not many people in the society would read histories of garbage collection or sewage disposal (though they might well be advised to) in order to overcome "identity diffusion" or "identity confusion." But the larger culture is political, and political history has a following. Literary history illumines the whole past of the same society.

In a guided tour or a cartogram of recent American religion it is only natural that we take a moment to point to the overlooked importance of religious history. One would expect that the world of religion would occupy a privileged place in American storytelling. One would not think of going deep in the study of Buddhist, Islamic, or Hindu cultures without making attempts to become familiar with the religions that form and inform them. The United States Supreme Court similarly spoke for the national majority in 1951 when it concluded that "we are a religious people."[8] A national motto, "In God We Trust," appears on coins and currency. Nine out of ten citizens at least profess belief in God. Three out of five claim to be members of churches. Millions would say that religious faith offers them the central and even ultimate meaning in life.

These survivals and contemporary expressions have historical dimensions. Western religion is time conscious and regards history itself as a decisive category of experience and revelation. Its symbols and myths are recognized at many crucial turns in the cultural past.

The public at large gives little evidence of any perception of the complex bonds between religious expressions and their histories. They might share some of the scholars' awareness that in worlds that we often call "primitive" almost no line could be drawn between the sacred and the secular, and that this fusion of the spheres lasted through the years of Christendom down into modern America. But to study the fate of Catholicism or Judaism today or to explore the spread of occultism and Civil Religion in the 1970s often seems to be only a diversion, a hobby for experts on subcultures, a distraction from society's main business. A way of looking at "secularization" or "modernization" in Asian and African cultures assumes that the West has originated, experienced, and exported these trends.[9] Yet after secularization and modernization, whatever they might mean, America still does not draw rigid lines between religion and nonreligion.

Americans "separated church and state" but left the churches in privileged tax-exempt positions and subsidized denominational chaplains in the armed services. They have told pollsters that they remain overwhelmingly opposed to Supreme Court decisions that ruled devotionalism out of public schools. They blend religious and political symbols in both the sanctuary and the public square, in churches' calendars and at civil observances. They live simultaneously, and often without much sense of abrasion, in overlapping and interacting spheres of religious and secular order.

Yet *something* happened to the story and the storytellers of religion in the West and in America in particular. As I tell a story of a complex episode of the 1960s and 1970s in America, I cannot live in the world of Bradford or Mather. Few readers share the world views current when Shea and Schaff wrote. In modern times, religion, or at least an agreed-upon version of it, has lost its place as the prime mode of explaining reality. Most official ties between representatives of religious and other establishments have been broken. Religion must make its way by persuasion and not by coercion. It has become escapable and has been relocated on the cultural landscape.[10]

Despite their own varieties of commitments, the historians experienced many of these changes in common. Whatever their personal faiths, few professional historians make overt appeals to Providence for the purposes of historical explanation. They go about their business just as historians of labor and management or of the theater must do—engaging in research, creating narratives, summoning evidence, arguing, demonstrating, and then resting their cases.[11] They have moved from their earlier locales, from the campfire, the court, the cathedral close, the convent, the church, to the university or college, the research library or denominational archives. Even when, as is rarely the case, their salary is paid by a religious organization, they receive training in the university and their credentials and achievements are checked out there.

The changes of environment and sponsorship altered the historians and their histories. They often were segregated in the academy, victims of a division of labor that left them with too-clearly defined topics. They were placed in a corral, or chose to go there. They were to tell the story of particular religious institutions, leaving to others an accounting of life in the larger culture. Leaders in modern universities found it important to distance themselves from sectarian pressures and influences. Many of them found reason in their personal histories to try to forget or transcend their own religious pasts and religion itself. For most of the first half of the century after 1870, a symbolic date for the rise of the modern American university with its defined disciplines, religion was neglected in the historial fraternity.[12]

Our present researches, however, profit from at least a moderate change in climate during the second half century. Thus in the field of intellectual history, as a work by Robert Allen Skotheim makes clear, religious themes and inquiries again became prominent in the careers of Samuel Eliot Morison, Perry Miller, Ralph Henry Gabriel, and Daniel J. Boorstin, all dominant figures in the field. Skotheim quoted an essay written by Henry May in 1964: "The recovery of American religious history really began in the 1930's." "A 'recovery' occurred in the sense that there was a new interest in the history of religion and histories of religion evinced newly sympathetic attitudes toward their topic as well." Most of the new studies "allowed for some causal influence on the part of religious belief as well as some social environmental influence." While some of the works were in social history, more threatening to the dominance of progressivist-secular histories "were the studies of American religious thought which assumed that the ideas themselves were interesting and of intellectual worth, in additions to possessing certain causal power in the environment."[13]

Meanwhile what has been called "a quiet revolution" on campuses allowed for a larger element of religion in secular college curricula. Many students during and after the academic revolt of the 1960s claimed to find missing the kind of talk about values and ideals that they needed. It was present in religious studies, and such studies prospered. The American Academy of Religion, one of many scholarly societies in the field, numbers scores of historians among its thousands of members. In the culture at large three "revivals," one of institutional religion in the Eisenhower era, one of public expressions of faith in the early 1960s, and a third—the subject of this book—through the mid-seventies, at least helped prepare a climate favorable to religion, if not always to religious history. Religion, in short, had not disappeared. It had been relocated. The time had arrived for historians to approach their subjects with both new self-confidence and new self-consciousness.

Four Models in the American Religious Tradition

The present effort to map the American religious scene during or after an episode of change in the 1960s and 1970s relates to and builds on other histories— as virtually all historical writing would do. Changing circumstances call for different approaches and concentrations; this call for more accent on religious social behavior is based on a perception of neglect and a belief in the promise of such an accent. In a sense it calls for a somewhat different model of approach than those now current. To use a more fashionable term, it would employ a changed paradigm. The word, popularized by Thomas S. Kuhn in *The Structure of Scientific Revolutions*, includes two concepts.

The first is what a critic of Kuhn, David Hollinger, calls a "disciplinary matrix," which consists of "the entire constellation of beliefs, values, techniques, and so on shared by the members of a given community"—in this case the company of historians of American religion. The other is the concept of "exemplars," "concrete puzzle-solutions which, employed as models or examples, can replace explicit rules as a basis for the solution of the remaining puzzles of normal science." Hollinger's discussion has import for the tradition and community of historians of religion. He says that "activities are defined and controlled by tradition," and

> tradition consists of a set of devices, or principles, that have proven their ability to order the experience of a given social constituency. An operative tradition provides a community with criteria to distinguish one activity from another, sets priorities among those activities, and enables the community to perform whatever common activities make it a community at all. Insofar as the community's experience is contingent that experience presents itself as a series of "problems" to be solved by that tradition, which validates itself by transforming the contingency of experience into something comprehensible and subject to maximum control. Tradition, then, is socially grounded, and its function is that of organization. Organization may be achieved through a number of modes and devices, ranging from formal institutions to informal habits and from codes of abstract principles to concrete examples of how problems of a given class have been solved in the past. Whether it is conduct or perceptions that require organization, whether the task is

prescriptive or cognitive, the organizing devices have enough flexibility to sustain them through successive, contingent experiences.[14]

Three successful paradigms to date have dominated American religious history, providing both disciplinary matrices and exemplars in the tradition of a community.

The first and most durable has been intellectual history. Just as Skotheim observed its reappearance in the 1930s, it characterized the efforts of Bradford, Mather, Edwards, and most of the lesser figures in the colonial period. Governor Bradford related the mundane existence of early New England settlers to the cosmic themes of biblical exodus and exile. Jonathan Edwards, the age's great theologian, intended to write theology in the historical mode and set out in thirty sermons in the *History of the Work of Redemption* to provide a background for interpreting the American experience. Before him, Cotton Mather summoned examples from world history to show how his worlds of Cambridge and Boston fit into the larger story.[15] In our time, Perry Miller, who did not share their faith, by acts of empathy and understanding tried to share their concerns and viewpoints in order to deal with them seriously.

Intellectual or theological history notices in particular the cognitive dimensions of American religion, the "belief *in*" and "belief *that*" elements. People believe that gods will act in certain ways, that humans have this or that destiny, that certain interpretations of meanings are necessary, that doctrines and dogmas are true or false, that some philosophies can be supportive of faith, that some ideas may be dangerous and some salutary. They may not always use terms of formal theology to express all this, but they know that somehow ideas have consequences, and they regard ideas as being important.

Whether the historians have taught the public to take religious ideas seriously or whether they simply enlarged upon the peoples' instincts is not easy to determine; some sort of interaction and symbiosis must have occurred. In any case, no one need apologize for the number of impressive histories of theology or religious thought, particularly those of monographic character, even in America where, Europeans charge, formal theology is rare and second-rate. It is natural that intellectual historians would converge on the thought world of Puritans, of New England theology, and of the intellectually respectable Mercersburg theology, at the expense of less formal systems. Thus they miss the story of the religion of most Americans while dealing capably enough with one level or strand of religion.

To this intellectual-theological model was added a rather fully developed institutional paradigm, chiefly in the nineteenth century. Robert Baird, Philip Schaff, John Gilmary Shea, and their counterparts all found the history of the churches to be vital for what it revealed about American life as a whole. They judged the value of the denominations, classified or graded the sects, explained their workings, and convinced publics that the spiritual strand in American life was largely confined to formal organizations. This approach and subject matter have not been exhausted and will not disappear. They represent the meat and potatoes of historical research and point to the most concrete and durable expressions of faiths.

The typical citizen who might on a rare occasion have to consult library shelves for books on American religion would be surprised and disappointed not to find works on religious bodies. But before long he or she would learn the limits of the institutional approach. So far as thought, taste, and commitment are concerned, a certain type of Presbyterian will differ more from another type of Presbyterian than he or she will from many a Roman Catholic. Across denominational lines people display similarities in political or theological preferences, in their appreciation of tradition or innovation, in their observances or delinquencies.

At the same time, public curiosity about all but the more exotic or eccentric groups has diminished. Writers may hold attention with accounts of "kidnappings" by or from the Children of God sect, polygamy among earlier Latter-day Saints, or snake-handling among rural Pentecostalists. But written histories of mainline groups like Episcopalianism, Reform Judaism, or Methodism will at best attract the attention of a few members in each. These institutions represent too little threat, promise, or fascination to alert a public to the need of becoming familiar with their histories.

The third paradigm, which might be called the political, came increasingly on the scene as people saw the limits of what they had regarded to be the normative approach, the institutional. The political model is associated with the professional or academic period, just as the theological has roots in colonial establishment and the institutional in the time of denominational self-consciousness. In the midst of an ever more perceived religious pluralism, it became necessary to look for common strands. When religion was segregated, both on and off campus, from more respectable inquiries because of its sectarian ties, historians found it important to show how religion infused and suffused other fields.

First the institutional historians began to show how relevant to the larger public were the stories of their clienteles or subjects. Thus John Tracy Ellis and Abdel Ross Wentz, in turn, showed how Catholics and Lutherans were on the scene with positive contributions at each basic change in American life—for example, in the struggles for religious freedom. The later historians of the *religions* of the republic, like Sidney E. Mead and Sydney Ahlstrom, built on theological and institutional paradigms but moved ever more to the political theme, to the story of the *religion* of the republic. So did most of their contemporaries who were full-time writers on American religious history.[16]

In this period, especially during the middle third of the twentieth century, practitioners of the discipline were eager to show the past significance of religion in the American *polis*, the "human city," the sphere of public affairs. Such pre-occupations had long been present, but the new generation made them virtually normative. They wrote on issues of church and state, civil religion, democracy and faith, Abraham Lincoln or Woodrow Wilson as theologians, public and private spirituality, sacred and profane America. Hardly any of them shunned theology and belief or disguised their base in religious institutional history—why should a historian throw anything so valuable away?—but these became secondary questions for many of them.

The political paradigm and its products have the advantage, then, of building on and profiting from the earlier two "first words," to use Goebbels's phrase, to the society. The extent to which the achievement has always been recognized as being truly religious is questionable. The public has only slowly begun to learn of the relocation of American religion beyond the simple borders of denominations. To many the history of religion in the *polis* may simply look like a subtheme or subplot of political history. Many citizens seem to work with a division of labor. Presidential inaugurations are political, in no way religious, events. For religion, "go to the church of your choice," but see American Legion or Fourth of July rites as merely patriotic. Despite some cultural lag and some conceptual blocks, the political paradigm has met ever wider acceptance. It became a third "right" word to the society. Our generation, and I include myself, gravitates to it reflexively. It will remain sufficiently secure that it can be built upon and supplemented. But often in history something new stirs and takes shape or awaits more voices just at the moment when the arrival or maturation of its predecessor movement is announced.

In that context, the fourth and emerging paradigm deserves notice in the mapping of American religion. A species of social history, it would concentrate on habit and conduct and practice, on religious social behavior. An announcement of

the discovery of social history as a genus should be greeted
with nothing but a yawn; it can hardly be the great new salvation for historians in quest of new angles of vision or new
subject matters. Lest anyone receive the impression that its
novelty is here being touted, it may be well to note the focus
on "peoples' history" from the pen of John Bach McMaster
in his *History of the People of the United States*, an eight-
volume work that he began almost a century ago. McMaster
wrote:

> In the course of this narrative much, indeed, must be
> written of wars, conspiracies, and rebellions; of presidents,
> of congresses, of embassies, of treaties, of the ambition
> of political leaders in the senate-house, and of the rise
> of great parties in the nation. Yet the history of the
> people shall be the chief theme. At every stage of the
> splendid progress which separates the America of Wash-
> ington and Adams from the America in which we live,
> it shall be my purpose to describe the dress, the occupa-
> tions, the amusements, the literary canons of the times;
> to note the changes of manners and morals; to trace the
> growth of that humane spirit which abolished punishment
> for debt, which reformed the disciplines of prisons and
> jails, and which has, in our own time, destroyed slavery
> and lessened the miseries of dumb brutes.[17]

Already in 1937 in *A History of Historical Writing*, Harry
Elmer Barnes, while he could speak of "social history" as
"another of the relatively recent additions to the achievement
of making history more inclusive in scope and more vital in
content," noted that in Europe "this movement started nearly
a century ago."[18] Of course, there are trends and transformations in social history, the most significant of these perhaps
being, in the words of David Hackett Fischer, from social
history as "merely an interest in all the discrete happenings
which political historians had ignored" to "social history . . .
becoming a sophisticated study of the lineaments of society
itself, as they have changed through time." "This new work

appears not merely in manifestos but in monographs. It is sustained not by mere aspiration but by solid achievement. And it is happening in every historical field." He notes that "the new history seems to be moving very fast in France, the United States, and also the developing nations."[19]

In our subsequent mapping of a transformation in American religion at the turn between the second and final thirds of the twentieth century, we shall argue that the theological paradigm will fail us at almost every point. Ideas, of course, were implicated, but they were not central. No significant theology motivated or issued from the turn. The changes of the period left all religious institutions altered, but the heart of the change had little to do with development of fresh structure. In a political society it can be argued that everything that occurs has political significance, but the alterations that characterized this episode often had only negative or parapolitical import. Concentration on the kind of social history that turns to the subject of group behavior and practice best contributes to the "study of the lineaments of society itself, as they have changed through [that] time."

Historians live with jumbled mental attics, cluttered junkyard minds, and randomly cataloged libraries as they set out to order their thinking and their narrative. They are reluctant to throw anything away and have become somewhat wary or cynical in the presence of those who tout wholly new ways of looking at history, embracing "new histories." But they can and do welcome new light and better tools. They also know that previously neglected aspects of the past can be unearthed and held up to view. Before Americans developed theories to explain their ways, before they invented and nurtured homegrown institutions to house their spiritual strivings, before there were intricate social mechanisms to which they had to relate these ideas and institutions, they were already practicing religion and expressing it in personal and social behavior. Such a story is so old that it effectually places Americans among the primitives, for whom practice and behavior were more important than particularized theologies, discrete institutions, or problems of relating to non-religious orders of reality. It is so ecumenical that it links American religion more than previously with Asian and African spirituality, both of which accent behavioral correlates to their systems of meaning. It is so familiar that it can be the subject of Everyman's observation, just as it has provided subject matter for scholars in cognate disciplines such as sociology.

Locating Religious Social Behavior

Historians, reluctant as they are—and here they share notions with most writers of fiction—to begin accounts with too many definitions, usually prefer to let fences grow around concepts in the course of a narrative.[20] Yet terms have to be used with some sense of conceptual propriety. Our first word, "religious," is employed in rather broad terms—but not so broad that, as in the practice of some overreaching theologians, it becomes too inclusive; nothing is left out, so that "if everything is religious, nothing is religious." "It is necessary to let everything be what it is," protested Bishop Gustaf Aulén of the Church of Sweden, on another subject.[21] At least the historian allows for the possibility of a secular order, an agnostic profession.[22] Nor is the present use so narrow that it is confined to the religion that occurs under the tutelage of the priests alone.

In my informal observations of middle-range defining by historians, it would seem that they tend to regard an entity or event as religious if it displays a combination of three or four of the following elements:

Religion would have to manifest something like ultimate concern. But ultimate concern by itself is of little interest to social historians; it may be represented in a private agnostic philosophic viewpoint that falls short of most historical definitions of religion. Normally, then, one also looks for a social expression of this concern. Religion, of course, can be a private affair—we shall with Thomas Luckmann again speak of "invisible religion"—but it is of special interest when it is born socially and sustained in the conditions of community.

To these add the predilection historians have for calling something religious if it is expressed as part of a nexus of myths or symbols. Reality is not grasped head-on. It seems to come to most people as an at least partly prefabricated package deal through "given" symbols and myths. In slightly more complex religions, including some in the primitive world, one also expects a ritual expression. Forms develop and become part of the rhythms, patterns, and cycles of community life. In literate societies people expect more; they expect interpreters to claim that "there is more to all this than meets the eye." Behind the perceived mundane world is a more important order of being, one that demands explanations that might be called more or less metaphysical. The package is complete when certain behavioral correlates or consequences (or, perhaps, inspirations and triggers) appear on the scene.

Little more need be said on the theme of the term "social," since we have already regarded the genus "social history" and the social dimension of religious definition. The term here points to the fact that the historian has a different interest than does the biographer, since his focus is on human beings in society. The maverick or misfit makes history; religious founders tend to be charismatic exceptions or mutations. The historian as a student of social behavior is more interested in repeatable, sustained, imitable, and widely shared practice or conduct than in eccentric, idiosyncratic, or unrepeated expressions.[23] (I prefer the milder "social behavior" to the term "collective behavior," which appears in much sociological literature. Ordinarily "collective" connotes mob activity. The two do overlap and interact; much of the literature on collective behavior informs the present subject).[24]

Since this book maps religious behavior, or, sometimes, practice, it is behavior that most demands prior definition.

Henri Desroche, dependent largely on the work of Gabriel Le Bras, has issued a typical call, the kind to which this book is a partial response:

> We need a history of religious practices as much as, or more than, a history of religious theory, doctrines, theologies, and dogmas. We need this history of religious attitudes to serve as the basis for a further exploration of the forms they have taken. And a field study like this would gather its data not from the actions of great men or virtuosos, not from the turbulent moments in the history of great events, but from everyday living, . . . 'We know of a thousand different doctrines and a thousand great men. Let us study together the religious practices and faith of a whole people.' (Le Bras).[25]

In that paragraph, practices, attitudes, forms, everyday living, and faith all point to the phenomenon called behavior. The term here, and in social scientific discourse in general, does not attract to itself the adjectives "good" or "bad" as it might in parental or other moral discourse, nor does it refer to simple manners or civility.[26] Further, most connotations of the philosophical and psychological schools of "behaviorism" do not receive too much special notice here. The work of people like John Watson and B. F. Skinner has a bearing on the topic of social behavior. But to most historians it might carry a too heavy ideological note of determinism, and would be seen as only one among many modes of accounting for human actions.

At the same time, mention of the behaviorist school alerts us to a problem that is at least tangentially addressed but is not the main topic of this effort to map the American religious scene. That problem is extensively and effectively addressed by Robert F. Berkhofer, Jr., in *A Behavioral Approach to Historical Analysis*, a book that shows much awareness of behaviorism. Berkhofer presses on every historian the need to take a self-conscious stand on the question whether one can write history without making up his mind about one or another explicit doctrines or ideologies having to do with why people behave as they do. "The basis of the problem lies in the possibility of studying the internal component of human action as opposed to the mere external manifestations." "[T]he historian is forced to fall back upon implicit or explicit hypotheses in order to discover the actual behavior the social scientist can see in person," since the historian is ordinarily dealing with inaccessible and not infrequently dead people, while the other social scientists may find them available for probing, interview, examination, and maybe even psychoanalysis! Not every piece of historical narrative will or can go extensively into all the connections between "ideation" and "behavior," though it is likely that some assumption about the nature of human being and action at least implicitly colors every historian's work. Thus in the following pages, again and again it is assumed, not without some evidence, that in a pluralist modern society significant numbers of people will have and will want to deal with the problem of identity and meaning.[27]

Simpler definitions of behavior course through this book's usages; they are informed canonically by the historically based Oxford English Dictionary. Translate the first two uses of "behavior" into the plural: "1. Manner of conducting oneself in the external relations of life; demeanour, deportment, bearing, manners. 2. Conduct, general practice, course of life; course of action *towards* or *to* others, treatment of others." Gabriel Le Bras thus speaks of behavior or practice as "the accountable element of Christianity," since belief and thought are invisible and in some ways beyond scrutiny, while behavior is at least visible and external.

The insertion of the word "human" into Elliott McGinnies's definition in his behaviorist psychological text makes a contribution. Social behavior *"is evidenced whenever two or more [human] organisms, either directly or indirectly, serve both to prompt and to reinforce one another's performances."*[28] Richard T. LaPiere in 1938 referred to social behavior as *"the interaction which occurs between two or more socialized human beings for the duration of the particular situation in which that interaction occurs."*[29] The historians turn their attention to such interactions in the past, not the present, but they share with other social scientists an interest in external behavior patterns that represent "(a) observable and measurable, (b) frequently recurring action, (c) shared in by many people, and (d) possessed of some social significance." These can be measured in part according to how universal they are, how much social pressure they exert, what social value they can be demonstrated to possess. In descending order of compulsion they include "mores," "folkways," and "usages."[30]

The accent on behavior places the work squarely in the traditions of cultural history as well as social history. In *Culture and History* Philip Bagby, in a summary, brings his argument to the point at which we are:

> Culture, then, is a particular class of regularities of behaviour. It includes both internal and external behaviour; it excludes the biologically-inherited aspects of behaviour. Cultural regularities may or may not recur in the behaviour of individuals, but, to be called 'culture', they should recur (or fail to occur) in a regular fashion in the behaviour of most of the members, and ideally in that of all the members, of a particular society.

(We should also note that Bagby applies this definition to what he calls "sub-cultures," "the aggregate of cultural regularities found in any society or class of human beings smaller than the group of local communities which serves to define a culture." The mapping in this book often concentrates on such subcultures, as in the case of occult groups, Hasidic Judaism, and the like.)[31]

One naive but effective way to begin to move beyond definition toward pointing is to scan the index of an aging volume like LaPiere's and simply indicate the kinds of topics that preoccupy historians who work with the social behavioral paradigm in religion. They can evoke the outlines of a more formal study. For example, one might cull: advertisements, agitation, audiences, best-sellers, censorship, clubs, conferences, committees, colloquies, confessionals, crazes, crusades, dance, dress, etiquette, fads and fashions and fanaticisms, funeral customs, gambling, games, gestures, kinship, law, medical practices, mobs and panics, rebellions and riots, revels and ritual and rumor. All these belong to the zone of inquiry.

So familiar are all these to observers and participants in contemporary religion that one might safely assume that their story has long preoccupied the historians. But one would assume wrongly. Astonishingly, these show up only tangentially and incidentally in historical writing. One can think of an occasional title having to do with behavior at camp meetings or religious revivals. But most historians turn instantly to the question of revivalists' theology, the institutional consolidation of an awakening, the political consequences of mass conversions. Rarely are the experiences of the experiencers the main subject of the stories.

Despite the probability that the behavioral elements are the most widespread, popular, firmly grasped, and disputed aspects of religion and despite occasional monographs by historians and some forays into the past by sociologists, the behavioral paradigm carries its users into relatively undiscovered or undeveloped territory. It is hard to think of a single volume that has treated the subject on either a chronologically sustained or culture-wide basis. Surely no general histories of American religion have treated the subject in anything but casual and haphazard fashion, though eighty-nine years after John Bach McMaster stated a programme for general social history, Sydney E. Ahlstrom, in his extensive narrative that so well fuses the three developed paradigms, began to move toward the fourth. His title significantly points to his intention: *A Religious History of the American People* (1972).[32]

In Ahlstrom's extensive bibliography the reader will find only a score of behavioral titles out of hundreds of possibilities. These deal with, for example, the culture of the European shtetl, the Protestant establishment, the laziness of the South, deviance among Puritans, the faith *and* practice of Puritans, character and social order in Connecticut, the social and intellectual history of enthusiastic religion in New York, moral stewardship, the camp meeting, social ferment in Vermont, individualism and conformity on the frontier, character in the Old South, and the like. Despite the excellence of many, together they can be called only a beginning. In a twenty-three-page essay on American church historiography in the mid-twentieth–century decades, James Hastings Nichols turned up not a single title that begins to meet the description of religious social behavioral history.[33]

This obvious field may have been neglected because historians and the public have been content with the three other models or approaches. Only as they began to fail to inspire satisfying stories or accountings of inherited reality was there motivation to move further. It may be that practice and behavior are so "up close" that they can be taken for granted and do not always seem to merit inquiry, so far as their pasts are concerned. Certainly their diffusion represents problems for historians, and the disappearance of many traces raises problems not so readily confronted in disciplines that restrict themselves to study of the present. Cultural inferiority may have afflicted some historians. Could they not discover records of a theology sufficiently distinguished that it might be held up for comparison with Europe? Or might they at least not write the history of religious thought in order to show its deficiencies? Whatever the reasons, curiosity about the subject has increased and historians are working to satisfy the curiosity.

Corollary Disciplines, Fields, and Methods

The central problem for historians who are alert to the importance and revelatory potential of social behavioral studies in religion has to do with finding and organizing traces. Most of them are lost. Some social scientists can often, in effect, "create traces." They can take polls or field trips, set up interviews or experiments; their subjects are alive and can "sit for the camera," or be eavesdropped or kibitzed upon.

Most of what has happened has been lost from view. Historians, not free to write fiction or engage in pure guesses, have to fall silent unless they have substantial surviving clues as evidence that something occurred in a certain way. As already noted, they have especially difficult problems when they try to connect external with internal behavior, practice with ideation. Can they trust their sources to be telling the truth? May not people of the past have suppressed true self-knowledge and disguised their motivations from themselves?[34]

No one claims that we have no traces in the American past. What inhibits full-scale social behavioral history may instead be the embarrassment of riches in selected cases. Any reader who thinks back to the profusion of throw-away posters, bumper stickers, tracts, and mimeographed handouts in the counter cultures of the 1960s, will immediately recognize that even the most recent past creates problems for this story. The intellectual historian may be satisfied with tracing the history of ideas in Paul Tillich's formal *Systematic Theology*.[35] The institutional chronicler can report on statistics, conventions, and jurisdictional changes in the Presbyterian church. The political historian can be content largely to recount Supreme Court decisions and summarize legislation in the period. The leather-bound, gilt-edged but not necessarily representative election day sermons of colonial Massachusetts are apparently more accessible than are the church bulletins from the Christian churches of America two Sundays ago!

Some specialties within the historical profession have been brought to the rescue. Most notable of these is that practiced by cliometricians, an unnecessarily controversial group. From one point of view, they use quantitative methods that have long been appreciated, but render them more efficient by the use of computers. Controversy ensues when humanistic historians fault them for depersonalizing the past or concentrating only on the easily measurable and quantifiable. Or they may be at fault when they make extravagant claims for their subdisciplines. It would be injudicious to embark on a full review of the merits or flaws of both sides, given the small space that could be allotted the theme here. Suffice it to say that some critical revision of quantitative (sometimes, confusingly for us, called behavioral history as well) approaches will almost certainly survive and be developed in a new generation, which can more readily learn its special techniques. And to say that even those of us who are not competent in the field or not curious about its detail are profiting from findings by its experts. Thus it is now easier than before to measure Sabbath practices or to trace demographic facts in the longer past than it had been when a historian had to count observances laboriously while reading diaries.[36]

Similarly controversial is the approach called psychohistory, in which various psychoanalytical models—most frequently those of Erik Erikson but often some derived from Sigmund Freud or Carl J. Jung—are employed to explain past behavior. This usually has more importance for biographers than for historians, though books dealing with, say, the psychohistory of Zionists or white racists have begun to appear. Some of the difficulties in using psychoanalytic approaches to the unresponsive dead seem insurmountable. But insofar as historians informed by these approaches develop and improve their techniques, it is quite possible that they can make some contribution to that most nagging question of the nexus between ideation and behavior, or between internal and external behavior.[37]

Literary historians in recent years have been helpful as they sophisticate their approach to the use of fiction and poetry as special kinds of evidence about the past. It is the artists' task to see (in Goethe's sense of *schauen*, really to see to the heart of things) what others may overlook. The Nathaniel Hawthornes and Herman Melvilles and Mark Twains have had eyes to see what historians have often overlooked, and serve as at least one kind of guide to some traces of past behavior.[38]

Beyond the historical profession, the sociologist will be the most important colleague, and behavioral studies may do much to bring the two disciplines closer together. While sociologists have been less curious about development and change and have needed to show little disciplined interest in narrative, they have long been asking behavioral questions about the present. Those presents have receded into the past, and they provide data for historians. Meanwhile, some sociologists have been critical of their discipline for the general lack of historical concern of many practitioners, for the one-dimensionality that plagues their work. C. Wright Mills complained that most sociologists have been content with "the dull little padding known as 'sketching in the historical background' or with the reckless *ad hoc* procedure of 'giving an historical explanation.' " Mills had a positive intent: to show that history is "the shank of social study." Without history it is not possible to grasp "the problems of our time—which now include the problem of man's very nature." "All sociology worthy of the name is historical sociology." Mills did not convert everyone in his discipline to this point of view, but he both stimulated and represented an appreciation of history in it.[39]

Historians, who owe many a card of thanks to sociologists, will not content themselves simply with writing histories of past sociologists' findings. Nor would they see their study simply as being "sociology projected backward." While they share preoccupations, historians are more interested in development, evolution, sequence, surprise, and change; sociologists are concerned also with "snap shots" of the present,

with the nomothetic and the regular, whether change is pre-
dominant or not. Historians will instinctively gravitate to narrative, the characteristic way of ordering reality by giving
attention to chronology. Sociologists do not need that mode.

To speak of narrative is not to suggest that historians do
all their ordering chronologically, telling "one damn thing
after another," as Arnold Toynbee was said to have dismissed
simple annalism. The use of narrative is evolving in recent
times. Just as it has changed in the modern novel (for example, in James Joyce, William Faulkner, and the like), so
historical exposition may also be transformed. Robert Berkhofer properly says:

> In the works of innovative novelists, plot began to reflect
> the multiple viewpoints of many human consciousnesses
> and many different time scales rather than the first- or
> third-person narration of sequential events on a single
> time line. . . . If storytelling has changed so radically, then
> should not history telling also change? The multiplicity
> of human consciousness that plays a part in the life of past
> men called history must be represented in the historical
> narrative if it would be true to current knowledge of
> behavior and contemporary standards of explanation.[40]

In the ensuing story of an episode in contemporary history,
therefore, we shall not simply order things by saying something like this: "In 1960, this happened in Pentecostalism; a
year later the following occurred in civil religion; then in
1962, Hare Krishna advocates did this or that; and in 1963
. . ." Instead there will be prehistories and flashbacks inter-
spersed with simple narrative and nonnarrative analysis—all
in the interest of better ordering the map.

Finally, the combined disciplines of anthropology and history of religion are interacting with "ordinary" history on the
behavioral front. To take but one illustration, in 1974 there
appeared an 837-page collection of essays called *Religious
Movements in Contemporary America*. There in almost thirty

essays almost thirty approaches to phenomena were displayed. Straight narrative, studies of ritual structures, psychological probings of ritual, structural studies of language and tonality, and the like were employed. Many of these can be effectively used on traces left from the groups who inhabited, say, nineteenth-century America.[41]

The history of religion has connections with anthropology, sociology, psychology, phenomenology, and what used to be called comparative religion. Those who are not at home in these fields may be justifiably confused at this point. Those in the historical fraternity who study religious history or the history of religion in America do not follow exactly the methods taken up by those who work in the comparative and phenomenological history of religion fields!

Historians of religion have begun to teach Americans to see their bonds with the primitives or their ties to African or Asian religion. They have taught our contemporaries to think in terms of myth and symbol and not only of doctrine or dogma. They alert historians to the need for seeing patterned behavior as being prior to theology and not always rendered formal in enduring political or spiritual institutions. Thanks to their discernments, some scholars have begun, for example, to see religious revivals as initiation rites for the larger American society.[42] Such a vantage can lead scholars to regard Roman Catholicism as a complex or nexus of hundreds of apparently trivial behavior patterns, whose whole may be more important to the faithful than are dogma or the political experience of institutions.[43]

The history of religions approach informs the present study, not always in acknowledged ways, at the very least by the questions it imposes and the angles of vision it proposes. Today's historian has the luxury of sharing in a fresh address to realities that are on the minds of his contemporaries without carrying the burden of arrogance that goes with the claim that something wholly new has waited for the moment when he or she might discover it.

Connecting Beliefs and Behavior

One special problem confronts the historian of religious social behavior, a problem hinted at in previous comment on the relation of internal to external behavior, or of the ideational to the behavioral in general. Without some reference to it, it is impossible to proceed to the task of mapping, for readers may well ask what justice is done to religion if priority and primacy are not given to the discussion of belief. After all, in the lives of most people, is not belief absolutely central? And is it not most difficult to relate behavior to belief in a sphere wherein the beliefs seem all to be unverifiable empirically, since they have to do with an unseen world?

These are serious and valid questions. In passing we might say that belief is not central, at least not in conventional senses, in many religions of the world. The West makes more of both "belief in" and "belief that" than do many religions of Africa and Asia. Some have also seen that Westerners seem to be moving "beyond belief" into a religious style that accents experience over the cognitive dimensions.[44] And we recognize the special problems induced by religious as opposed to, say, political beliefs. Also it will be necessary to fall back here somewhat on hypothesis and assumption, though I have confidence that a careful examination of evidence will substantiate the assumptions.

At this stage it may be important only to say that while talking about behavior one is not denigrating belief but only holding it in some suspension while something else is being examined, all the while seeing the two to be profoundly and even integrally linked. Suzanne K. Langer, a philosopher who is uncommonly informed as a scientist and psychologist, summarizes the meaning of this link. She notes that humans' symbolic behavior has roots which "lie much deeper than any conscious purpose . . . in that substratum of the mind, the realm of fundamental ideas."[45] Conversely, with intellectual historian and philosopher George Boas we observe that "when an idea is adopted by a group and *put into practice*, as in a church or a state, its rate of change will be slow [emphasis mine],"[46] because it connects belief and behavior in especially solid ways.

A fruitful way to speak of the nexus, but one which demands some translation, is to see the link between what José Ortega y Gasset as philosopher and, in a sense, historian of culture saw as a connection between what he called *creencias* and *vigencias*. *Creencias* are the kind of ideas or beliefs that count most in an exercise in mapping. *Creencias* are *Grundideen*, fundamental ideas; "they are not ideas which we *have*, but ideas which we *are*." They may not be the dogmas of Christianity held by a young person who is a "Jesus freak" for two weeks in passage from the drug culture to belief in the Maharaj Ji. They would more likely be longer lasting if more diffuse beliefs about community and purpose, for which the succession of commitments are but passing "fillings in" of prior outlines.

A student of Ortega, Karl J. Weintraub, says that "*creencias* share some of the characteristics of usage and custom, since the latter are the actual forms in which societies express their basic convictions." Another spokesman for Ortega, Julián Marías, carries the discussion further, making a sharp distinction between ideas and these deepest beliefs. When beliefs are expressed, argued over, refined and honed as doctrines or ideas, something fatal happens to them. (Anyone who has tried to spell out and then impose the content of, say, "the American Creed" for practitioners of a civil religion has learned this.) "We could say, paradoxical as it may seem, that the explicit affirmation of beliefs is the first step in their weakening."[47] In any case, it is often beside the point. The Presbyterian Confession of 1967, we may safely surmise, is an articulation that is hardly known by Presbyterian lay people and would not explain them nearly as well as would their liturgical tastes, political commitments, or locations in suburb or ghetto. The contentious Missouri Synod Lutherans during their controversies in the early 1970s gave every evidence that the *fact* that one party possessed an articulated set of beliefs about biblical inerrancy was more important to it than the content of those beliefs, about which most of them knew little. Books explaining and justifying the details of the teachings on the basis of the seventeenth-century scholasticism from which they derived attracted almost no notice at all. Catholic behavior went on as before for both Roman Catholic parties, despite the familiarity of the few with Hans Küng's book-length questioning of the key dogma of papal infallibility. Controversies about birth control and abortion practices were more vivid. People on both sides of these conflicts acted as if the over-definition of doctrine was irrelevant and maybe even disintegrative.

How various Presbyterians, Lutherans, or Catholics characteristically behave as a group in their subcultures are called *vigencias* by Ortega; they are connected to the primal beliefs or *creencias* in subtle ways. *Vigencias* are binding social observances that do not present themselves to us "as something that depends upon our individual adherence but, on the contrary, is indifferent to our adherence, it *is there*, we are obliged to *reckon with it*" and, contrariwise, "at any moment we can resort to it as to an authority, a power to which we can look for support." They therefore include laws, customs, language, extant social obligations, taboos.

The historian is interested in these not as once-and-for-all statements about life in society but as ever-changing, however subtly. Reference to change also suggests that neither *creencias* nor *vigencias*, neither beliefs nor "binding" behavior patterns and customs, wholly determine life. Marías says that the individual need not necessarily yield to the demands of current customs, "but he does have to be aware of them; he must confront them in order to accept or reject them."[48]

In the fluidity of American culture and subculture one must also notice behavior that is less profoundly rooted than are the *vigencias*. A president may choose to announce a one-time-only Day of National Humiliation and not be criticized if he neglects to follow it up a year later. He would create considerable stir if he departed from a time-honored custom of naming a national Thanksgiving Day each November, since it is locked in to Americans' notions about their past, their relation to God, and their attitude toward their possessions, called "blessings."

The connection between *creencias* and *vigencias* as here perceived also serves as an alert against anti-intellectualism. The historians who would argue that what preachers preach, theologians write, scholars discover, and philosophers think have little or no bearing on their fellow believers' behavior patterns, engage in an artificial act of disjunction between two modes of being that can be and are exemplified in the lives of countless humans. He prejudges the case or confuses the issue of the effect of belief on behavior with the issue of precisely which beliefs effect what behavior and in what way. A church-goer may attend services because he wants to be seen at worship or because it helps his business or because his grandmother instilled a habit in him. But there are few reasons to be suspicious of the consistent profession of numerous people that they truly believe *in* what the church teaches or believe *that* what it says is true, and in some complex way or other put selective parts of the religious idea system into action and practice.

The Uses of "Peoples' History"

John Bach McMaster spoke of the whole enterprise of social history as being "peoples' history," and most social and behavioral historians would argue that they are also contributing to the subject. This does not necessarily place them in the camp of those who, in the "conflict" (as opposed to "consensus") school of historians in the 1960s, professed to have discovered the peoples' history on ideological grounds. Often these claims were founded on Marxian principles; they may well have served as a corrective to established modes and conclusions. They did leave a legacy of questions and some clues about methods for those who bring less formal ideological commitments.

The familiar complaint of the radical or leftist historians was that only conservative elites are in position to leave traces and documents. If we knew more of what nonelites were thinking, history could be rewritten. This charge is partly true.[49] On the other hand, something can be deduced from establishment documents. In the familiar case of the American Revolution, had there been a "revolution within the revolution," had there been a true proletariat, would it not show up in the nervous reactions of those in power? One would not need mimeographed documents from the Students for a Democratic Society or in-house communications between the Weathermen of the 1960s to know that they induced fear and reaction in the larger official culture. One cannot, of course, draw a full or accurate picture on the basis of "someone else's" documents, but they provide some indicator.

The controversy serves as a reminder that basic problems remain for anyone who would deal with longer pasts in the field of social behavior. While my own inquiries usually focus on eighteenth- and nineteenth-century America, it is also significant that this first venture deals with the immediate past. One regrets that there were no tape recorders on the scene to preserve the opinions black slaves had about the religious practices on the plantation. But Eugene Genovese has shown in an extensive volume on the subject that historians should not have so readily despaired of finding anything from the lips of slaves or from within slave culture.[50]

Yes, it would have been fortuitous if more nineteenth-century chroniclers had had Henry Mayhew's skill and staying power as he interviewed and published the opinions of Victorian "common people."[51] But attics and archives are full of happy accidents of preservation, exemplified in the book *Children of Pride*, based upon a trove of letters from a southern Presbyterian family's experience.[52] The researcher can take comfort from the fact that the American past included so many literate people; middle-class and bourgeois folk are also people in "peoples' history." But newcomers have a right to be nervous about the reliability of the haphazardly preserved records we do have. How representative are these?

The nervousness may be part of the dues paid in the historians' profession. "Welcome to the club. You are now learning something about the relativity of historical research and construction. You are coming to see that narratives about the past, however intensively researched they may be, however objectively they be recounted, *are* constructions of reality, fabrications—as factually based as possible—of a world whose whole can never be grasped, was never grasped. History does not encompass total reality; it addresses significant parts of it."

Turn the question around: why should historians put as much confidence as many of them seem to do in a New England sermon, written by a minister who may be skilled in the art of self-deception, and yet be worried about the unrepresentativeness and inaccuracy of a diary by someone who comments on it? Suppose we had tape recordings of entire conversations through periods of many months, we would not have an undistorted view of reality—as anyone who heard the famed Watergate tapes of the Richard Nixon era will be likely to testify.

Regret for what has been lost will and should always exist. This can be compensated for by new curiosities about the kinds of documentation that had long interested few about events that they once considered of secondary importance. One of the uses of peoples' history is to teach a new respect for the wider range of such traces. We know that throw-away literature (comic books, bills of sale, Sunday church bulletins, private memos) often are more revealing than are formal, unmarketable, never-read tomes that fall into the hands of librarians and historians alone. Where nothing is left, there can be no story; where traces are left, there can be outlines of a story.

Elite leaders' writings and relics do inform peoples' history, and they should also be respected. In religion especially, because of the voluntary pattern of religious life, leaders and agitators have had to be extremely sensitive to the responses and reactions of congregations, masses, crowds, cells, or individual potential converts. The spokesmen cannot so easily throw posterity off the trail with side comments as could clerics in societies where the church had been established, where spokesmen could say roughly the same things whether or not people responded. The fact that people could turn their back on a potential or actual leader in American religion adds a note of realism and inspires confidence in many of these documents.

If social behavioral history is useful for what it teaches about history, it has other uses, most of which need not here detain us. Those who find in history a simple esthetic delight can find in this kind of history one more sphere for enjoyment. Those who think history has some sort of social purpose will have available a history that discusses prime modes of living in the American past.

Others may, with Adolf Harnack, *"study history in order to intervene in the course of history. . . .* To intervene in history means that we must reject the *past* when it reaches into the *present* as a hindrance; it means further that we must do the right thing in the *present*; and it means finally that we must prepare prudently for the *future."*[53] Some readers of a book like this may feel that religion has taken a right or wrong turn, one they may have overlooked had they not, through it, noticed the social behavioral dimensions and what they revealed. Our only claim along the way has been to suggest in advance that theological, institutional, and political paradigms or models did not suffice for the story that waited here to be told, whose uses are left to the people who read it, who might walk where the map only describes a terrain.

3

Mainline Religion

Every change in a map is made at the expense of what was outlined there before. If the change is demographic and accounts for the arrival of new people, the map will show either crowding of populations or the removal of the people who had earlier occupied the space. If the change is topographic, symbolically as the result of seismic, glacial, or erosive forces, this means that the old landscape has been altered and the hachures have to be redrawn.

At the turn to the last third of the twentieth century both new people and metaphoric changes in topography altered the American religious map. They did so at the expense of the people who had been previously established, who had produced the terrain of a map that had satisfied its users for some years after mid-century. If much of the attention of this book is to be given to the new people and new forces or to the old ones that drew new attention, we should not overlook the fact that perhaps the highest drama of the decade occurred in the displaced, acted upon, or threatened religious forces.

In the course of telling the story of their vicissitudes and reactions, reporters, journalists, clerics, social analysts, and historians progressively if instinctively began to speak of this complex as "Mainline Religion," and the name seems to be destined to prevail. To my knowledge, by 1975 no scholarly attempts had yet been made to trace its rise to prevalence, attempts comparable to those devoted, say, to the acronym WASP,[1] the White Anglo-Saxon Protestant component of "the establishment."

The term "Mainline" may be as unfortunate as the pejorative-sounding WASP, but it is no more likely to fall into disuse and may as well be lived with and enjoyed. I say unfortunate because in the day's argot a "mainliner" is "a drug addict who takes his narcotics by intravenous injection."[2] (Let prophetic critics who see established American religion as a soporosed and sedated entity make of that what they will!) Or the word connotes "The Main Line," "the traditionally aristocratic district just outside Philadelphia, Pa., served by the main line of the Pennsylvania Railroad," back when there was a Pennsylvania Railroad.[3] Hence its connotation is somewhat more elite than is the whole complex of majority religion in America. Its aura in that case grows from money and refers to "collectively, wealthy people, socially prominent elements in any community."[4]

Something far more neutral has been intended by most people who use the word. The word is not classic English, and does not appear in the Oxford English Dictionary. It arose chiefly from railroad usage, where the main line is the principal route as opposed to a branch line, a sideline, or a sidetrack. Mainline religion was thus thought of as the traditional, inherited, normative, or median style of American spirituality and organization, over against the "marginal" or "fringe" or "curious" groups that drew so much attention in the story-telling of the late 1960s and early 1970s.

While the aquatic imagery of the "mainstream" or the market metaphor of "standard brand" religion occasionally appeared, we may safely speak of the term "Mainline" as a product of the period when the central feature of its story was the picture of at least relative decline in America—decline in statistics, in its proportionate share of citizens' loyalty and attention, in its ability to quicken curiosity, in its power to provide people with group or social identity and to inspire stereotypical behavior patterns.

Mainline religion had meant simply white Protestant until well into the twentieth century. At mid-century, however, the pace of change in Catholicism and Judaism had been so rapid that they joined Protestantism as being part of the normative faith in pluralist America. Projections of religion over public media had to give "equal time" to the three faiths; Religion in American Life, related to the Advertising Council, knew that its billboards would have to suggest Jewish temples and Catholic cathedrals alongside visualized Protestant churches when it enjoined people to "Go to the Church of Your Choice." The military and public institutions devoted attention to the three as being typically American, to the neglect of Eastern Orthodoxy and black Protestantism—to say nothing of the smaller sects and marginal cults.

Americans entered the sixties with the inheritance of a generally accurate map drawn by a large number of sociologists of religion, but most effectively by Will Herberg in the book to which we have already referred, *Protestant-Catholic-Jew*. Herberg's description plausibly detailed the lay of the land for another ten years, through the end of what was called the Revival of Religion in the 1950s and the period of social activism and ecumenical encounter through 1965. Not all would have agreed with Herberg's attempt at explaining the "triple melting-pot" that contained essentially one religion; he attributed much to what he called "Hansen's Law," after Marcus Hansen: "What the son wishes to forget, the grandson wishes to remember." The son wishes to forget many features of ethnic inheritance, but the grandson, who needs to but cannot retrieve them all, reacquires at least the fading legacy of his grandparents' religion. But if the explanation did not satisfy, the depiction of present-day realities did.

Herberg's summary statement was this:

The outstanding feature of the religious situation in America today is the pervasiveness of religious self-identification along the tripartite scheme of Protestant, Catholic, Jew. Within this comprehensive framework of basic sociological change operate those inner factors making for a "return to religion" which so many observers have noted in recent years—the collapse of all secular securities in the historical crisis of our time, the quest for a recovery of meaning in life, the new search for inwardness and personal authenticity amid the collectivistic heteronomies of the present-day world.

Self-identification in religious terms, almost universal in the America of today, obviously makes for religious belonging in a more directly institutional way.

... Not to be—that is, not to identify oneself and be identified as—either a Protestant, a Catholic, or a Jew is somehow not to be an American.   *Anabaptist /*

The reader of those words after twenty years and more would find them less than fully descriptive of later American life, in which it became increasingly respectable to adopt what might best be called secular styles; to be religious but not in any socially visible sense, as in the practice of "invisible religion"; to find one's identity through religions and movements that have little directly to do with Protestantism, Catholicism, and Judaism.

Herberg's key word was "identify" or "self-identification," clues that signal what became a preoccupying issue in later religion, a new search for identity in a changed culture. He had begun with moving personalized passages on the historic American problem of immigrants (and, thus, all but the American Indians, who acquired the same problem in response): "Who am I?" "What am I?"

This question is perhaps the most immediate that a man can ask himself in the course of his social life. Everyone finds himself in a social context which he shares with many others, but within this social context, how shall he locate himself? Unless he can so locate himself, he cannot tell himself, and others will not be able to know, who and what he is; he will remain "anonymous," a nobody—

which is intolerable. To live, he must "belong"; to "belong," he must be able to locate himself in the larger social whole, to identify himself to himself and to others. . . . The process of self-location and identification is normally a "hidden" social process of which the individual is little aware; only at moments of disintegration and crisis does it emerge to the level of consciousness and require some measure of deliberate decision.

Herberg could hardly have foreseen the extent and depth of "disintegration and crisis" that awaited Americans in the late 1960s. Nor was he able to envisage the extent to which many of them would turn to roots that he was dismissing, including the ethnic. "The perpetuation of ethnic differences in any serious way is altogether out of line with the logic of American reality." In the black, Chicano, Puerto Rican, American Indian, and to some extent "white ethnic movements" of the late 1960s there were to be revivals or rediscoveries of durable ethnic self-identifications. In 1955 he could say with considerable warrant that "being a Protestant, a Catholic, or a Jew is understood as the specific way, and increasingly perhaps the only way, of being an American and locating oneself in American society." "All other forms of self-identification and social location are either (like regional background) peripheral and obsolescent, or else (like ethnic diversity) subsumed under the broader head of religious community."[5]

This reductionist map was superimposed on the earlier territorial and denominational ones, but soon events would occur, both in religious demography and in the change of the spiritual landscape, that necessitated another map, another layer. The quest for "self-identification and social location" endured and even intensified in the midst of cultural upheavals. But people invented (that is, they found or they fashioned) new ecological niches in which to find themselves, to which to belong. A final backward glance at Herberg reveals how much he noticed the mainline of the Mainline; only a couple of pages then needed to be devoted to the alternatives.

He remembered the Protestant "fringe" sects, but did not envision a day when prosperous, affluent, highly educated Americans on campuses and in suburbs would gravitate toward latter-day versions of these or even of non-Christian alternatives. In 1955 the fringes' appeal was "largely to those sections of the urban and rural poor who feel themselves rejected in contemporary society, deprived of status and prestige, devaluated, 'proletarianized'." Although these sects remained strong, he observed accurately enough that their members tended eventually to "become more prosperous and socially accepted and move up in the social scale," to "leave the sects and join denominations more congenial to their new status." At the same time, many of the former lower-class sects also became respectable middle-class churches. He could dismiss them, however, because "they become very minor denominations, hardly affecting the total picture."[6]

Seventeen years later a book appeared that became an event, just as Herberg's had been an event in 1955. Dean Kelley's *Why Conservative Churches Are Growing* captured the sense of change in his own period. While discussion of Kelley will be generally reserved for our notice of Protestantism below, one sneak glance ahead at what he called "the Exclusivist-Ecumenical Gradient" indicates to observers of American religion how times have changed. While Herberg may have been correct in his prediction that the "minor denominations" would not replace the Mainline churches, *something* was new. Public curiosity had shifted to the exclusive sects. They were looked to with more of a sense of both promise and threat than they had been in 1955. Books, magazines, college courses, television programs devoted to them would be attractive as attention given to the Mainline Religions would not. He grades the groups from the top, where they were seen as most exclusivist and antiecumenical, least a part of Herberg's "American Way of Life" religion, as follows:

Black Muslims
   Jehovah's Witnesses
      Evangelicals and Pentecostals
         Orthodox Jews
            Churches of Christ
               Latter-day Saints (Mormons)
               Seventh-day Adventists
               Church of God
               Church of Christ, Scientist

Then come the generally large churches of ambiguous status; they were newcomers to the Mainline but still were intact enough to provide social identity for members:

Southern Baptist Convention
   Lutheran Church—Missouri Synod
      American Lutheran Church
      Roman Catholic Church
      Conservative Jews
      Russian Orthodox
      Greek Orthodox

His last section was made up of the kinds of churches that were more typically main stream:

Southern Presbyterian Church
   Reformed Church in America
      Episcopal Church
         American Baptist Convention
            United Presbyterian Church
            United Methodist Church
               United Church of Christ
               Reform Jews
                  Ethical Culture Society
                  Unitarian-Universalists

Kelley properly notes that "fine scaling . . . will have to await empirical testing." He knows that counting ecumenical memberships may slightly mislocate some churches; thus the Orthodox may appear to be more exposed than they truly are. And Roman Catholicism represents a special case for reasons that will be seen below. But Kelley's list can suffice for the broad purposes to which it is here being put; he went on from there to point to what Herberg was less ready to see. "To put it in its grossest, most simplistic form: other things being equal, *bodies low on the list will tend to diminish in numbers while those high on the list will tend to increase.*" To the degree that that is true, it points to the fact that millions of Americans were not satisfied to identify or to find their identity in the Mainline.[7] The story of this change, as we have already suggested, may be the most dramatic event in recent American religion, though it has been obscured by the colorful rise of alternatives. Here that story cannot be fully told; it can only be pointed to, referred to, summarized as part of a sixfold division.

Judaism, Herberg's newest-comer to status, embodies many of the problems and some of the attempts at solution in one people's identity-search in the late 1960s. From having chosen to accept Mainline status, Jews suddenly reversed themselves after the "Six-Day War" in 1967 and had to preoccupy themselves not only with the psychological questions of identity but also the deeper physical corollary of survival. Would there be a Jewish people in several generations unless today's Jews took steps to help assure their survival?

To his credit, Herberg anticipated the new Jewish problem in his final paragraph on the subject:

> And yet among some American Jews there was perplexity and restlessness. Was this all there was to Judaism after all? Had it no higher purpose or destiny? What was it, in the last analysis, that made the Jew a Jew, and kept him a Jew? A young Jewish sociologist [Nathan Glazer],

at mid-century point, formulated his perplexity in a way that was bound to find an echo in many of the third generation: 'A social group with clearly marked boundaries exists, but the source of the energies that hold [it] separate, and of the ties that bind it together, has become completely mysterious.[8]

That young sociologist wrote the most widely received history of American Judaism in 1957 and updated it in 1972 with an epilogue wholly devoted to a discussion of the changes worked in Jewish life by response to the war in 1967. For convenience's sake I shall seem to be engaging in the breaking of a sacred rule among historians and draw upon a secondary source, for the simple reason that in contemporary history such sources become primary and have to be regarded as events. In this and in other cases my own reading and research confirms the outline of reformulated materials; to detail and cite them all would be to distract us from the main pointing and mapping intention.

"When one considers Jewish experience in the United States in the years since 1956, one year stands out as a dividing line: 1967. The periodization of Jewish history is not the periodization of general history, nor is the periodization of American Jewish history that of American history." He suggested that the assassination of President John F. Kennedy, the Vietnamese War, the year of assassinations might loom larger in general accounts. But the threat to Jewish survival posed by the war in Israel had interrupted the Jewish drift and evoked memories and fears that American Jews thought they had left behind as they became accepted in the Mainline religion and culture.

The war was not the only cause. Jews had been closer to blacks than other whites had been, remaining with their businesses as Jewish ghettos became black ghettos, and generally supporting civil rights causes as part of their liberal political programs. But around 1967 the black movements, he noted, took ugly turns and became overtly anti-Semitic. Jews found it necessary to reinforce a boundary that had been eroded. Political radicalism among Jewish youths had also disturbed the larger community, since they questioned both American and acculturated parental values. "The postwar excitement over a 'Jewish revival' [had come] to an end in the late 1950's. Interest in Jewish religion and in Jewish issues among young Jews seemed to have reached a nadir in the early 1960's." But then came that "one overwhelming event, the Israeli war of 1967," leading them to "a new intensity of self-consciousness."

The revival had been superficial, unmarked by high theology or deep education or piety. Synagogue building in suburbs was the main phenomenon, as parents resisted overly "ethnic" expressions. After 1967 it was Orthodoxy, the least Mainline of the three main branches, that was most aggressive and attractive because it stressed boundaries and focused on the source of energies that bound Judaism together, to use Glazer's earlier terms. But Conservative and Reform groups also drew back from endorsing and blessing intermarriage with non-Jews. In addition to growing concern for the content of Judaism and the threat of intermarriage, Glazer cited the "survival" issue and the search for a soulful community as energizers of Jewish reconstructions. These four topics were partly academic until "in 1967 something happened that suddenly sharpened their consciousness of being Jews."

Glazer knew that "it is hard to document a sudden reversal of feeling. Yet everyone who lived through it has attested to it," not least of all the young Jewish leftists who began to "come home." Before that war, neither the Holocaust of the Hitler period nor the birth of Israel had really shaped American Jewish consciousness. Now *ex post facto* they left their mark. Attempts to formulate appropriate theology may have come too late; it may be that the fresh traditioning of Jewish education and community life may not have enough resources. But the question of survival at least motivated Jews to reexamine what life in the Mainline meant even as those further from that "standard brand" concept of religion prospered most. One is almost tempted to relocate Orthodox, Hasidic, and various communal styles of Judaism, because of their accent on conversion to their approach or to experience within it, as "evangelicals" (see next chapter); only the historic connotations of that term's substance prevent one from doing this sociological shuffling.[9]

Almost any other recent accounting of Jewish reappraisals would confirm Glazer's. In Henry L. Feingold's *Zion in America* a final chapter on "The American Jewish Condition Today" begins "At the heart of contemporary American Jewry's consciousness is concern about its continued ability to survive as a distinct group in America." Survival anxiety surfaced in reaction to black anti-Semitism, intermarriage, and the Protestant efforts in "Key '73" in 1973 to "call a continent to Christ." These were all overlays on the anxieties occasioned by the 1967 war and public opinion polls taken during the "energy crisis" of 1974, when some anti-Israeli reaction appeared. But Feingold also saw that the survival question did not necessarily lead to a recovery of institutionalized Judaism. "When one peers behind . . . impressive statistics one cannot help but note a loss of vitality in American Judaism" (in 1974). The youth, by and large, did not return. "Jewish secular and religious organizations no longer seem to encompass the whole of Jewish life in America." At the edges of the Mainline alone, "Orthodoxy, which showed few signs of being able to find a practical accommodation at the turn of the century, is today revealing many signs of vitality." In the past Judaism had superimposed religious layers over folk traditions, institutions, languages, and cultures. "That extra insurance against erosion seems to be waning in America."[10]

Locating troubled Judaism in and at the edges of the Mainline depends very little on theology and Jewish intellectual life. Judaism has always regarded formal theology as a kind of adaptation to Christian modes and terms. Its theology has tended to be a reflection on the life of community and thus locked in to the experiential and behavioral references as Christian theology has not. Reflections on the meaning of the Holocaust and the rise of Israel in both theological and anti-theological terms[11] came late and, according to the historians, had limited impact.

A second model for discernment, the institutional, would have turned up little, since Jewish denominationalism remained the normative pattern and there was little improvisation in the 1950s and 1960s. A single exception was innovation in small communes or other experiments in community living. Politically, the war in Israel and the black anti-Jewish expressions were important, but not nearly so important as the subtler psychological reactions to these. Here as ordinarily before, the history of Judaism is best seen as a history of social behavior. This is no surprise to Jews, who have always made as much of Halakhah ("that by which one walks"), the binding rules, as of Haggadah, the narrative that expounds or interprets scripture. Further studies of Jewish popular culture alongside elite culture will illustrate more dimensions of the problems survival-minded Jews have in Mainline religion.[12]

If Judaism is conveniently grasped from the behavioral side, Roman Catholicism has been less regularly seen from that point of view. It is possible and necessary to see Catholicism's Mainline traumas and Catholics' search for identity and social location in intellectual and theological terms, for the late 1960s saw this church, "the only *the* Church," according to the comedian Lenny Bruce, experience the most drastic theological revision in centuries. There were fewer formal institutional changes to hold attention, since the basic Catholic structure held. But some experiments with "underground" churches, enlargements of lay spheres of power, major alterations in the roles of priests and religious, and the like, have a bearing on the story. And there were political changes that began with the election of the first Catholic president in 1960, through the Second Vatican Council's declarations on religious freedom or ongoing domestic debates over church-state relations to disputes about abortion and the law. They all have to be kept in mind, but the great Catholic changes were best experienced in the most observable but also most difficult to account for zone, social behavioral responses.

Will Herberg's parting glance at Catholicism in 1955 found it securely in the Mainline, as one of three main melting-pot expressions of a single religion of the American Way of Life. "By and large . . . American Catholicism seems to be successfully coping with the difficulties and perils that its changed position in American society has brought."[13] Then, unlike the Jewish case where Nathan Glazer said "something happened," one could say of Catholics, "everything happened." It is difficult to conceive of more unforeseen changes —and who, after all, *did* foresee them?—than those that occurred in America's largest single religious group in the decade of the Second Vatican Council (1962–65). Posed on entirely different grounds than those that inspired Jewish "survivalism," there was in Catholicism a similarly urgent question of identity and social location.

Edward Wakin and Joseph F. Scheuer tried to describe the changes with the title *The De-Romanization of the American Catholic Church* in 1966. Their opening lines already then were almost ritually followed in subsequent chronicles:

> The label *American Catholic* expresses ambivalence and implies conflict. *American* and *Catholic* are two demanding identities, each supported by an environment of values, attitudes, and relationships which surround the individual. Though the pressures of each identity often reinforce each other, they can also be centrifugal, sometimes pulling the American Catholic away from his Catholicism, sometimes drawing him away from the *mainstream* [italics mine] of American life. As an American he reflects his Catholicism and as a Catholic his Americanism. Each makes a difference; each has consequences for the other.[14]

The Catholic "ghetto culture" ("which all seem to agree is dying," says John Cogley in *Catholic America*), had its own style of intellectuality, denominationalism, and politics, but it thrived chiefly "in the realm of behavior." Cogley noted the boundaries between Catholics and other Americans over birth control and marital practices, parochial schools, the system of internal social structures ("Catholic debutante balls . . . Catholic bowling leagues . . . Catholic travel agencies . . . . and even . . . comic books."[15]) The formation and retention of a social identity there was rather simple, and the Catholic Church therefore, while fulfilling its functions, grew consistently into the 1960s.

On the identity diffusion and behavioral blurring that followed the Vatican Council, liberals and conservatives could agree. Thus James Hitchcock, who wrote as a more traditional scholar of *The Decline and Fall of Radical Catholicism*, quoted with favor two people he would have cited as radicals, Michael Novak and Garry Wills. Their concurrence came over the issue of what happens to identity and purpose when a people is disintegrating. "Michael Novak once quoted Dostoyevsky with approval, 'When a man leaves the people he becomes an atheist,' and it is clear that many reformers, who despised the folk religion of their youth, are now much closer to this condition than they had ever anticipated." To him the connection between custom or behavior (*vigencias*) and belief (*creencias*) was clear.

He also quoted Garry Wills, whose *Bare Ruined Choirs* mourned or attacked all kinds of Catholics (but whose praise for the dissenting Fathers Berrigan put him, in Hitchcock's eyes, in the radical camp). Wills had described the folk culture well enough:

Bingo, large families, fish on Friday, novenas . . . clouds of incense . . . car blessings . . . *Dies Irae* on All Souls . . . the sign of the cross before a foul shot . . . food-chiseling in Lent . . . tribal rites, superstitions . . . and, all of them, insignia of a community. These marks and rites were not so much altered, refined, elevated, reformed, transfigured as—overnight—erased. This was a ghetto that had no one to say 'Catholic is Beautiful' over it. Men rose up to change this world who did not love it—demented teachers, ready to improve a student's mind by destroying his body. Do we need a culture? Only if we need a community, however imperfect. Only if we need each other.

Professor Hitchcock agreed that "within this folk Catholicism there was a great deal which was narrow, superstitious, petty, even pernicious and anti-religious." But the reformers removed much of the cement without building something new. "The death of this community has meant for a large number of people the death of their religious faith as well." For even more, "it has meant a weakening of belief—a loss of certitude, a diminution of joy and serenity, an unaccustomed cynicism and vague spiritual malaise, an embarrassment about expressing beliefs."[16] With the end of intact Catholic culture and community came the end of Catholic growth and an inability for it to help provide people with a social identity or guides for social behavior.

Libraries are being written about the Catholic change, and even rather large details are not needed in the present task of mapping and designating. For present purposes an ideal place for taking a sounding appears in a Catholic counterpart to Nathan Glazer's book on Judaism, John Tracy Ellis's revision of *American Catholicism*. As dean of Catholic church historians, Ellis knew more and had longer perspectives than almost anyone else; his book had been the best-received modern accounting of its subject when it appeared in 1956. His epilogue, "The Changing Church, 1956-68," matched Glazer's in mood and effect, and it bears a brief revisiting for comparison of the main themes.

If Mainline Jews had been shocked into survival and identity questions by the War in 1967, Ellis's Catholics had had a similar though more positive counterpart in the Second Vatican Council shortly before that. Ellis, of course, does not see the Council as the only cause or occasion for change, but places it in a continuity. Yet the Council did make possible most dimensions of Catholic change. "The 'ripples [have] run far." The results affected "a new mood, a new style, often an entirely new school of thought."[17]

While Catholics in America "have not been in the fore of speculative thought," they were sensitive to preconciliar stagnation, had shown signs of vitality, and after the Council came forth with far-reaching proposals for theological change. The laity had new opportunities, and priests' organizations were formed. The Kennedy election and radical dissent around 1968 were changing the political aspects of Catholicism; bloc voting was waning. But the most decisive change came when Catholics decided to remove some of the behavioral and ritual props that had helped people forge identities—just at a moment when many in the cultures were signalling a need for the kind of social location that Catholicism still provided. Says Hitchcock of the new "worldliness" of the reformers: "It is by now almost a law that religious liberals will discover and espouse various aspects of American culture just as true secularists become disenchanted and begin looking for realities which the religious progressive is trying to forget."[18]

In any case, ever after, a generation of young and middle-aged Catholics began to bemoan "the identity crisis" the Church had given them; their sometimes drearily regular recitation of this problem obscured the fact that the Church had at least been able to give them an identity to have a crisis about, while much older Protestantism no longer could do that. And older church members often found that they underwent a crisis of confidence when behavioral changes were allowed and even prescribed too suddenly. After looking at the searing black-white issue that tore Catholicism, Ellis also judged that "even more generally divisive than the race issue —for all Catholics are not confronted by that problem—have been the liturgical changes which were adumbrated in the pontificate of Pope Pius XII but which received thorough and effective treatment only in Vatican Council II." After it the liturgical constitution went into effect. Indeed, it is not highly capricious to suggest that the First Sunday in Advent, 1964, the official chartering day, could be as symbolically important for Catholic popular life as the Israeli War was for Jews. "Few branches of the Church . . . have been under more tension because of the language and form of public worship than the American church."[19] True, later surveys consistently found that the majority of those who still came to Mass did welcome most of the changes. But these changes also had a "ripple effect" throughout private and social observance of the Catholic way.

Historian David J. O'Brien summarizes the ritual changes:

In 1960 the suggestion that perhaps some of the liturgy of the church might be translated into English stamped one as a 'kook' in Catholic circles. By 1970 not only had the entire liturgy been transferred to the vernacular, but laymen were demanding drastic reforms in the parish structure and free experimentation in the Mass. Singers and dancers appeared, and guitars, brass ensembles and bongo drums sounded forth from beneath dusty organs in neo-Gothic churches. Small groups of suburban Catholics followed their teen-age children to services in the inner city church that had become a center for community action, liturgical excitement and general religious and social nonconformity, while other ghetto churches stood nearly empty. Suburban churches no longer bulged with people and expanded their plants, and dissatisfied laymen began their own 'floating' or 'underground' parishes, meeting in private homes, club rooms or storefronts for community religious celebration, discussion of social and theological problems and development of *avant garde* sunday schools for the young.[20]

A few years later some of the wild experimentation had quieted and there were signs of some return to tradition in worship and structure, but it was impossible to go back to the patterns of 1960. Old behavioral injunctions that included diet, laws about marriage, divorce, days of obligation, and the like, also were changed, again with effect on the more liberated but also more confused laity. When on July 25, 1968, Pope Paul VI issued *Humanae Vitae*, a formal attempt to insist on old views of birth control, he created an even deeper crisis of confidence as most theologians questioned his argument while bishops found it important to assent to it. The old presumed monolith could not be leaned upon with the old security.

Ellis and other intellectuals greeted the changes with varying reactions, but all of them found it easier to adjust than did the majority of the millions of pew-sitters. They had sophisticated means of doing so and could quote, as Ellis did, John Henry Newman: "In a higher world it is otherwise, but here below to live is to change, and to be perfect is to have changed often." "The change is seen and experienced in every aspect of Catholic life: in the Church's approach to the world, in the style and manner of her apostolate to those outside her fold as well as to her own members, in the attitude of those members of the Church itself."[21]

There were losses from both left and right, from those who felt the Church moved too slowly and from those who were shocked by rapid change. What Ellis called "the psychological enclosure that surrounded the Catholics had remained practically unshaken" during the half century that Catholicism was becoming part of Herberg's "three-religion" but one-faith country. Now the enclosure was broken open. Suburbanization in the 1950s had begun the blurring. Attempts after the Vatican Council to repeal the changes were led by conscious traditionalists, but they generally failed, so implausible did they seem to the majority. Changes in attitude, location, and financial patterns brought trouble for the Catholic parochial schools, where the old behavioral styles had been nurtured. An intense but brief "generation gap" led to youths' defections from "the establishment." Ellis considered the old Catholicism to be irretrievable, though as an agent of change he kept some optimism about what survived.[22]

In *American Catholicism: Where Do We Go from Here?* George Devine summarized: "The average American Catholic no longer 'knew where he stood,' and the staggeringly complex and rigid superstructure of certain moral questions-and-answers seemed gone, probably to stay for good. Nothing could hope to duplicate it, but something would have to replace it."[23] One did not have to be a conservative partisan as was James Hitchcock to agree that nothing would replace it unless there would be some institutionalization of tradition: "Without institutionalization—of belief, of piety, of organization, of love—the Church can never be more than an ineffective, ephemeral reality."[24] Catholicism was in no danger of leaving the Mainline, but its place and the Mainline's place were less commanding and more challenged than before.

Until almost the middle of the twentieth century "Mainline" almost equalled Protestant and, at that, a certain kind of Protestant. This circumstance resulted from the facts of chronological priority and statistical dominance through most of American history, as well as Protestantism's power—which included the power to name what was in the main stream and what was not. Mainline Protestantism, acculturated, accommodated, acclimatized, after experiencing almost artificial prosperity in the 1950s, suffered relative losses ever after. Observers who lack historical perspective have made too much of the declines and setbacks, since many of them have as their only point of comparison the booming activities in the period of postwar expansion and religious revival.

One may as well note or argue that from the beginning or almost the beginning Mainline Protestantism has suffered relative decline as it regularly had to yield space to each new religious phenomenon. The colonial "Big Three," Congregationalism, Episcopalianism, and Presbyterianism, enjoyed the privileges and took on the burdens of establishment. But during the first half of the nineteenth century they lost out to the more successfully evangelistic Methodists, Baptists, and Disciples of Christ. The Southern Baptists and the right-wing Churches of Christ alone still grow from this family of religious forces, while other Methodists, Baptists, and Disciples were less successful at growing, in the late nineteenth century, than were the Catholics and the Lutherans, as immigrants arrived.

Mainline churches always have the advantage that in the years in which the official culture is secure and expansive, they are well off. On these terms, the Southern Baptists, doctrinally and morally more conservative than many, are certainly Southern Mainline; the Church of Jesus Christ of Latter-day Saints, sometimes called "the typical *Reader's Digest* religion," dominates in and around Utah, where it is the culture religion, and is socially acceptable elsewhere. These two groups have the best of both worlds, remaining "cognitively distant" with some theological norms while both producing and then embracing very worldly looking cultures. Mainline churches suffer in times of cultural crisis and disintegration, when they receive blame for what goes wrong in society but are bypassed when people look for new ways to achieve social identity and location. So they looked as good in the 1950s as they looked bad by the 1970s.

No one expects Mainline Protestants to be sidelined or to disappear, though some may remain demoralized and may dwindle into relative statistical insignificance—even as others remain at least locally strong, and recover when they find themselves with the help of cultural shifts. They were part of the ideology with which Americans "passed the hump of transition" to the approved social order that still binds them. Ernest Gellner has pointed out that such ideology "is likely to remain [the society's] nominal doctrines, thereafter,"[25] however transformed and ambiguous it may become. The churches that were identified with early America retain that status. Taken for granted, they cannot gain at the expense of the culture into which they merge. And they are too merged and blended to be needed by people who cannot find who they are or how to act while following the signals emitted by the larger culture.

To tell the story of the Mainline Protestants in the 1960s and 1970s would almost be to tell the story of the culture in travail itself. Because it was a period of polarization between at least two political forces, Protestantism divided. Thus competing attitudes about both black and white church involvements in the Civil Rights movements tore these churches apart, as did dissent over the Vietnamese War, the other decade-long preoccupation. Debate over "new morality" in the more intimate zones of life—sexual and family existence in particular—found acculturated Mainline members on both sides. If there was a brief "generation gap," the churches that looked too parental and established were victims of reactions.

Mainline Protestant vicissitudes and minor victories can all be appraised along the lines of all the surviving models of inquiry or zones of approach. The intellectual or theological set of questions applies to Protestants of these stripes, for they had been heirs and custodians of the longest and richest theological lineage in American history. But the last giants were dying now in America—Reinhold and H. Richard Niebuhr and Paul Tillich were all three to die in the sixties— and no one arrived to take their place, even as the influential Europeans who also were read in America were disappearing.

Meanwhile the theological school that prevailed with the breakup of Neo-Orthodoxy until around 1967 or 1968 could hardly have been designed with better genius to offer what the churches did not or did not long need: more means of fusing with the culture. Winthrop Hudson, in *his* revision for the seventies (compare Glazer and Ellis), looked back in 1973 on an ecclesiastical and theological movement that had only been taking shape when he had written the first edition of *Religion in America* in 1965. That earlier edition had had to end with comment on the tail-ending religious revival and Neoorthodoxy. But now he could already see in perspective their successors:

> The new 'secular' emphases and programs of the churches were scarcely calculated to stimulate church renewal and augment religious interest. The reductionism of 'secular theology' had scant appeal and little compelling power. Its most provocative slogan—'the death of God'—appeared at face value to be an announcement of the irrelevance of religion. Psychological therapy, moreover, was no monopoly of the church and required no return either to church or to 'religion.' Therapy groups were everywhere available to those who wished to embark upon the process of self-discovery. The 'secular city' (Gibson Winter's 'metropolis' as 'the new creation') thrust was more preoccupied with action than reflection, more interested in power than piety, more concerned with effecting political coalitions than with communicating Christian insight. Small wonder that these emphases were more productive of apathy than renewal, of dissidence than growth.[26]

The theologians soon moved on from the secular-worldly emphasis to new accents on "transcendence,"[27] but they were often outdistanced by the fundamentalist and non-Christian groups that advertise transcendence at the expense of the worldly commitments that Mainline Protestantism could not leave behind without denying its very character.

The period was not particularly creative institutionally, as denominationalism reemerged as the basic structure and ecumenism survived but suffered setbacks. Were one to concentrate on form and structure, the late sixties and early seventies would reveal little important change and the religious map could remain as it had been decades before. The institutional content or substance was, however, much directed to the political order, and some of the drama was there.

Hudson, again: "Most major Protestant bodies, including Episcopal, Methodist, and Presbyterian churches, experienced widespread dissension centering around social issues that was often referred to as a 'gap between clergy and laity.' "[28]

Debate about the degree to which this dissension contributed to the problems of the Mainline church will continue for decades. Empirical studies suggest that it was a major but not decisive contributor to the difficulties. Jeffrey Hadden, in the midst of the gathered storm, successfully demonstrated its existence by 1969 in *The Gathering Storm in the Churches*. He began, "The Christian churches today are in the midst of a struggle which has every evidence of being the most serious ferment in Christendom since the Protestant Reformation." He could still speak—too late, I believe—of residual "liberal euphoria" over ecumenism. But the church-unity people had turned their backs on developments *"which are threatening seriously to disrupt or alter existing church structures."* He quoted Gibson Winter who argued that the religious congregation was missing its mission. "The search for identity in the churches seems to be a grasp for traditional symbols by an uprooted and alienated social class." How, asked Winter, could an "inclusive message be mediated through an exclusive group?" Winter may have been theologically appropriate, from classic Christian points of view. But at that moment some Mainline Protestants were drifting from the churches because these had become too inclusive; they sought more exclusive congregations. Hadden found crises of "meaning and purpose," "belief," "authority," and the like, but concentrated on the gap in social postures.

Hadden did not carry the question of social location to all the Mainline Protestant members, but he did conclude with long passages on the clergyman's crises of identity: "Who am I?" Identity emerges, Hadden said, as a product of social interaction whereby the individual internalizes the attitudes and values of others toward the world around him as well as toward himself. This was now difficult to do because his communal values were in too much flux. Others lack a sense of who he is and what he is to do. The clergy had become too heterogeneous to be definable. His message: firm up, check your beliefs, relate better to the laity.[29]

The gathered storm broke. Five years later, when it was all over and everything had quieted in the political side of the churches, Harold E. Quinley followed up with a study of the aftermath. As Hadden had done before him, he piled graph upon graph to document the distances between the social activist clerics and their congregations. (Later, Mainline Protestants as a whole were regularly accused of having been too liberal or radical; no one seems to remember that in the surveys of the sixties the lay majority was unable to be differentiated from the American populace as a whole.) Quinley could only show that the political stance was one among many factors that led the California clerics in his sample to see their congregations dwindle, their youth head for society's new and more exotic religions.[30]

Hadden and Quinley both connected institutional losses and political tensions to theological disarray and showed how there was not enough cognitive distance between Mainline Protestant professions of faith or actual belief and the secular or pluralist culture around these churches. They did not devote as much systematic attention to the diffusion of identity that occurred because these churches could no longer prescribe or even describe distinctive behavior patterns, anything visible that might set people aside and give them the social location that other religions provided.

Once upon a time these behavioral marks were highly visible. Methodists had revivals and class meetings; they did not drink alcoholic beverages and they wanted to reform the world. Baptists insisted on immersing adults. Baptists and Disciples embodied the simple life and aspired to reproduce the moral codes of earliest Christianity. Episcopalians favored sedate liturgies. Not only did being a Mainline Protestant set you off from Catholics, Jews, and "the fringe," but being of one species of Protestantism distanced you from another species and provided habit, manner, custom, rule, and ritual.

No longer. It is true that, cognitively, enough difference remained between Protestant groups that, when members thought about it, they could think up something that removed them theologically from their ecumenical partners. Sociologists Charles Y. Glock and Rodney Stark even spoke of "the New Denominationalism" after having taken doctrinal soundings in California. They found so many differences on dogmatic points that they thought "we spin statistical fiction" if we speak of "Protestants" in social sciences at all. But they made less of the behavioral congruities between the denominations, congruities based upon the fact that most held little distinctively.

On the question whether "drinking liquor would definitely prevent salvation," eight Mainline groups answered "yes" with the following percentages: 2, 4, 2, 0, 2, 2, 9 (American Baptist), 1; the Southern Baptists' sample included 15 percent, and the sects, 35 percent! On whether the same salvation would be denied those who practiced birth control, the percentages were 0, 0, 2, 2, 1, 3, 1, 2, 5, 4, 2, and Roman Catholics stood out with what was then considered to be a very low figure, 23. This is a small survey, to be sure. The Mainline Protestants have grown quite tolerant and cannot picture much of anything preventing salvation. Neither drink nor practicing birth control may be the central behavioral tests they would have been in the same groups in the nineteenth century. But nothing has taken their place; on almost any other conceivable question of conduct and practice they will be found to be similar.[31]

Just as we saw the revisions of three basic histories to be events, so the publication in 1972 of Dean M. Kelley's book *Why Conservative Churches Are Growing* was symbolic of many particular studies and more uneasiness. The formal systematic sociologists tended to be condescending about the book; it was methodologically flawed, superficial, historically imperceptive, philosophically lacking. The strenuousness with which people had to work to ignore the book and the popularity of the same book with clergymen and lay leaders, however, indicate that Kelley had addressed their needs and much of what he presented was based in statistics and psychological studies. Rather than criticize the book, it is well to appraise it and see why it spoke to its moment.

The book, it was often said, could better have been titled *Why Mainline Churches Are Declining.* Conservative church leaders did not need it, except when they wanted to boast or warn. They did not need it as a manual of arms, since Kelley took lessons from them and not vice versa. The work helped them in advertisement; whereas once they had certified the truth of their faith because it was rejected by the world, now it became a sign of truth that so many accepted it.

Kelley's study had most impact in the nervous or demoralized Mainline Protestant churches, where it was read as a means of discerning what went wrong or for the clues as to what others were doing right. They were to learn that there was little they could imitate from the most successful, most strict sects. These were organized around what to Mainliners were outrageous and absurd doctrines that could not be appropriated even in transformation. And their behavioral exactions—think of Black Muslims, Jehovah's Witnesses, and Seventh Day Adventists and their limits as models of suburban Episcopalian or Methodist styles—were implausible. The Mainline people learned categories but not how to fill them.

Kelley began with depressing graphs about relative statistical decline in the established and conventional churches in contrast to the dramatic rise in percentage growth among the former "fringe" sects—a trend few had foreseen in that very decade when church people taught themselves to be relevant and modern and secular, in order to attract moderns and especially the young. It was especially the young who were drifting away toward Fundamentalism, Pentecostalism, or Eastern religions.

Kelley argued that churches, in order to attract, had to offer "meaning" and "belonging." Meaning came best through the world-views of "cognitive minorities" who shared little with those around them. And belonging, the expression of social identity and location, came when specific and rigid behavior was expected of every member of the group. Relativism in standards of conduct, diversity of permitted alternatives within, appreciation of dialogue, tolerance or lukewarmness, individualism, and reserve about one's religion were all marks of declining churches, while commitment, discipline, missionary zeal, absolutism, conformity, and fanaticism benefited those who embodied them.[32] Kelley's message was at least a lukewarm, "Go and do thou likewise!" to Mainline members.

If the record of Protestant, Catholic, and Jewish mainliners through the previous quarter century was any guide, it might be possible that they would buy this advice just at the moment when it would no longer be appropriate—just as they had styled themselves to blur boundaries at the very moment when everyone else wanted boundaries. In the prophet's eyes, the members should pay no attention to the psychosocial indications of a particular moment. Yet Mainliners and others alike do share the spirit of the times. The "sects" may have profited from cultural changes in the late 1960s and early 1970s just as the more established churches had exploited the moment Will Herberg had described during the revival in the 1950s.

Whether or not the question of social identity and location—in the fields of both meaning and belonging—would or could remain so intense over a prolonged period, or whether people would turn to religion at all to face them, are issues that must be left to predicters or future historians. Whether these questions are in the acute form of these years or in the chronic form displayed often in the history of religion, there does seem to be something permanent about the need for distance between traditions or institutions and their counterparts and competitors, as people ask "Who am I?" or "What am I?" Certainly, in a free society where religion is escapable, it is questionable whether many would take pains to continue to belong to groups that give them few reasons for adherence. When the Mainliners minimized their reasons, Americans began to take their quests to other locales on the map; these zones are the subjects of the rest of this book.

4 Evangelicalism and Fundamentalism

To look at American religion and to overlook Evangelicalism and Fundamentalism would be comparable to scanning the American physical landscape and missing the Rocky Mountains. The movements are large, rugged, commanding attention. To look at the two and to think of them as one on a religious map would be similar to drawing a physical features map without making topographic or ecological distinctions between Midwest farmlands and the Great Plains. For that reason it should seem foolish to suggest with any breathless sense of discovery that the Evangelical-Fundamentalist nexus is one of six main zones of religiosity in America. Yet one must exercise great care in discussing its survival, its transformations, and most of all the distinctions between the two forces within the combination.

Evangelicalism-Fundamentalism is the only one of the six elements that is only Protestant, a fact for which one need not apologize, given the Protestant provenance of so many features of American life. (Formally, structurally, and stylistically, one could point to an "evangelical" mode in Catholicism, in non-Christian sects, and even in Judaism, but that could bring with it many confusions because of the connotations or the historical and substantial differences.)

The American visitor equipped only with a map of denominations would have difficulty finding this conservative part of the spectrum. The *Yearbook of American and Canadian Churches 1975* lists only three or four "fundamental" denominations, including the Berean Fundamental Church, an almost invisible outcropping headquartered at North

Platte, Nebraska; the Fundamental Methodist Church, Inc., with a national membership of 724 in 14 congregations; and a Cicero, Illinois, organization of Independent Fundamental Churches of America, which towers above the others with up to 80,000 members.

The word "evangelical" signals the presence of Evangelicalism in few denominations. The Evangelical Church of North America, the Evangelical Congregational Church, the Evangelical Covenant Church of America, the Evangelical Free Church of America, the Evangelical Friends Alliance, the Evangelical Lutheran Church in America, the Evangelical Lutheran Synod, two Evangelical Mennonite groups, and the Evangelical Methodist Church taken together number only a couple hundred thousand members. There is listed also a cooperative National Association of Evangelicals which claims to service congregations and individuals in sixty denominations, but membership in the thirty-three complete denominations that make it up includes only two or three million citizens.[1]

If only two or three million people were involved, Evangelicalism would still rate attention, but it would have to be ranked not much larger than "the New Religions" on the religious map. The N.A.E., however, claims to represent indirectly about fifteen million people. Since so many Evangelicals and Fundamentalists are members of Mainline churches, one can only estimate wildly as to how many there are. One effort was made by Father Robert Campbell in 1968. He included a category called "Confessional," which would be at home in the Mainline groups, but many of whose members would probably have Evangelical sympathies. His estimate:

Fundamentalists	23.5	million
New Evangelical	15.5	million
Confessional	8.0	million
Liberal	20.0	million
Radical	0.1	million

He also reproduced an estimate by John Warwick Montgomery, a theologian strongly identified with Confessional-Evangelical movements; Montgomery's subdivision according to vocation is also of interest:

	Theologians	Pastors	Laity	Total
Fundamentalist	1%	20%	25%	17 million
Evangelical	55%	24%	20%	13.5 million
Confessional	20%	30%	30%	20.5 million
Liberal	20%	25%	25%	17 million
Radical	4%	1%	0.01%	5 to 10 thousand

These guesses were made on the basis of localized surveys such as those conducted in California by Charles Y. Glock and Rodney Stark. Regional differences may vary. Definitions in the minds of pollsters or interviewers and certainly of respondents are blurry. The predispositions and biases of the estimators cannot be disguised; witness the much larger group of Confessionals in Montgomery's than in Campbell's list.[2] Later surveys by Jeffrey Hadden and Harold E. Quinley do tend to confirm the general sense of Evangelical-Fundamentalist shares of the market, though each uses some different categories in his inquiries (for example, Neo-orthodox).[3] An overall assessment of polls, estimates, and guesses would leave the combination at least comparable in size to the Roman Catholic Church.

The Evangelicals and Fundamentalists, then, were located in a few small denominations, a number of large inter-church agencies, and throughout church bodies of conservative temperament as well as in Mainline churches. They are generally committed to what they perceive to be traditional Protestant points of view and styles of living. They have been generally resistant to most of the ideological features of modernity, having opposed theories of evolution, the practice of historical and critical methods of Biblical interpretatation, and the like. If it is easier to define them in the light of what they oppose, it is also possible to say that on the positive side most of them are united by their accent on a conversion experience and on the personal experience of salvation in Jesus Christ. They couple this with a concern for doctrinal orthodoxy and a generally conservative view of personal morality unaccompanied by much passion for churchly engagement with social issues. To those wholly unfamiliar with the American lay of the land it often suffices to provide a first clue: the Evangelicals are people who find evangelist Billy Graham or his viewpoints acceptable. The Fundamentalists would agree with most of his doctrine but separate from him on most other grounds.

Evangelicalism and moderate Fundamentalism occupy curious places in American religious mythology. In the proclamations of evangelists who stimulated conversion and pastors or theologians who would distance the church from "the world," their movement is a force of massive resistance against the world and the culture. "Be not conformed to this world, but be transformed by the renewal of your mind"; this biblical text from Romans 12:2 would typically be cited as the norm and the goal for Evangelical-Fundamentalist attitudes.

In practice, as far as students of both political and social behavior are concerned, anything but such distancing occurs. The combination belongs to the American "old family album" along with Fourth of July celebrations and ice cream cones. Despite the calls to people to come out of the world to Christ, being converted and joining an Evangelical church securely places the new members in a safe American-world context. They withhold consent from features of life that manifestly run against their theological or moral convictions; to illustrate, they would regularly speak out against pornography. But on the macropolitical scale they cannot be sorted out from the rest of the population. Every survey confirms what Franklin H. Littell observed in 1962:

Many of the groups which continued to use the language [of classical mass evangelism] without standing for the context of the message of repentance and conversion have become impassioned champions of the American way of life. . . . In the present controversies the heirs of the liberal tradition of culture-religion have frequently carried the message of prophetic discontinuity, while avowed "Fundamentalists" justify the *status quo*.[4]

For Evangelicals to feel at home in America should not be a surprise, since they built so much of it. As long ago as the Second Great Awakening of the early nineteenth century, according to the researches and suggestions of Jerald C. Brauer and his students, evangelical revivals were initiation rites into the larger culture, not exit ceremonies from it.[5] The acceptance in the polls of Billy Graham as the perennial "second most-admired man in America" and his appeal to non-Protestant and even non-Christian "Middle America," added to his base in Evangelicalism, suggest the absence of what Littell calls "prophetic discontinuity."[6]

In the late 1960s, in the midst of the rise to prominence of what we shall later call the New Religions (occult, Eastern, African, American Indian), after an early period of disengagement from the culture, many young people "came home" to Christianity. Significantly, their access was through "Jesus freak" and other Jesus movements. The counter cultural phase lasted only a couple of years or so; by the time the media began to lose interest most of these young people had settled back not into liberal forms of Protestantism, designed to be relevant to them, but to Evangelical, Fundamentalist, or Pentecostal styles.[7]

In order to point to the transformations in both Evangelicalism and Fundamentalism in the late 1960s and early 1970s, it will be necessary to discern their roots. Both feel that they are fully incarnating the general shape and intention of the Bible and especially of the first generation of the Christian church. Both want to be seen as sharing the sixteenth-century Protestant evangelical witness, though some of them (for example, Christian Churches and other heirs of nineteenth-century "primitive Gospel" causes) try to be non-traditional or ahistorical in outlook. They all share lineage in eighteenth- and nineteenth-century American revivalism.

By the middle of the nineteenth century, although no one would have been called Fundamentalist, most Protestants called themselves Evangelical, which then could have been equated with "Mainline Protestant." Robert Baird, in *Religion in America*, simply divided his map into "Evangelical" and "Nonevangelical" spheres, relegating only a few minuscule Protestant churches like Unitarianism and Universalism to the latter camp.[8] During the second half of the century Evangelicalism began to split into liberal and conservative forces, both of which could claim that they were drawing on authentic features of a common heritage. But the differences were institutionalized by 1908, when the Federal Council of Churches was formed to bring together the social endeavors of the more liberal churches. The conservatives counter-organized and began to harden into a Fundamentalist movement.

The lines of division were never completely clear. The liberals were more interested in social issues, while the conservatives ruled out all but the private—unless a public issue directly fell into the orbit of earlier Evangelical interest, as was the case with prohibition of alcoholic beverages. The liberals wanted to accommodate to or interpret and transform evolution, criticism, and some socialisms. The conservatives resisted all these efforts, though most of them did turn out to be Social Darwinists without the overt help of Charles Darwin. By 1913 the circulation of some booklets called *The Fundamentals* gave the hard-liners a name and a battle line for the celebrated denominational controversies of the 1920s. The Modernists, as they were called, won most of these, and the Fundamentalists either remained to sulk in the old churches or they moved off to found new churches or a parallel set of Bible colleges, missionary agencies, and the like.

Many observers of American culture seemed to think that Fundamentalists would not be heard from again. They were obscurantists, victims of cultural lag, deviants from the main line of historical development, and often boors. But the dismissal was ill-grounded and certainly premature. For one thing, the Modernist party had been misnamed; there were only a few overt and militant "Modernist" theologians. Even "Liberal" may be a false categorization. The liberal churches were based in the older evangelicalism. Many people of undisguised evangelical sentiments remained in their churches. Meanwhile, splits were occurring between the apparent losers of the 1920s. Many found that they did not really belong with the noisier Fundamentalists; other Fundamentalists learned new manners or underwent experiences of change.

When they again surfaced in the 1940s the split was institutionalized. The American Council of Christian Churches, made up of the more intransigent elements, organized on "militantly pro-Gospel and anti-modernist" lines on September 17, 1941. What became the National Association of Evangelicals grew out of a meeting held on October 27–28, 1941. Much of the difference from the first was best discerned on behavioral grounds; even the intentions of the N.A.E. showed this. Its leaders were "determined to break with apostasy but . . . wanted no dog-in-the-manger, reactionary, negative, or destructive type of organization." (They had Fundamentalism in mind.) They sought instead one that was "determined to shun all forms of bigotry, intolerance, misrepresentation, hate, jealousy, false judgment, and hypocrisy."[9]

After World War II more nonpartisans began to become aware of a separate party, then called New Evangelicals or Neo-Evangelical, as named by a Boston minister, Harold Ockenga. Then came Billy Graham to give it more visibility, and editor Carl F. H. Henry and *Christianity Today* to provide a cultural and theological rallying point. The generalized revival of interest in religion during the Eisenhower era worked to the benefit of people holding these positions. When their movement first crested after the mid-fifties, it was difficult for outsiders to separate the two sometimes overlapping but often conflicting conservative Protestant strands.

Charles Clayton Morrison, doughty warrior and leader of the Modernist troops in the 1920s, came out of retirement to write an editorial (unsigned) for *The Christian Century*. The editorial merits citation today because it is so representative of the people who saw the Fundamentalist revival to be at the heart of the new surge; the better manners looked like a disguise or a public relations stunt. Morrison saw in Graham's New York revival and its accompaniments a "portentous development to which the nation's press and most of its churches are curiously blind. . . . The narrow and divisive creed which the churches rejected a generation ago is staging a comeback." With some prophetic skill he predicted that "if their effort succeeds it will make mincemeat of the ecumenical movement, will divide congregations and denominations, will [and here he signals his progressivist philosophy of history] set back Protestant Christianity a half-century." He properly knew that not only the Evangelicals had a claim on evangelicalism:

> The historic Christian concern for evangelical outreach
> is being assigned to partisans whose interpretation of
> their aim leaves out our equally historic, equally Christian,
> equally evangelical concern for societies, institutions,
> cultures. . . . Protestants, rightly eager to let every opinion
> be heard, are letting themselves be identified with a
> discredited and disavowed version of Christianity.

In a rather long passage he then quite accurately showed how on the cognitive level the New Evangelicalism differed not at all from the old Fundamentalism, which he associated with belief in "(1) the virgin birth of Jesus; (2) the in-

fallible inerrancy of the Bible in every detail; (3) the resur-
rection of the physical body of Jesus and of the saints at the
end of history; (4) the substitutionary blood atonement;
and (5) the imminent return of Christ in person to establish
his kingdom."

Morrison foresaw prosperity for the discredited Fundamentalists because of Billy Graham, the emergence of conservative Protestant groups moving out of ethnic isolation
(presumably chiefly Lutherans), the climate of "superficial
religiosity," and new organizations of Evangelicals.

> It is instructive to note that increasingly fundamentalism
> seeks to press the good word "evangelical" into its service.
> Having by its dogmatism made a once favorable term
> obnoxious, it is trying to appropriate a designation
> which is in better repute. . . . By changing its name to
> "evangelical" yet holding on to its unevangelical creed,
> fundamentalism unchurches the church.[10]

The battle over the name continued for some years and
sounds of mopping-up operations are still heard. Many participants in and observers of church life, I among them, have
only grudgingly yielded them their chosen designation, having long preferred the earlier term Neo-Evangelical. This
attitude was based not on a theological judgment that they
were in no way evangelical but rather that it is confusing
to allow them a monopoly on a word locked in validly to so
many histories of so many churches and movements that
are not part of their outlook. Eventually, however, one gives
in to sociological necessity; the term has won acceptance
as a handy if still confusing and not always appropriate
name.

In the early 1960s the conservative force continued to
grow, but it moved out of the spotlight with the end of the
Eisenhower revival. Now curiosity and media attention
shifted elsewhere: to the Catholicism of President John F.
Kennedy and the Second Vatican Council of Pope John; to

Martin Luther King and the Civil Rights struggles as these absorbed the churches; to social activism in general; to radical theological experiment; to religious identifications with the New Frontier and the Great Society; to the beginnings of dissent against increasing involvement in Southeast Asia; to liturgical and artistic experiment; to "the new morality" in *The Secular City*; to theologians who wanted to be *Honest to God* but ended with *The Death of God*. In this heady atmosphere Billy Graham endured and prospered, but he looked like "the same old thing." Political Evangelicalism and, more, Fundamentalism tied themselves to the discredited conservative Republican cause in the Barry Goldwater campaign of 1964, and seemed to have been compromised thereby.

Just as *The Christian Century* editorial provided a Distant Early Warning signal in 1957, another journal article manifested a mid-decade view of a sober analyst and prepared one to understand the more enthusiastic prophecies of advocates in the liberal camp. The article appeared in a historic issue of *Daedalus*, where it was upstaged along with other pieces by Robert N. Bellah's now classic essay on Civil Religion, about which we shall have occasion to speak later. While the journal appeared in winter, 1967, it reflected mid-decade views propounded at conferences held at Boston in 1965.

The author was William G. McLoughlin, regarded as the historian best equipped to tell the story of Evangelism and Evangelicalism. To speak of sober analysts is to point to people like McLoughlin, who had impeccable scholarly credentials and were well-trained to protect themselves against too broad generalizations or wild projections. He chose to ask, "Is There a Third Force in Christendom?" As we shall see in the next chapter, *Life* magazine in 1958 had published an article on new Pentecostalism; its author, Henry Pitney Van Dusen, also included some "fringe-sect" and fundamentalist groups in that category, but McLoughlin chose to speak much less of Pentecostalism and much more of Evangelicalism and Fundamentalism in the context of a "Third Force."

McLoughlin noted, as we already have, that in the broad sense Evangelicalism is often seen as a kind of normative American faith or, better, it is even regarded as what people "get" when they really "get religion." (To get religion, according to H. L. Mencken, was an American act that inspired that new term.) Americans, wrote McLoughlin, have always measured faith in terms of the "activistic, enthusiastic self-commitment exemplified by the fringe sects. Not even the Liberal Protestants seemed to question these criteria." He then presented his perspective on the conservative forces:

> Americans have unquestionably been going through a major reorientation in religious outlook during the past twenty years. We are still too close to this shift to see it in historical perspective. But it seems apparent that the pietistic upthrust by fringe-sect dissenters and come-outers does not in itself constitute the creation of a significant new religious movement in Christendom. Rather, the fringe sects appear to be the usual and inevitable emotional and institutional effluvia of a major alteration within Christendom. They may be a comment upon the confused state of religion and world affairs in this generation, but they do not constitute a dynamic new force capable of replacing or seriously threatening the old order.

More important were the flexibilities and vitalities of Mainline, including post-Vatican II Catholic, churches. "The fringe groups . . . refuse to face reality and try to deny or thwart change. And their appeal seems limited to those least willing or capable of contributing to a new religious or social order." Ten years later the promoters of Evangelicalism and Fundamentalism could boast that they were succeeding. They saw themselves as a "dynamic new force." Whether or not

McLoughlin is correct in his long-range projection—and there are good reasons to see that the conservatives are exploiting a particular *Zeitgeist* that may itself be ephemeral—on the short range they were securely establishing their place on the American religious map in ways that he and most other observers did not or could not perceive in 1965.

Professor McLoughlin tried several means for measuring the conservative efforts; there were few clear outlines. Theologically they were divided within, and many distinctions which they claimed were held as well by Roman Catholics and high-church Episcopalians who could "be as dogmatic as any pentecostalist about the miraculous or 'mysterious' in Christianity" while "highly sophisticated theologians can be very dogmatic about the Trinity or the Virgin Birth." A second measure, the psychological, is unsatisfying. Many liberals, even the extreme Transcendentalists, experience the mystical; and many Fundamentalists are sedate and not ecstatic. Sociological class distinctions still inform, but are not completely helpful, nor are definitions of "church" and "sect." Church polity tells almost nothing.

His fifth measurement, which sees the continuum "within a specific historical framework," the "moving main stream of America's pietistic culture," satisfies him best. He locates the nexus in a subculture and does not see it as its spokespersons do, as "a force that is capable of significantly altering a culture or that is symptomatic of a significant new shift in the dynamics of a culture." "Probably the high-tide of this neo-evangelical 'third force' was the selection of Barry Goldwater as the Republican candidate for the Presidency in 1964."[11]

Hardly ten years later the Neo-Evangelicals claimed to have captured Washington. James C. Hefley and Edward E. Plowman boasted in *Washington: Christians in the Corridors of Power* (1975) that Evangelicals had swept away other religious styles and could claim most actively religious Protestant politicians from President Gerald R. Ford on down. The authors quoted Illinois congressman John Anderson, who, before he set out to criticize the evangelicals for their failure to live up to their new status, described that status in triumphal terms. Anderson had said:

> It was *they* [the liberals] who denied the supernatural acts of God, conforming the gospel to the canons of modern science. It was *they* who advocated laws and legislation as the modern substitutionary atonement for the sins of mankind. . . . It was *they* who were the friends of those in positions of political power. *They* were the 'beautiful people,' and *we*—you will recall— were the 'kooks.' We were regarded as rural, reactionary, illiterate fundamentalists who just didn't know better.
>
> Well, things have changed. Now *they* are the 'kooks'— and *we* are the 'beautiful people.' *Our* prayer breakfasts are so popular that only those with engraved invitations are allowed to attend. *Our* evangelists have the ready ear of those in positions of highest authority. *Our* churches are growing and theirs are withering. . . . *They* are tired, worn-out 19th century liberals trying to repair the pieces of an optimism shattered by world wars, race riots, population explosion, and the spectre of worldwide famine. *We* always knew that things would get worse before the Lord came again.[12]

If this is the kind of pride that goeth before a fall, his audience at the National Association of Evangelicals convention in Boston in 1974 may not have recognized it. In their eye the McLoughlins and the other scholars had been discomfited, along with the hated Mainliners whom Anderson called "liberals."

Between 1965 and 1975 the new Evangelicals and many of the Fundamentalists experienced a new resurgence while the Mainline churches suffered setbacks. The characteristic book-titles about Protestantism in this period were *The Gathering Storm in the Churches; To Comfort and to Challenge: A Dilemma of the Contemporary Church; The Prophetic Clergy; The Jesus Revolution; The Evangelical*

Renaissance; and, best known, the already mentioned *Why Conservative Churches Are Growing*.[13] "The gathering storm" favored the conservative factions who were the "comforters" against the disfavored "challengers." The prophetic clergy had been dispersed or were in disarray; the Jesus revolution led to Evangelical prosperity. Harold E. Quinley, as he watched the prophetic clergy dwindle, saw chiefly "the continuing lay backlash," "a spiritual revival," "liberal losses," and "retrenchment and decentralization."

Dean Kelley looked back on the prophecies of the midsixties:

> we have noted three assessments of obsolescence in the churches: (1) modern man no longer needs religion; or (2) even if he wants religion, he no longer needs churches; or (3) even if he wants religion and churches, he doesn't want those with (*a*) absurd beliefs, (*b*) unreasonable requirements, (*c*) irrelevant preoccupations, or (*d*) invidious distinctions between those who belong and those who don't.

Yet these axioms of the prevailing wisdom *"are directly contrary to the evidence." "Not all religious bodies are declining."* He then listed Evangelical, Fundamentalist, Pentecostal, and even a few non-Christian groups that were growing.[14]

Not all of them were growing for the same reasons, nor were they all like each other. Pentecostalists will be isolated in the next chapter; here it is necessary to map the differences between the two multimillion member camps. Charles Clayton Morrison, using the first model for analysis, the intellectual or theological, saw none—and he was correct. William G. McLoughlin, experimenting with the same paradigm, thought that the lines were far too blurry for theological analysis to be of much help, and he was equally correct. Partisans, as we shall see, agree. Both sides share central cognitive features of the faith with each other and with outsiders so far as both are concerned.

The second or formal institutional approach offers little more help. To the narrative historian it is interesting and valid to trace the new denominations, interchurch agencies, crusades, Bible colleges, missionary sponsors, and publishing ventures. But these are not structurally distinctive; they do not define, since they are variations on each others' and on others' themes.

The third or political angle of vision begins to be of more help because it has to do with attitudes, styles, conduct, and manners. While both are normally seen to be conservative (though many Evangelicals and Fundamentalists through the years have voted for the New Deal and for progressive legislation, as citizens and not as representatives of their churches), Evangelicals are closer to the political mainstream, while almost all radical rightists and those dismissed by others as demagogues come out of Fundamentalism. Erling Jorstad speaks of their efforts as *The Politics of Doomsday*. The American Council of Christian Churches, the American Council of Christian Laymen, Edgar C. Bundy, the Christian Anti-Communism Crusade, *Christian Beacon, The Christian Crusade*, the Church League of America, Billy James Hargis, the International Council of Churches, Carl McIntire, and the rest of his indexed roll call are or attract Fundamentalists, not Evangelicals.

Just as the Evangelicals are embarrassed by the extremism, so are they criticized by the Fundamentalist doomsdayers and doomsayers. According to Jorstad, "the new evangelicals, made up primarily of members of the National Association of Evangelicals are, in McIntire's judgment, 'more abusive and do more harm to the cause of the Gospel and the purity of the Church than do the liberals themselves.' "[15] The Evangelicals preferred the politics of Dwight Eisenhower, Gerald Ford, and—until the last days of the Watergate scandal—Richard Nixon. Lowell D. Streiker and Gerald S. Strober better described their mood in *Religion and the New Majority*.[16]

The two orthodoxies have different orthopraxises; that is, while Evangelicalism and Fundamentalism share the same cognitive propositions, they practice their beliefs in such different ways that one must go beyond their inherited dogmatic formulations to find what they really believe. And they do turn out, in the end, to believe on "non-Fundamentals" vastly different things about conduct, relation to other Christians, the social posture of churches, and even cultural expressions—almost anything not codified in the proverbial five points of Fundamentalism or the fourteen that historian Ernest Sandeen isolated.[17]

Scholars and spokespersons in Evangelicalism are aware of the basis for most distinctions. Thus Donald Bloesch in *The Evangelical Renaissance* spoke of the new Evangelicalism as "a mood and not a theological system." His treatment displayed so many differences from Fundamentalism that mood overwhelmed vestiges of kinships.[18]

In *The Young Evangelicals* another advocate, Richard Quebedeaux, correctly observed that "varieties of Orthodox Christianity have undergone modification to some degree in the finer points of theology, and, *more profoundly, in their attitudes toward culture.*" [italics mine] He complained that

> for too long it has been the fault of mainstream Ecumenical Liberalism to lump together with pejorative intent *all* theological conservatives into the worn Fundamentalist category. In general, Evangelicals resent being called Fundamentalists, and Fundamentalists likewise do not usually appreciate the Evangelical designation.[19]

Carl F. H. Henry, one of the older new Evangelicals and the man least likely to slight the cognitive features of faith, as early as 1957, the year in which Charles Clayton Morrison was leading a counter attack, noted that "by mid-century, fundamentalism obviously *signified a temperament as fully as a theology.*" [italics mine] While some Evangelicals had "courageously" stayed with Fundamentalism through the lonely years of its age-old battle against unbelief, others, "weary of the spirit of strife," declared that "fundamentalism is dead." Evangelicals should repent of the excesses of Fundamentalism just as Neo-Orthodox leaders had had the decency to regret the excesses of antecedent and sometimes still strong liberalism. He called for a new "mind-set and a new method in ecclesiastical life."[20]

Nine years later Henry was to criticize the liberties some Evangelicals took with their new freedom from Fundamentalism. Too many of them were finding more congenial company among the once-despised liberals than they were with each other or with their old kin, the Fundamentalists. He warned that "it would be naive to argue . . . that liberals and evangelicals need each other for complementary emphases." Alliances might alter biblical doctrine and produce Christian support of the welfare state. To him, Evangelicalism represented catholicity, all that the Church was or needed.[21]

If the Evangelicals did not always link up with representatives of the Mainline, they did copy many features of the liberal and moderate church life that they had once scorned— to the universal consternation of the Fundamentalists. The best illustration is their copying of the ecumenical style they had shunned previously. From 1941 to 1973 they tried to live up to the N.A.E. motto reproduced in a book title, *Cooperation without Compromise*.[22] Gradually they learned that there was no such thing, even if compromise meant no more than agreeing to disagree, than being silent over volatile matters. Many Mainline Protestants, for instance, considered sacramental definitions to be integral to the life of the church, to be "fundamentals." The Evangelicals disagreed with each other so much on these that they rarely brought them up and accented other fundamentals. Their common efforts led them more and more into what looked to all the world like the compromises they had abhorred.

In 1973, after several years of preparatory effort, they launched "Key 73," with the slogan, "Calling a Continent to Christ." Generally a failure as an evangelistic enterprise, it succeeded in familiarizing many Evangelicals with ecumenical goals and practices, as Mainline Protestants and even conservative Roman Catholics shared the common effort. While the Evangelicals gerrymandered their polities and made a point that they were theologically uncompromising, the Fundamentalists regularly charged that they had adopted the ecumenical style.

In explicitly moving forward in ecumenical life, as they did again in Switzerland at a conference that came to be known as "Lausanne '74," where they engaged in theological compromise over their statement of biblical inerrancy, Evangelicals were resuming their nineteenth-century postures. Much of the antecedency of the movement had grown out of what one historian called "an errand of mercy"—a layled, intercontinental and inter- or non-denominational network of reform, benevolent, and evangelistic forces.[23] There had already been an Evangelical Alliance in 1846. Evangelicals had been behind at least the missionary side of the twentieth-century ecumenical movement's launching in 1910 at Edinburgh. They lost interest as the movement in most of its forms adopted theological positions or took social stands with which they did not agree.

Fundamentalists consistently opposed the renewed ecumenism by Evangelicals. They were proudly separatistic and even schismatic. They would cooperate for joint defense or aggression but only on pragmatic grounds. Pragmatic grounds could justify no churchly association with non-Fundamentalists, especially with the Evangelicals, since more confusion could result from some alliances than from engagements with more remote styles and forces. In a manual on Fundamentalism, Thomas E. Baker attacked "new evangelicalism" because it "violates the plain teaching of scripture" in its "departure from the truth of separation from unbelief."

Taking the attack, Baker said that Evangelicalism itself had "brought a major 'division' in the ranks of Fundamen-

talism as well as a minor division in the philosophies of
Liberalism and Neo-Orthodoxy." He was puzzled as to how
to handle the erring Evangelical, for the Fundamentalist "is
not dealing with an unbeliever, but one who believes most of
the basic fundamental truths of scripture." He could not dis-
associate himself doctrinally from their general position. But
when they dealt with Pentecostals, non-Calvinists, and clergy
from Communist countries, as he saw them doing, they "revealed the same attitude that prevailed in Liberalism." "Cooperation of belief with unbelief in Ecumenism would produce ecumenical babylon." Indeed, "this is exactly what took
place." Fundamentalists dared not allow Evangelicals to
share their pulpits. Such practice was unscriptural. It was not
necessary. No benefit ensued. "The invisible line must be
drawn and kept drawn at all times between fundamentalist
and New Evangelical, even when the fundamentalist feels
strong enough through growth spiritually, numerically or fi-
nancially."[24]

A New Evangelical founder, Harold Ockenga, has always
answered in kind. "The order of the day for fundamentalism" is "fragmentation, segregation, separation, criticism,
censoriousness, suspicion, solecism." Millard Erickson la-
ments that Fundamentalists have forgotten that "there are
only two justifiable grounds for separation from an existing
denomination: eviction or apostasy." Yet they split off "on
the basis of personality or minor creedal items." "The new
evangelicals are not separatists in the sense of seeking to
withdraw from any slight taint of heterodoxy or worldliness."
Bruce Shelley criticized, along with Fundamentalism's "wow-
ser" worship, its cultural isolationism, its sectarian separat-
ism, its monastic ethics, its theological hair-splitting."[25]

Here is a first instance where consistent behavioral change
(vigencias, conduct and binding customs) was having an effect on creencias, the deepest beliefs. As Evangelicals had
more practice at ecumenism, they began to express a theology of church cooperation and unity that differed from Fun-

damentalism's. Or one could argue as readily that they were reverting to nineteenth-century beliefs from which Fundamentalists departed, beliefs that had been long suppressed or repressed but that could not permanently fail to find expression in practice.

The second field where belief and practice divided the two conservative clusters, beyond the bounds of their five or fourteen doctrinal points but not far from the center of theological affirmations in general, is social attitudes and activities. Thanks to men like Carl F. H. Henry in the first wave of New Evangelicalism in the 1950s there was at least a beginning of talk about ethical responsiveness beyond the merely private sphere. His *Christianity Today*, while criticizing liberal church people for taking political stands, also took them. "Not to take a stand is a stand," but the magazine was more positive than that statement implies; its stands were often conservative, but they were rich in commitment. Fundamentalists, on the other hand, often because of their premillennial views and the expectation of Christ's early return, kept their corporate distance from the social field.

Many Evangelicals are also premillennialist, but they do not let their belief on this point keep them from making social comment. Millard Erickson attacked Fundamentalism: "During its long history orthodox, or conservative, Christianity had stressed the application of its message to social ills. . . . As the twentieth century moved on, however, fundamentalism neglected this emphasis. . . . The fundamentalist seemed to be . . . passing suffering humanity."

Pioneer Harold Ockenga in the first generation had written:

> The new evangelicalism embraces the full orthodoxy of fundamentalism, but manifests a social consciousness and responsibility which was strangely absent from fundamentalism. The new evangelicalism concerns itself not only with personal salvation, doctrinal truth and an eternal point of reference, but also with the problems of race, of

war, of class struggle, of liquor control, of juvenile delinquency, of immorality, and of national imperialism. . . .
The new evangelicalism believes that orthodox Christians
cannot abdicate their responsibility in the social scene.[26]

Sherwood Eliott Wirt and Leighton Ford, both closely associated with Billy Graham, regularly spoke up on this
theme, to the consternation of Fundamentalists. But it was a
group small in size but effectively vocal in second generation
Evangelicalism that converged with fresh emphasis on social
themes. Richard Quebedeaux, Richard V. Pierard, Richard
J. Mouw, the editors of *The Reformed Journal*, the Southern
Baptist Convention's Christian Life Commission, the authors
of the (1973) Chicago Declaration of Social Concern, a
more radical group that edited *The Post-American*, and
others, took up the theme that helped part the two conservative camps. Both sides were proud of their stand. Each accepted the other's depiction of that stand.

Evangelicals had a style distinctive from that of Mainline
churches. They were more mistrustful of lobbies, of denominational pronouncements, of elitism in leadership ranks, of
bureaucratization of the social impulse, and of reflexive resort to legislation. They proposed more individual responsibility, voluntary initiative, prophetic criticism without programs. But the differences came to be more those of degree
than of kind.

As in the ecumenical instance, one must ask at some stage
whether doctrinal unity in the orthodox camp has not died
the death of a thousand qualifications. Admittedly, the focus
here has been on elites, and the followers of both may be
nearer each other than are the leaders. But the leaders gave
expression to different views of the human *polis* and the
divine intention for it; theologically they were here again
divided.

The line is somewhat more eroded in the fields of literature, the arts, and cultural analysis. In general and with some impressive exceptions (including some features of life at the Fundamentalist stronghold Bob Jones University, which encourages the arts) the Evangelicals take more positive interests and aspire higher in these fields than do the Fundamentalists. Despite all the efforts, however, it must be said that the larger public takes no notice of the artifacts, paintings, sculptures, poems, dramas, or novels of the Evangelical subculture. The extent of the attention paid the convert C. S. Lewis, favored by Evangelicals, suggests the general poverty in the camp beyond Lewis. (These are also, however, not decades in which to boast about what has been coming from Mainline religion, either.)

Fundamentalism, while it has been spelled out by some people of learning and scholarship, is professedly more anti-intellectual than cultured Evangelicalism at its best. G. B. Wurth, on the other hand, saw Fundamentalism falling into "a morbid and sickly enthusiasm." It embodied, added Carl Henry, "an uncritical antithesis between the heart and the head," a "belittling" of the intellect. It "neglected the production of great exegetical and theological literature," and reprinted only works from the past. Therefore, "if modernism stands discredited as a perversion of scriptural theology, certainly fundamentalism in this contemporary expression stands discredited as a perversion of the biblical spirit."[27]

While Fundamentalists built the Bible colleges, Evangelicals did their best to nurture several liberal arts schools, and progressively more gained doctorates at prestigious European and American universities. Their scholarly societies became comparable to many secular ones, except for their creedal demands on members.

When people start speaking of each other's cultural attitudes as "a perversion of the biblical spirit," their speech also signals different theologies. These show up finally in what might be called styles or ways of life, codes of conduct, habits and manners. Some within the Evangelical camp felt that their fellow-believers had gone too far in their embrace of worldliness; Fundamentalists were more able to resist it. With the successes of the fifties and sixties came cultural responsibilities and opportunities that led to many accommodations to the world as it was, accommodations often glossed over with a few quoted passages of the Bible.

A. W. Tozer saw emergent Evangelical culture-religion to be "fascinated by the great, noisy, aggressive world with its big name, its hero worship, its wealth and garish pageantry." A Fundamentalist minister made national headlines by allowing his daughter to wear a bathing suit in a beauty contest and by then being reprimanded by his congregation. Evangelicals, on the contrary, pushed their daughters forward and boasted about their witness for Christ in their bathing suits. Donald Bloesch, a responsible spokesman, was disconcerted by

> the carnality and frivolity in much modern-day popular
> evangelical religion. This can be seen in the glorification
> of beauty queens and athletes who happen to be Christian.
> It is also noticeable in the fascination of many evangeli-
> cals with public relations and showmanship. In some
> schools and churches technique and method are valued
> more highly than right doctrine, and group dynamics
> is given more attention than prayer and other spiritual
> disciplines. The popularity of gospel rock groups that
> appeal to the sensual side of man is yet another indication
> of accommodation to worldly standards. Culture-religion
> is also evident in the camaraderie between some evan-
> gelical leaders and right-wing politicians.

The Tozers and the Bloesches sometimes tried to link the ideational and the behavioral, or to connect internal and external behavior. Why the worldliness? Could it be that millions of disappointed persons who never found worldly glory sought to gain their heart's desire in the realm of social acceptance, publicity, success in sports or business or entertainment? "All this on earth and heaven at last. Certainly no insurance company can offer half as much." Nor could Mainline religion.[28]

Fundamentalism was less celebrity-conscious, perhaps because it attracted fewer celebrities. But it did indulge in showmanship and public relations, as a glance at Saturday newspapers in any "Bible Belt" city would show. But Fundamentalism was more uneasy about its covert carnality and leaned more toward what H. Richard Niebuhr called models associated with "Christ against Culture," as Evangelicals leaned toward "Christ Transforming Culture."[29]

Evangelicals came to criticize the more codified moralism of their counterparts and competitors. Daniel Stevick, in a book significantly titled *Beyond Fundamentalism*, quoted Carl Henry:

> "The Fundamentalist catalogue of 'sins' is small and specific: commercial movies, dancing, gambling, card-playing, drinking beer or wine or liquor, and smoking. No 'spiritual Christian' will presumably do any of these things, and generally will have little to do with anyone who does do them. Everyone who grows up in this tradition finds that it has a vise-like grip on him. His conscience has been made sensitive to these things by the never-ending tirade against them."

Evangelicals are not entirely nonlegalistic and certainly not libertarian, but they feel that instead of a "childish reaction into a uniformly opposite pattern of behavior," there should be a "variety of practice that indicates life, color, and the freedom for each person to be himself." The Fundamentalist, believing that his or her practices alone are scripturally grounded, has to believe that such variety represents apostasy.[30]

Bloesch summarized the Evangelical self-criticism: "When evangelicalism becomes respectable and even fashionable, then the temptation to accommodate to the values and goals of the world becomes almost overwhelming."[31] And Carl

Henry made the final judgment on Fundamentalist style and conduct, saying that "the real bankruptcy of fundamentalism has resulted not so much from a reactionary spirit—lamentable as this was—as from a harsh temperament, a spirit of lovelessness and strife contributed by much of its leadership in the recent past. . . . It is this character of fundamentalism as a temperament, and not primarily fundamentalism as a theology, which has brought the movement into contemporary discredit."[32] While Henry minimized theology as an offense, one must again ask whether the deepest behavior patterns are not also rooted in differing views of order and meaning. If they are, as we are consistently hypothesizing, then the second question is: are not the doctrinal similarities between the two systems only partial descriptions of their whole theological outlooks? And are not even these parts held so differently that they alert us to look for competing world views so opposed that the distinctions again have to be called theological?

These are questions whose answers will unfold more clearly in the years ahead. Even if "the pietistic upthrust," as McLoughlin spoke of it, downthrusts soon and fails to provide an alternative ordering of the world, after ten years of a second resurgence the combination of Evangelicalism and Fundamentalism has reestablished itself on the map as a nexus, but one that is itself almost broken within.

In the meantime Evangelicals seem to have the better of it. They offer much of what Dean Kelley observed churches needed in order to grow. They displayed much but not too much commitment, discipline, missionary zeal, absolutism, conformity, and fanaticism.[33] This may have kept them from growing as rapidly as the more extreme small Fundamentalist groups, but they were also able to be more protean, to reach out into more subcultures and to touch on the larger culture in some positive ways, as the withdrawn and belligerent groups could not.

Their success, in a sense, lies in their ability to offer prospective converts and members the best of both worlds. On the one hand, they provide meaning, belonging, and identity apparently *over against* other Americans while on the other hand they are taught to *fit in with the other Americans*, to be the real and true citizens. The Evangelicals address near majorities and then give them a sense of clear minority status. The continuing denominationalism of the member groups serves well here. Each one has something to which it adheres in particular, a way of baptizing or communing or observing the church calendar. All these are decided on the basis of variant readings of the Scriptures, which they all believe to be inerrant and clear. Yet they are also increasingly ecumenical and worldly, and can offer their clienteles the assets that go with such commitments. Their formula provides both identity and exposure; it is hard to match as a combination for tens of millions of Americans on this part of the religious map.

Pentecostal-
                     Charismatic
                     Religion

In 1959 no map of American religion would include anything called Pentecostal except at the margins or in the ecological niches. Pentecostalism then was simply a cluster of
lower-class denominations perceived as being a branch of
Fundamentalism. Pentecostalists were dismissed as hillbillies,
"holy rollers," and even as snake-handlers. That this status
was regarded proverbially and stereotypically was symbolized in a chapter heading used by the very popular sociologist Vance Packard in that year's best seller, *The Status
Seekers:* "The Long Road from Pentecostal to Episcopal." He
quoted sociologist Liston Pope on the fact that people in
the lower classes have turned to the new Pentecostal and
Holiness sects as "a protest (couched in religious form)
against social exclusiveness, and, on the other [hand], a com-
pensatory method (also in religious form) for regaining
status, and for redefining class lines in religious terms."[1] They
were far from the board rooms and country clubs populated
by Episcopalians, Presbyterians, and the like.

One year earlier Henry Pitney Van Dusen, then president
of Union Theological Seminary, New York's citadel of
Mainline religion, had made an effort to place Pentecostalism
on the map. In a famous article in *Life* on June 9, 1958, a
text that is quoted almost canonically now that Pentecostalism is less restricted to the excluded and those without status,
he chided the other churches for dismissing Pentecostalism
as a "fringe sect." Actually, it was what he called "Third

Force Christendom." He was prophetic—and too early.[2] Two things had to happen to give Pentecostalism a place in the perceptions of the larger culture. The older churches in the movement had to make some compromises and accommodations to the culture, and some people in the mainstream churches had to produce some advocates themselves.

Both occurred. An example of the former had been the founding, at Clinton's Cafeteria in Los Angeles in 1951, of the Full Gospel Businessmen's Fellowship International, an interdenominational lay Pentecostal movement headed by dairyman Demos Shakarian. The members, later over 100,000 strong, had a predilection for holding publicized meetings in motels and hotels, where their activity could become known and could gain respectability. From the other side, people in the movement date the rise of what they prefer to call the Charismatic effort to April 3, 1960, the day on which Rector Dennis Bennett of St. Mark's Episcopal Church in Van Nuys, California, announced that he shared pentecostal experiences. From that date the force spread into Lutheranism, Methodism, Presbyterianism, and after 1967 to Roman Catholicism, where it became most visible.

When Van Dusen and Packard wrote, the word "charismatic" meant little to most people—unless they heard it in connection with a senator who was being spoken of as a presidential candidate, John F. Kennedy. "Charisma" was a magical marketable political commodity. Half a dozen years later the term was familiarly applied to the churchly movement, in which connection its meaning was closer to that of its Greek original, *charismata*, the promised gifts of the Holy Spirit. The terms "pentecostal" and "charismatic" are often used interchangeably, with the old-liners slightly tilting toward "pentecostal," in part because it is in some of their denominational names; the newer-comers lean toward "charismatic." Sometimes a slight class difference is implied;

"charismatic" helps distance the members from lower-status and rougher-cut Protestant Pentecostalists. Here we shall hyphenate the two because of their easy interchangeability.

A fair-minded observer, Joseph Fichter, in *The Catholic Cult of the Paraclete*, captures well the sense of surprise and suddenness that has gone with the Pentecostal-Charismatic movement in Catholicism:

> out of the heartland of affluent, technological, success-oriented America, there has emerged a remarkable religious revival that goes counter to contemporary behavioral expectations. . . . [In hierarchical, stylized, liturgical Catholicism] there was no room for outbursts of spiritual enthusiasm, spontaneous prayer and prophecy, speaking in tongues, handclapping, or the joyful singing of hymns. . . .
>
> The chronicle is clear . . . : the movement got under way in 1967 at Duquesne University, then spread to the University of Notre Dame, the University of Michigan, and other centers of learning.[3]

Some thought that the movement drew attention chiefly because it was "the only show in town." After the social activism of the churches in the mid-sixties, nothing else seemed to be going on. Others dismissed the new trends as mere fads and fashions, part of a genteel counterculture as ephemeral as its secular counterpart. It may also be seen as an acceptable group manifestation of a widespread movement that would focus on experience at the expense of other features of religion. In the context of this book, it is also seen as a means of providing an identity in a pluralist society; demarcation or boundary-setting on social behavioral lines is one of its main attractions.

No one can measure accurately the Pentecostal-Charismatic movement. The records in the Pentecostal denominations may be fairly reliable, but it is not possible to know just how many hundreds of thousands of Catholic and Mainline Protestants are committed to it. Between these there is a kind of independent network of Pentecostal ventures, in the lineage of the entrepreneurship associated in the public eye with the careers of the best-known Pentecostalists before 1960, people like Aimee Semple McPherson or, later, the healers Oral Roberts and Kathryn Kuhlmann. Firms like Logos, a New Jersey publisher, market single titles in the hundreds of thousands. Even if trends go against the movement, and as the certain institutionalization of its perplexing forces occurs, perhaps at the expense of visibility or effervescence, enough has occurred to assure Pentecostalism-Charismaticism a safe territory on the American religious map.

Through behavioral observation, lay and professional, it gained this status. The non-Pentecostal church-going public, if the records it leaves are to be trusted, knows almost nothing about Charismatic theology, but very much about the practices: holy rolling, snake handling, prayer meetings, healing, and most of all, speaking in tongues are the familiar marks. The historian of theology would have to content himself with noticing how people in the movement lift out neglected elements in Christian witness to the Holy Spirit. But they are often quite antiintellectual, demonstrably so. A special burden is placed upon them to sound orthodox, and they go out of their way to show that they are not doctrinal innovators. They do not want to be interesting on that front— though Joseph Fichter found that in practice Catholic Charismatics tend to be heterodox in their beliefs about the literal Second Coming of Christ, the certainty of salvation, and the notion that the Holy Spirit speaks to the heart and not to the mind. Bibliographer David W. Faupel surveyed the whole literature and made an unassailable judgment: "A Pentecostal Theology has never actually been written."[4]

Pentecostalists, like Pietists often before them, tend to coast on interpretation independent of their special accents, adding only their own chapters about the experience of the Holy Spirit. They are not all anti-intellectual, of course; some Mainline Pentecostals in particular try to counter the tide.

The older denominations have upgraded their seminaries. There is a sophisticated Society for Pentecostal Studies, made up of participant observers. They have reason, however, to smart under stigma of Ronald A. Knox in his classic critique, *Enthusiasm*, as repeated by Catholic humorist Kieran Quinn. They "do not trust scholarship, biblical or theological, and well they should not. Reason and scholarship have always been the nemesis of enthusiasm. Under rational inquiry pentecostalism falters." But most followers would not care. Those who care would answer in something equivalent to Paul Tillich's suggestion that enthusiasm and ecstasy transcend but do not negate the structure of reason.[5]

The folk hero of Pentecostalism and author of books that sell in millions, David Wilkerson, speaks for the masses in his complaint that "often experts deplore and criticize those who speak with tongues and then protect themselves from being judged or criticized themselves by hiding behind research charts and special degrees."[6] Dennis Bennett compensatorily takes pride in his having attended major theological schools but does not make much use of special theological vantages in his many writings. Perhaps the theologians give Pentecostalists good reason to back away, especially if they have to listen to linguistic barbarisms like this:

> If we wished to be unacademically schematic in making our point we would suggest that, in generally christocentric Protestantism, alongside of particularly chariscentric Lutheranism, theocentric Calvinism, ecclesiocentric Anglicanism, kardiocentric Anabaptism, and hagiocentric Methodism may be ranged the most recent significant arrival on the stage of Protestant church history—what may somewhat awkwardly be called pneumobaptistocentric Pentecostalism.[7]

Correct. Or "never mind." Yet non-Pentecostalist theologian Frederick Dale Bruner is correct in his focus. Pentecostalists do have distinctive ideas, beliefs, behavioral roots in perceptions of a world, *creencias*; these center in what they call "Baptism in the Holy Spirit" or *pneuma*. The Spirit is elusive, beyond sociology and intellectuality, say many leaders. Thus Joseph Fichter found many resistant to his researches. Pentecostal theologian Edward O'Connor was sure that "a survey would miss the essence of the Pentecostal movement;" "the very point . . . is the personal intervention of God in the lives of his people."[8] In Vincent M. Walsh's *A Key to Charismatic Renewal in the Catholic Church* the catechizing priest makes every effort not to look antitheological and even is mildly kind to biblical critics.[9] But he is essentially bored by it all, and considers intellectuality in effect to be as beside the point of his experiential movement as is programmed social action. No historian of high-culture intellectuality or of formal systematic Christian theology would need to look up from his researches, and none would put Pentecostalism on the map for its theology.

The second paradigm for locating and describing American religion might be slightly more familiar and useful in this case. Yet there has been, as already noted, little novelty or intricacy in Pentecostalism from the structural point of view. It started as revival movements that became denominations like unto all others. Exactly like. Using a brush as broad as theologian Bruner's, we may say that old-line Pentecostalism (1900–) had always been in the process of moving from being sectarian to being churchly, while newer Charismatic movements (1960–) were always in the process of moving from being churchly toward becoming sectarian. Pentecostalism denominationalized, and the Charismatics largely stayed in the old churches. Both could be seen as having a sectarian tendency; Fichter definitely locates Catholic Charismatics in a "cult."[10]

The movement is sectarian, in Ernst Troeltsch's classic term, insofar as and because it represents "subjective holiness," but sectarianism does not always breed sects, and most Mainliners "stayed in." Their meetings differ little structurally from those of non-Pentecostalists. The suggestions that Spirit-people could transcend institutionalism are denied by discussions of ministerial pensions or advertisements in Pentecostal newspapers.[11] If anything, Pentecostalists do succeed in slightly undervaluing inherited institutions before they form their own—which by the summer of 1975 were in the news for occasional scandals brought on by rigidity and power-seeking. Short of that, and in their view of existing forms, they echo the sentiment of Walt Whitman, who was "neither for nor against institutions."

The movement is equally overlookable on political grounds, if again one keeps an eye out for innovation. Fichter found members quite passive about and uninterested in the social realm.[12] Walsh was quite open about the lack of concern. "There does seem to be some basis for [the] complaint . . . that Catholics involved in social action withdraw from their attempts to correct injustices as they become interested in Charismatic Renewal." Many non-Charismatics also have withdrawn. He was writing in 1974, long after the activist urges of the 1960s had disappeared. Further, people had been naive in the 1960s; they needed a new look. "Some withdrawal from these works resulted from an experience of their futility." Yes, it would be detrimental if the renewal were deliberately turning people from social action, but the turn is accidental and secondary. Spiritual needs now take priority. Some day people will find that Charismatic Renewal has something, at least, to offer social activists.[13]

The casual observer would probably classify old-line Protestant Pentecostalists as political conservatives, maintainers of the status quo. But their leaders have not taken care to line them up politically, or have taken care not to line them up politically. They may take negative stands in the legislative realm against liberalization of laws on personal vices: drinking, gambling, pornography, and the like. But they are not notably prescriptive or rigid beyond that and, partly because of the regional and economic make-up of their clienteles, they have often been progressive and populist. They do not shun the world and are extremely celebrity conscious, parading the Pat Boones and Johnny Cashes as prize converts. The only time any Pentecostalism is overtly involved in political issues is in the highly exceptional instance of snake-handling, where it is legally proscribed. Snake-handling is not a major preoccupation of Charismatic movements at Ann Arbor or among the Rotarians of the Full Gospel Businessmen's Fellowship International. For the rest, American political history would be largely the same with or without Pentecostalism.[14]

Perhaps because of an awakening to the behavioral nuance, historians of American religion gave increasing attention to the movements. Sydney Ahlstrom's 1158-page work devoted only three pages each to black and white Pentecostalism and a long footnote to the new Charismatic movement, but Winthrop Hudson in a revised *Religion in America* balanced this by giving two pages to Pentecostalists and four to the new Charismatics.[15] (The four pages were added; there would have been little to cover in the 1965 edition of Hudson's work.) Both authors improved on their predecessors; William Warren Sweet's standard history revised in 1950 allowed only one of his 423 pages to go to "Third Force Christendom."[16]

From the beginning the Holy Rollers and speakers-in-tongues attracted attention for their social behavior. Father Kilian McDonnell, a Catholic Charismatic, regretted, for instance, the fact that to the public the movement "conjures up images of emotionalism, fanaticism, religious mania, illiteracy, messianic postures, credulity, and panting after miracles." The new versions of the movement have replaced these images with more respectable but no less visible ones.[17]

On the other hand, friendly observers like Southern Baptist psychologist of religion Wayne Oates lauded members precisely because they behaved differently than other Christians. They were not shy or inarticulate about their faith.

They were ready to look nonrespectable, fanatic, sick, and foolish in support of their cause. Their vulnerability and risk made them attractive.[18] And, while the experience must be personally appropriated, the behavior is highly social. Thus Bruner writes of the "center of the Pentecostal secret":

> contrary to general expectation, highly individualistic Pentecostalism is remarkably corporate and congregational in its life. The Pentecostal church-meeting or assembly where the individual gifts are principally exercised is close to the center of the Pentecostal secret. Here the experiences of the many merge into the one and by this confluence the power of the Spirit is felt in multiplication.[19]

So it has been from the beginning. The prehistory of the current outbreak begins precisely with the twentieth century. This is not to say that other religions of the world lacked the features of Pentecostal behavior: speaking in tongues (glossolalia), prophesying and interpretation, healing, ecstatic dancing and the like appear almost everywhere phenomenologists look. Early Christianity displayed them—as Pentecostalists never tire of pointing out by reference to Acts 2 and some passages in Paul's First Letter to the Corinthians. There the apostle had embarrassed them by placing their most visible gift, speaking in tongues, at the bottom among charismata, but he *had* placed it and allowed for it, and they wanted to overcome the neglect.

Out of nineteenth-century British and American Wesleyan, Holiness, and other revivalist roots came the settings and the sparks. Then on New Year's Eve of 1900 in Topeka, Kansas, Agnes Ozman received the gift of speaking in tongues, and the next morning the congregation resolved to stay together. *The Kansas City World* grasped at once that "these people have a faith almost incomprehensible at this day."[20] Six years later in the Azusa Street (Los Angeles) revival of W. J. Seymour, a black evangelist, urban America began to notice the new thing on the map. Born racially integrated, the congregations soon segregated. Born in a ferment, they soon adapted to denominationalism. Phase II, as already noted, began with speaking in tongues in 1960. By the time of the Fifth Pentecostal World Conference at Toronto in 1958 keynoter J. A. Synan boasted: "They say Pentecost [alism] is the *third* great force in Christendom. But it is really the *first* great force."[21] Pentecostalists, who use images of wildfire for their cause, like to quote a Methodist professor in 1913: "The present day tongues movement is likely to run its course in a few months or a few years."[22]

Instead it prevailed, and is the fastest-growing part of Christian expansion in the southern hemisphere, especially in Africa, Latin America, and Indonesia. Pentecostal historian Walter Hollenweger even complained that growth in the so-called developing nations was so dramatic that "sophisticated people in Europe and America" felt that Pentecostalism was "of importance only for the poor and for the Third World,"[23] a notion he set out to correct. The best known ecumenical Pentecostal leader, South African David du Plessis, could boast in the 1960s: "At the turn of the century there was no Pentecostal Movement. Today it consists of a community of more than ten million souls that can be found in almost every country under the sun."[24]

How could the two Pentecostalisms, old and new, low-status and Mainline, Protestant and largely Catholic, be part of "a community?" Theologically the differences in dogma remained, said Catholic Walsh.[25] Few would disagree. Institutionally there were differences based on denominational traditions. Politically there were radical differences based on who lived where and what they sought. Father Donald Gelpi, S. J., faced the question, especially as it related to the Protestant/Catholic line: "Doesn't it seem possible that there is a relation of potential complementarity between Catholic and Pentecostal piety?"[26]

Piety was the place where complementarity would show; doctrine could not be on the agenda. Ecumenical tensions

were to grow over life style, as when Protestant Pentecostalists were offended by the beer-drinking that went on at inter-
missions during summer Charismatic rallies at Notre Dame.
The Catholics were even vastly more distant from the many
Black Protestant Pentecostal churches that shared their experience. Even a catalog of the names of the black denominations, provided by Joseph Washington, will suggest how remote in status they are from Duquesne and suburban living
rooms:

> The Fire-Baptized Holiness Church of God of the
>   Americas
> Church of God in Christ
> Church of God, Holiness United States of America
> Triumph the Church and Kingdom of God in Christ
>   and Spiritual House of Prayer, Incorporated
> The Latter House of the Lord for All People
>   and the Church on the Mountain, Apostolic Faith
> Church of the Living God, the Pillar and Ground
>   of Truth
> Apostolic Overcoming Holy Church of God
> The National David Spiritual Temple of
>   Christ Church Union
> The House of God, the Holy Church of the Living
>   God, the Pillar and Grounds of the Truth, House of
>   Prayer for all People.[27]

And yet? And yet many of these shared "Baptism in the
Holy Spirit" and accompanying signs, so they were in special
ways members of that ten-million souled community inside
the Christian Church.

The signs: sooner or later, and usually sooner, under special conditions certain behavioral responses must mark the
individual or the group—or else there is nothing Pentecostal-
Charismatic. The behavior must be evidential, manifest, and
visible. It was a non-Christian Pentecostalist, Father Divine,
who provided the best term for what is claimed, when he
once said, "I visibilate God! I tangibilitate! I materialize

every assertion, for God is the materializer of all of His Earth's Creation!" (The visible-tangible metaphor was extended when "Prophet Jones" said, after a visit, "I know that the chassis of your divine mind has been lubricated with divine lubrimentality.")[28]

Manifestness is the hallmark of all Pentecostal books, tracts, sermons, testimonies, appeals, street-corner sermons, magazines, and denominational reports when they come to the question of effects. The second blessing or the Baptism in the Holy Spirit must be accompanied by certain complex signs and gifts. Almost at random one can cull these: linguistically, there must be "a definite act"; "initial evidence"; recipients seek an "objectively observable act," an "evidential sign." This baptism offers the "empirical evidence of salvation"; the second blessing is "tangible"; glossolalia is "visible evidence"; the Topeka revivalist-founder Charles Fox Parham had sought speaking in tongues as "the only evidence" of Spirit baptism; there must be "manifestations, powers, and services," an "externalization."[29]

All Christianity implies some sort of practical responses. But in the course of time the responses have come to appear in generalized and not always predictable terms. The ancient prayers of the church ask that lives of believers exemplify "good behavior." Many moral codes are spelled out as part of good Christian behavior. Rites and ceremonies may be canonically prescribed. But only in highly focused and articulate groups like Pentecostalism is there such a stereotyped set of responses programmed into the appeal.

Sometimes Charismatic spokespersons act as if the visible marks and habits are a kind of burden, a barrier to communication—but, then, they must be borne. Conventional pictures of Charismatics in their congresses show them praying or singing with both hands upraised. Walsh asks himself, "Why do members of Charismatic prayer groups lift their hands and arms while praying?" He does not answer that it is unnecessary.[30] No, it "signifies the freedom of praise" present in the group and "most importantly, it allows prayer to be part of the whole person,—mind, heart, lips, body, arms, etc." Biologically or anatomically Walsh would be hard pressed to show that kneeling would not effect the same— but then everybody kneels, and Pentecostalism needs and finds behaviorally demarcating signs. Anthropologist William J. Samarin in a scholarly study of the movement reinforces Bruner's concept of "the center of the Pentecostal secret."

> What is a validating experience for the individual, . . . is a demarcating one for the group; it symbolizes the group's differences from others. In this respect glossolalia serves the same function that any form of speech may have, like the in-group languages of students (slang) or secret societies. The latter, of course, also have communicative functions in the strict sense of the term. . . .
>
> Symbols can become frozen, but when a movement is new, they are especially significant. Thus, the demarcating function of glossolalia is more important for neo-Pentecostal groups than it is for the established ones which perpetuate themselves biologically (where children are born into Pentecostal homes) rather than sociologically. (However, where Pentecostalism is spreading rapidly, as in Brazil, we can expect glossolalia to retain its symbolic demarcating function, unless other symbols have superseded it.) In these groups, then, it is not enough for a newcomer to identify himself as a Christian. The members will want to know if he has had "the experience." One of the best answers is simply, "Yes, I have spoken in tongues." This marks solidarity with the group. Indeed, reliable reports indicate that some groups will not integrate a person unless he gives evidence of being a tongue speaker. The expression is not theirs, but this is their "requirement for membership."

Symbolic demarcation is not all that occurs in the Charismatic circle, of course. Interviewed Pentecostalists would say they are part of the movement because there the second blessing of the Holy Spirit is sealed and enjoyed. Samarin knows this. But the members who recognize nothing of themselves in this portrait have not been listening to themselves. This "is unquestionably suggested by the way they talk about tongues and the way they treat the interested participant in their meetings."

Speaking in tongues "helps the members to reaffirm their difference as often as they will. . . . It achieves a pragmatic purpose. . . . As a manifestation of the divine . . . [it] contributes a sacred note to a meeting." Running across the spectrum from Appalachian sects to high Anglican life, "this use of glossolalia clearly illustrates how speech not only helps realize the ethos or way of life of a society but also the ethos of a social occasion."[31] No wonder that Werner Skibstedt, who claimed that the Pentecostal experience meant nothing less than "the rediscovery of Christianity," added that "the reception of the gift of the Holy Spirit" occurs "in an extraordinary, yes, in an eye-catching way."[32]

So much has been made of praying in tongues and, more important, the special gift of speaking in tongues, that at least the latter sign of the "second blessing" needs some elaboration—at least to the outsiders who are across the line of demarcation from it. Donald Gelpi calls it a kind of *"pons asinorum"* of the Pentecostal movement. Non-Pentecostals were repulsed, while Pentecostals thought it was the *sine qua non* of spiritual being.[33] He was right. Already in 1906 the Los Angeles *Times* eavesdropped and reported, "Weird Babel of Tongues. A new sect . . . is breaking loose."[34] Advocate Don Basham asked whether one could receive the baptism in the Holy Spirit without speaking in tongues? Well, maybe. But "SOMETHING IS MISSING IN YOUR SPIRITUAL LIFE IF YOU HAVE RECEIVED THE HOLY SPIRIT YET HAVE NOT SPOKEN IN TONGUES."[35] Even Dennis Bennett's stentorian phrasing shows how he regarded the phenomenon: "The Holy Spirit did take my lips and tongue and form a new and powerful language."[36]

To the Charismatic member, in Walsh's catechism, the un-intelligible and unrepressed speech called glossolalia "is a passing manifestation of the Holy Spirit to an individual (usually a mature member) during a charismatic prayer meeting, whereby the person is prompted to speak aloud in tongues, which must be followed by the companion gift of interpretation." He cites I Corinthians 12:10 in support.[37] Debates have raged over the character of glossolalia. Pentecostalists will not permit use of the term "ecstatic speaking." They would probably regard as "anthropological tongues speaking" the definition of Felicitas Goodman, who found nothing distinctive about the phonetics and syllables of Christian glossolalia. It is, she says,

> a vocalization pattern, a speech automatism, that is produced on the substratum of hyperarousal dissociation, reflecting directly, in its segmental and suprasegmental structure, neurophysiologic processes present in this mental state.[38]

More acceptable to many both within and without the movement is Samarin's conclusion, based on linguistic and psychological studies. Pentecostal speech was not the ex-pression merely of dissociated, irrational, or neurotic types, or of people who reflected lower-class origins. Recorded snatches of speaking in tongues were

> *strings of syllables, made up of sounds taken from among all those that the speaker knows, put together more or less haphazardly but which nevertheless emerge as word-like and sentence-like units because of realistic, language-like rhythm and melody.*[39]

Glossolalia is anomalous, not aberrant, behavior of people who are not necessarily abnormal. Pentecostalists claimed that the activity is Holy Spirit–inspired because they want it to be and because they have no other explanation. Samarin could not grant supernatural status to an event so explicable on other grounds, but could see it as an authentic religious experience, a symbolization of God's immediate presence.

Here it is not necessary to elaborate on all nine charismata or gifts of the Spirit: tongues, interpretation, prophecy; faith, healing, miracles; wisdom, knowledge, discernment. Suffice it to say that they serve as demarcating boundaries for the movement when these differ from the practices of other Christians. Charismatics' "spontaneous" prophecy differs from more ordered preaching. Healing, especially in the hands of the flamboyant, sets them apart, though not absolutely, as did speaking in tongues. Of course, anyone who in the modern West insists on miracles or engages in exorcisms, as many Charismatics do, will stand out.

Curiously, Pentecostalists seek spontaneity and impose great order to arrive at it. The earliest revivalists and the more rural and lower-class leaders may still cherish the free-for-all, no-holds-barred approach. But the Mainline church Charismatic textbooks are enormously complicated and detailed prescriptions for prayer meetings. In a leisured world the old-time Pentecostalists favored "tarrying meetings" after church; there gifts could be sought and enjoyed. Modern Charismatics have taken these and transformed them into normative patterns of Bible study, small cell groups, and prayer circles. They write hundreds of pages of directives for spontaneous worship.

Kevin Ranaghan, for example, one of the best-known leaders at Notre Dame, called the prayer meetings "the principal public manifestation and result of the charismatic renewal in the Church today. . . . It is unique . . . [and] . . . we are truly unique."[40] James Cavnar follows up with a chapter on "Dynamics of the Prayer Meeting." Leaders must be conscious of the fact that first-timers would feel strange. There must be order, a "definite length of time" set. The meeting "can have structure . . . it needs some structure."

> Let the prayer meeting be explicitly "pentecostal" from
> the very beginning so that all persons are aware that we
> are here to seek the gifts of the Spirit. . . . It is sometimes
> impossible to move a whole group together to Spirit-
> filled worship and prayer if they have first grown
> accustomed to a non-charismatic form of prayer meeting.

When a prayer meeting "grows too rapidly, the new people
often dominate and set the tone of the meeting." "It is important not to allow classical pentecostals to dominate the
meeting. Most Catholics are simply unprepared for the style
of classical pentecostals. . . . The problem is mainly cultural,
but it is nonetheless a problem." St. Paul is always cited for
seeking that everything be done "decently and in order."[41]

Much less attention is paid to prescription in private conduct, perhaps because it would be hard to fashion patterns
for demarcation there. In general, Pentecostalists in the Protestant churches share the conservative Evangelical moral
outlooks, while Mainline Protestants and Catholics manifest
slightly more conservative or "straight and square" ethical
patterns than do their non-Pentecostal fellows. But both tend
to resist codifications. The old Holiness churches, non-Pentecostal, were sometimes called "no hogmeat, no necktie"
religions because of their attention to details. Not so with
most in the newer movements.[42]

Anthropologist Gary Schwartz, who studied a Pentecostal
group, generalized that

> Pentecostal ideology lacks an ethically binding,
> comprehensive pattern for secular conduct. It defines
> proper behavior but . . . does not direct the believer to
> specific secular goals. . . . Of course this does not mean
> that Pentecostal ideology does not invest the boundaries
> of permissible behavior with considerable import.[43]

Members of the movement work strenuously to preserve
its and their identity. To be told that someone is a Catholic
or an Episcopalian does little to set boundaries or define

groups. But being a Catholic Charismatic or an Episcopalian Pentecostalist establishes behavioral expectations and lets one know precisely to whom and to what some described person belongs.

A distinction might be made between "soft" and "hard" Charismatics. The soft one is basically a Christian renewalist responsive to the language about and the experience of the Holy Spirit. He or she follows the prescriptions and patterns of the movement, but is gentle with non-Pentecostal Christians, more or less hoping and praying that they will seek the gift, but not looking on them as second-class Christians. The hard Charismatic makes the second Baptism or the blessing in the Spirit into a sign of qualitative difference and cannot help but rule that those who do not have it and seek it are truly unfinished Christian products, more or less "half safe." The former have the problem of being assimilated back into more nondescript renewal styles. The latter risk dividing the church and in almost every case they cause conflict and tension—which, to many of them, are signs of the validity of their witness.

The growing favor of the upgraded Pentecostalists and the successful Charismatics in the eyes of other Christians is sometimes rued as a sign that the good old days are gone. Persecution helps define a group and helps it fulfill its bonding roles. A latter-day historian looks back on the days when in Tennessee

> heavy persecutions could be counted on. An important reason for the widespread hostility . . . was the suspicion that everything odd and erroneous was believed and practiced by them. Whenever a pentecostal meeting took place in a community, rumors were rife about "magic powders," "trances," "wild emotion," and "sexual promiscuity." . . . These rumors eventually entered the folklore of the nation and stamped anyone claiming to be "holiness" or "pentecostal" with the epithet "holy roller." Those who engaged in this "religion of knockdown and

dragout" were considered to be uncultured and uneducated "poor white trash" who inhabited the outer fringes of society. A member of one of the traditional churches who joined a pentecostal church was generally considered to have "lost his mind" and to have severed his normal social connections. Within this framework, it is not surprising that the relationship of the pentecostals to society has been marked with mutual hostility and even violence.[44]

Now everything has changed. David Wilkerson's father had been a Pentecostal minister.

We were called "holy rollers," and people looked down their spiritual "noses" when they referred to the poor tongue talkers. I grew up feeling like a second-class Christian, unwelcome by quiet, dignified kinds of churches. . . . But now tongues have moved uptown. Orthodox Catholics, staid Presbyterians, dignified Episcopalians, and dispensationalized Baptists are now among those in the middle of the charismatic movement.[45]

Tongues have moved uptown—a dangerous place to be. Thirteen years after Vance Packard mapped a long road between Pentecostalism and Episcopalianism, William J. Samarin could say that "it no longer appears appropriate . . . to characterize Pentecostalism as arising from or being nurtured by sociocultural disruption, low status, and dissatisfaction." There is now even "a kind of Pentecostal 'Establishment.' "[46] Whereas once it was "true" because it was small and pure, now it is "true" because so many are drawn to it. Steve Durasoff, a partisan, boasted, "While one major denomination after another report declining memberships and incomes, and even as their overseas missionary staffs are hit the hardest, Pentecostal churches, to the contrary, have made impressive and even startling gains."[47] The claim has become routine and ritual.

Such language caused resentment just as the hard Charismatic line threatened schism or at least formation of new denomination-like structures. John T. Nichol pointed to the long roots of the separatist growth in his story of a southern California pastor who led his people in repetitious singing of

Out of the rubbish heap the Lord lifted me!
Out of the rubbish heap the Lord lifted me!

He interpreted the rubbish heap as "the Baptist Church . . . from which he had been drawn into Pentecostalism."[48] The movement is torn between enjoying its position of abrasion in the "rubbish heap" of disorganized and random Protestantism and Catholicism, and withdrawing in separation. Caught there, the members of the movement manifestly gain sufficient benefits from the cause. Demarcated by their behavior, they have gained a place on the map.

6   The New
         Religions

"The New Religions" is the most convenient and inclusive
name for a cluster of groups that represents new territory on
America's religious map. Their arrival and entrenchment
came about as part of a quiet revolution in the 1960s, and
they were rather securely established as a subculture or set
of subcultures by the mid-1970s. The term "the New Religions," which was used as the title of a book on the subject
by Jacob Needleman, encompasses the non-Jewish, non-
Christian faiths of Americans. The word "new" here can
refer only to the fact that they are new to America. Some of
the occult and Eastern representations are older than the
Jewish and Christian traditions; they were not widely recognized as an American presence until the 1960s.

The landscape of the New Religions is full of both pre-
carious and luxuriant growths. Needleman alone deals with
Hinduism, Buddhism, Sufism, the Occult, Zen, Baba-lovers,
Subud, Transcendental Meditation, Tibetan religion, astrology, reincarnation, nature religions, esotericism, drug-asso-
ciated religion and the like.[1] Another book that has gained
popular acceptance and has been used widely as a college
textbook, Robert S. Ellwood, Jr., *Religious and Spiritual
Groups in Modern America*,[2] includes these and adds others,
among them the Rosicrucians, Spiritualism, Theosophy, New
Thought—all of them longer-established in America, and
less "new"—"I Am," Unidentified Flying Objects Cults,
Guardjieff Groups, the Prosperos, Scientology, Abilitism,
Builders of the Adytum, the Church of Light, Neo-Pagan
groups, Vedanta Societies, the Self-Realization Fellowship,

the International Society for Krishna Consciousness, Nichiren Shoshu, and many subspecies. It is wearying to read catalogs of names, but this listing is necessary to help evoke a picture of the varieties of outcroppings and flowerings. Many of these are related to long-recognized world religions and will survive internationally even if they do not become strong in America. Others are novel or so transformed in transit to the United States that they might well be described as ephemeral.

The arrival of these groups was in many ways a surprise; they do not show up on the denominational map that prevailed until mid-century. They are not anticipated in the mid-century mapping done by Will Herberg and other sociologists who saw the broad categories of Protestant, Catholic, Jew then to be virtually inclusive. In terms popularized by Marshall Sahlins and his colleagues, the biblical faiths and their offshoots had spread "to just about every ecological nook and cranny" of the culture.[3] This means, to keep our metaphor of terrain, that wherever a bit of nurturant soil appeared, some sort of Judaism or Christianity would take root. Wherever little basins for the gathering of precipitation existed, there one could expect that biblical religion would be represented by some group or other. This genus had many species; here and there a stray seedling blown from the East by a west wind might luxuriate for its moment in the sun. Hardy ones might even survive, as esoteric exceptions on the landscape. They attracted curiosity because of their rarity. In the late 1950s few would have expected a change in the spiritual ecology of the nation.

Those who did looked in a different direction and had even more reason to be surprised by the growth of the New Religions. As late as the mid-sixties one of the most serious projections about the human future was associated with the concept of secularization.[4] In this envisioning, religion itself was progressively disappearing and would disappear. A new phyletic type or phenotype was appearing, one that would no longer be responsive to magic, mystery, myth, miracle. The culture at large would itself be termed only secular; religious survivals would be regarded as throwbacks to earlier stages of evolutionary development. They were on borrowed time in societies where the technopolitical styles were taking over the whole landscape. For both reasons, then, the survival of biblical faith and the secular assumption, the religious maps of the 1950s needed no outlines of what today are the New Religions in America.

So fascinating and engrossing are these phenomena that it seems frustrating to the reader merely to bring them up and in thirty pages to drop them. The temptation for the writer to make a whole book of them is almost overwhelming, because they can be so conveniently used to substantiate or illustrate the thesis of this book. They are almost entirely regarded as social-behaviorally interesting movements; it is hard to study them without some awareness of behavioral sciences old and new. But in order not to skew the proportions on the map, we shall have to leave unanswered and merely touched upon many questions to which researchers are now devoting themselves, questions about the reasons for the growth of these movements, their appeal for their members, and the like.

Statistically, few of these religions stood any chance of overtaking the historic complex of faiths, and even taken together they will no doubt remain a small minority, to be noticed because they are exotic growths on what can often be a drab and sere scene. Astrology, with its longer roots, and meditation movements, with their easily borrowed techniques, are rare exceptions to the generalization that Jewish and Christian heritages, coupled with aftereffects of the religion of the Enlightenment, are so bonded in the environment that they will prevail. They are taken for granted; citizens fall back on them even if they do not practice them; no one knows how the nation would look or function if they were wholly displaced and replaced.

If the new do not prevail, they will exert influences in two ways. One is as an intrusive presence, constantly attractive because they are intrusive and exceptional, an alternative to or judgment upon majority religion. The other is as what might be called suffusive forces; they offer some features that will suffuse, will cast a glow upon, will subtly soften or open or alter the Jewish and Christian faiths and the secular style. The reference to meditation above is an indicator of this tendency. One might remain a Presbyterian *and* practice Zen, might be a Catholic communicant who is absorbed in yoga, an orthodox Evangelical who sneaks a peek at the horoscope each day and thinks there just might be something to it. Thus the New Religions spread beyond their subcultures to others or to the whole culture. Picture the enlargement in a ten year period of the numbers of people who are familiar with words like "guru" or "transcendental," and some concept of the suffusive or osmotic understanding will become comprehensible.

Explanations of the presence of these movements and alternatives abound. At the very least one must say that they resulted in part from their new accessibility in a culture that was shaped by mass media of communications and that included mass higher education and mass mobility. "He who never visits thinks his mother is the only cook," a Bantu saying from Africa has it.[5] And the 1960s was a time of both physical and psychological travelling.

Within a period of ten years courses on these subjects had expanded in secular colleges. The camera's eye found devotees of Hare Krishna, in their saffron robes, more attractive than the Women's Auxiliary of First Methodist Church; Black Muslims seem to offer more threat and more "juices" to society than do the Black Baptists who vastly outnumber them. So television concentrated on the minority, not the majority outcroppings. Campuses, communes, "swingers' neighborhoods" in urban areas were all growing, and they are the locales where the psychically mobile congregate.

Newsmagazines bannered an "Occult Explosion," and commuters and bridge club members were soon "into" astrology and aware of witchcraft.

Most theorists connected the rise of the new groups to boredom or discontent with the existing tradition and to the search for identity.[6] California was especially studied as the home of "Protean man," of persons who embodied the assets and liabilities of that human life-style based on traditionlessness and open to bombardment by images from the media. Often cited in this context was William Glasser's picture of "the Identity Society," based on a line of Marshall McLuhan, a kind of guru in the period: universally youth is searching not for goals but for roles. In the sweeping style that characterized books of the era Glasser pictured the emergence of a whole new (fourth) stage of humanity. After periods of "primitive survival," "primitive identity," and "civilized survival" societies, "civilized identity" society is emerging.

> Less anxious about fulfilling goals to obtain security
> within the power hierarchy, people today concern them-
> selves more and more with an independent role—*their
> identity*. Arising from our need of involvement, identity
> or role is either totally independent of goal or, if goal
> and role are related, role is more important.[7]

Glasser accounted for the change by reference to affluence, political concern for human security and human rights, and increased communication.

Professionals in various disciplines will find it possible to fault Glasser's details. Economists and historians might find his view of a whole new culture a bit naive, based on ephemeral economic circumstances that hardly outlasted the first printing of his book. In their eyes, economic recession brought the Puritan Ethic, or goal- and purpose-orientations back to the culture with a vengeance, especially among senior collegians in quest of jobs on a tight market. But after all the qualifications have been issued, it is possible to see in Glasser's picture some of the quest that made new faiths attractive. One would think that at moments of upheaval people would return to their own traditions, but these often seemed to be expended, lacking in promise. The New Religions at least were highly cultic; they helped screen out confusing signals; they offered support groups of an intense character; traditions, in a way, became "prefabricated" for people. Almost instantly one could latch on or hook in to African or Eastern lineages that were millennia old.

In sociologist Emile Durkheim's term, these years can be seen as "moments of effervescence," one of those "periods of creation and renewal" when humans "are brought into more intimate relations with one another, when meetings and assemblies are more frequent, relationships more solid and the exchange of ideas more active" in the field of religion.[8] Such "collective effervescence" has appeared on a global scale, in the presence of and despite modernization, in the forms of new militant groups in the Muslim world, in *soka gakkai* and a hundred new religions in Japan, in the quasi-religion of Chinese Maoism, in nationalist and tribal religions in Africa.

While many of these were potent political forces, almost all of them converged on the idea of altering human consciousness. Most of the New Religions were obsessed with states of consciousness. Stanley Krippner, when he outlined a typology of altered states, made available a kind of checklist or catalog for observers and participants. These included the dreaming state, the sleeping state, the hypnagogic, hypnopompic, hyperalert, or lethargic states, and the like. More to the point of these faiths are the more religious "states of rapture," meditative states, expanded consciousness—most of them in opposition to the less spiritual " 'normal', everyday, waking state, characterized by logic, rationality, cause-and-effect thinking, goal-directedness, and the feeling that one is 'in control' of one's mental activity."[9] It was that state that was regularly faulted for having produced social problems, the Vietnamese war, and the modern shape of Jewish and Christian spirituality and institutions.

Anyone who takes notice of the episode by which the New Religions gained a beachhead will also pay attention to Durkheim's picture of a second stage after the "moments of effervescence." Crises would be faced or overcome, and everything would turn back to its ordinary level. "All that has been said, done, thought and felt during this period of fertile upheaval survives only as a memory . . . an idea, a set of ideas." If these memories and ideas are to survive, they must be wedded to practice, conduct, and group behavior, to be renewed by "festivities and public ceremonies, whether religious or secular." Through them people will "spontaneously feel the need to relive" effervescent occasions.[10]

By the mid-seventies, then, the effervescence had been bottled and bonded. The anti-institutions had become institutions, many of them looking curiously like the denominations they had opposed. The press, in which religion writers on Saturday afternoons had once published awed and awesome accounts of visits by the shaman or guru of the week, a few years later greeted many of these travellers as entrepreneurs and even approached some of them with tinges of humor or sarcasm. The magazine covers on the occult explosion were replaced with coffee table tomes on witchcraft in history. Freaks turned square. Black Muslims invited white Beautiful People to their affairs, and revised their myths and images about the white devils. One was free to yawn at the announcement of the opening of a new meditation center on a campus, to be bored in the face of exorcists and Satanologists on television.

By the time of the bottling of effervescence, a New Religions group must have offered its adherents a sense of demarcation ("the action of marking the boundary or limits of something, or of marking it off from something else"), the great boon of the sect or the cult in pluralist society.

Thus it contributes to the problems of an identity society or addresses the confusions of Protean man by providing boundaries and definitions. These usually appear in the form of a clear sense of who is in and who is out of the group of the true believers, and issues in detailed prescriptions for personal and social behavior. There is no danger that one might confuse a Scientologist with a Baba-lover, as one may a Methodist with a Baptist. People who belong to an Eastern cult will be aware of the limits of the group as members of a Catholic parish will not. The demarcating will not always follow cultic lines; Spiritualism, for example, is made up of ever-changing clienteles, most of whose people do not know each other.[11] In such cases the demarcating has more of a cognitive character: there are definite new boundaries to what can be known of the unseen world, a knowledge unshared by outsiders.

Before examining some of the New Religions more closely, a word about their prehistory in America is in order, both as a background for understanding and as a reminder that they are not really or wholly new in the culture; they had been anticipated or were available to elites and at the margins of the society. As we shall see, American Indians had always represented an alternative to biblical and Enlightened religion, but their faith was seldom positively appraised and almost never regarded as a choice for whites. So it was also with African survivals in black religion. Only the Christianized forms of Negro spirituality were approved, and black adaptations were regarded as curiosities or were simply rejected when they were known. At the time of the Enlightenment in the late eighteenth century, a few Americans became aware that some Europeans were urging a more sympathetic view of Islam and Asian faiths, but almost no one put any of these ideas to practice. Small elites among the New England Transcendentalists began to speak of some borrowings as Yankee Hindooism. So far as group life was concerned, these were virtually disincarnate ideas; they were invisible on the map of social groups. "Forget historical Christianity!" might be a slogan of some Transcendentalists, and some literary figures tried to do just that. They and a few communalists of the 1840s successfully, as groups, moved out of the Christian sphere.

Later in the century a few theosophists became well known, and Spiritualism through more than a century anticipated the New Religions. Some have noted an increase in public awareness of Eastern religion and the establishment of the centers to propagate it after the World's Parliament of Religions in Chicago in 1893. In the 1930s a number of British authors, among them Aldous Huxley, Gerald Heard, Christopher Isherwood, and Alan Watts, imported "the perennial philosophy" into intellectual circles; and there were, after all, the "Beat" poets of San Francisco, who advertised Zen in the 1950s.[12]

Then, suddenly, after a few years of expressed faith in secularity and control of the environment through politics and technology, came "the occult explosion," the announcement of "the age of Aquarius," "the making of a counter culture" that was saturated with the New Religions. The publication in 1969 of Theodore Roszak's best-selling *The Making of a Counter Culture* may well have marked the public awakening to the arrival of alternatives as well as a possible crest in their threat or promise. (One is tempted to ask, as we shall quote historian Sydney E. Ahlstrom asking in the context of our final chapter, "Is it possible that here we have evidence of a familiar fact—namely that we often study the history of something only after its demise?") Roszak spoke of a counterculture as being "a culture so radically disaffiliated from the mainstream assumptions of our society that it scarcely looks to many as a culture at all, but takes on the alarming appearance of a barbaric intrusion." Roszak compared this phenomenon to early Christianity, which also had begun "hopelessly estranged by ethos . . . from the official culture."[13] The disaffiliation, new assumptions, appearance, and ethos all signalled the visible behavioral differences that marked the movements.

The extreme forms did not last long. As already mentioned, the change in economic conditions by the mid-seventies may have removed the luxury of alternative styles from many who had to "turn straight" and who dropped new religious allegiances or rendered them covert. Cultural inertia no doubt played its part. As Morris Cohen says, "inertia is the first law of history, as it is of physics." "The dominant fact is that though people generally complain against the existing situation, inertia makes them unwilling to revolt or take other active measures to change the situation."[14] What Ernest Gellner calls the establishment's "danegeld" may have been too attractive, and discontent was bought off.[15] In any case, the more radical countercultural context disappeared, and the new faiths lived on either as isolated cults or as respectable and safe suffusive presences.

To the student of social behavior the most interesting feature is not the countercultural moment but the cultural (and subcultural) context of the enduring occult and metaphysical trends. While journalists often forgot the historical background to such phenomena and headlined the occult explosion, anthropologists, sociologists, and historians were more ready to see how these versions of the New Religions belonged structurally in a pluralistic society. On one hand, and the point is so obvious it hardly needs elaboration, great attention is paid to demarcating behavioral accents. One attends a seance on a wet afternoon just as others go to "the church of their choice." The rites of a witch coven or neo-pagan cults are diverse from and even sometimes the obverse of Christian worship. A certain conduct is expected of people in theosophical or Rosicrucian groups.[16] They may all be "gnostic," stressing secret and arcane knowledge, particular interpretations of reality, rich in cognitive implications— though to the larger society it is the behavior and not the ideas of the group that matters. The occult cult deals with what is anomalous in the larger culture's generally accepted storehouse of truths,[17] and offers both knowledge about it and a course of conduct.

On the other hand, most of these groups also take pains to remain acceptable, to let most aspects of their life appear ordinary in the mainstream culture. They are respectables who belong to many levels of "the establishment." Indeed, a kind of occult-metaphysical establishment exists, its members vastly outnumbering the more effervescent and extravagant members of radical groups in "the occult explosion." While admitting that one sounding is not sufficient evidence, I shall nevertheless review here the findings of an exploration of the face that occultists present to their own clienteles. The exploration was made by studying dozens of popular magazines in the field at the height of the explosion, in the winter and spring of 1970. (More empirical research must be undertaken and is being followed up in this area. While this question was not central to their inquiries, one gets the impression, in the essays collected by Zaretsky and Leone in *Religious Movements in Contemporary America*, that great numbers of occultists and Spiritualists are very safe and respectable middle-class people. The exceptions in life style were located largely in groups that appealed chiefly to society's outcasts or economically depressed groups).

Let me simply quote highlights from spokespersons in "the Occult Establishment."[18] They cherished psychologist Gardner Murphy's distinction between "lunatic fringes" and "normal fringes," taking pride in their fringe existence and stressing their normality. The reports of seances were banal and obvious; little of substance about the character of the afterlife or the nether world was offered. The editorialists complained that their movements were receiving a bad name because of countercultural extremism. They shared then–Vice President Spiro T. Agnew's view of the media. Thus in the case of Timothy Leary's religion of mind expansion through drugs, "if so much publicity had not been given" in the media, "it probably would not have spread so much and so fast," said the popular Dane Rudhyar. In the years of "the generation gap," writers like Rudhyar sanely and properly assumed that most of their readers were on the adult side; he could ask his clientele whether "we, their elders," might not give the young religious addicts a healthful alternative.

Drugs fascinated the writers and represented a challenge to them, since they seemed to offer some experiences similar to those advertised in many groups. *The Rosicrucian Digest* was typical in its call for patience with the drug taker, coupled with judgment on him:

> However, his *modus operandi*, or use of drugs, is quite wrong. He is impatient; he is not willing to resort to the *technique* of meditation to find illumination and inspiration. We may say that he is like a man who finds a door to a room which he wishes to enter to be difficult to open. Instead of taking sufficient time to properly open the door, he blasts it open with an explosive, thereby not only ruining the door but the contents of the room as well.

The dispute is not over the content of the illumination or inspiration but over a *modus operandi*, a use, and a technique—all behavioral, not cognitive matters.

Sex was another zone of inquiry. Respectable behavior was the norm. In *Prediction* magazine H. J. D. Murton told of four prominent psychics who resigned from a panel because their findings would have been published in *Penthouse*, surrounded by "nude photographs in luxuriant, something-colour," and by other reading matter that "appears to be concerned with a kind of free-for-all 'permissiveness' (euphemism for sex with everything.)" This is far from the orgiastic picture of the movement in explosion.

While the countercultural minority disguised its traces to white middle-class origins and outlooks, the occult establishment, whose journals far out-circulated the communications of the radicals, were as revealing about themselves in assumptions about race as they were about age and sex. Blacks almost never appeared on their pages. Nor did Orientals, even though Oriental wisdom from the past was prized. Nonwhite Americans were almost always "they." Ray Palmer in *Search* slipped into racist imagery as vivid as that practiced by imperialists at the turn of the century, when he expounded reincarnation: "The creator initially took a character of a principle and embodied it in special flesh form, the rosy human form. That's us. We are human. Our 'hue' is rosy red. We are also 'man'." Later the divine spirit will decide "what the next embodiment in rosy flesh will be."

Occultists boast about progress in a success culture. Thus witch Sybil Leek in her *Astrology Journal* bragged as much as Protestant evangelists ever have: "of America's 1,750 newspapers, more than 1,200 now carry a regular astrology column and most national magazines have their own astrologers." The heroes and heroines in these magazines were the heroes of what was then called "middle America." To risk a huge generalization: behaviorally, so far as the larger culture was concerned, one seemed to be reading the *Reader's Digest* except insofar as each cult or movement had to address the questions of practice and conduct issuing from its own stance toward the anomalous, the position that gave it a reason for existence and an attracting power.

What mattered throughout the occult and metaphysical movements was not new knowledge about the gods, new dogmas or doctrines. The movements did not come up with basic new structures, though the communes of the counterculture represented novelty to those who were unaware of their nineteenth-century precedents. Politically they tended to be withdrawn and noncommittal. They show up on the religious map, at least in the eyes of those external to all of the groups, almost exclusively because of their concentration on process, on practice. The public was interested in the focus on telepathy and the extrasensory as media, not as messages. Magic, hypnosis, healing, astral travel, levitation, clairvoyance, casting of horoscopes, following numerology, interpreting handwritings, reading palms, dowsing and water-witching, prayer with a hoped-for effect on plants—it was these that were preoccupying. In the occult establishment, further, behavior referred to ritual and not, except by casual implication, to ethics. Social activism was an alien concept; world-changing was highly secondary to other concerns.

Insofar as the public had contact with the literature of the movement, it would also come to know of the artifacts and products that went with the ritual life: mystic incense, astrological love secrets, directions for burning candles, commanding oil, fast luck power, lucky planet incense, and the like appeared on page after page, along with elaborate directions for their usage. Such wares accompany other complicated and full-blown religions, but appear in the context of dogmatic systems, institutional power, and political intentions—all of them missing here.

The occult and metaphysical half of the New Religions does not always issue in collective representations or group life. It is especially prone to producing advocates of what Thomas Luckmann calls "invisible religion." Much of it is propagated through mail-order or private purchase and reading of literature. Lonely people in apartments may never attend society or cult meetings, yet be informed by them. In all those senses it falls more or less outside the scope of a book on social behavior in religion or, as "invisible religion," belongs on its margins. Here the interest is on social dimensions: what happens when people convert to, attend, and behave in occult cults? What goes on in a Spiritualist seance, a coven, a Scientological gathering, a meeting of "I Am" members?

Similarly, as we move toward the kin of these groups, Eastern religions, it must be recognized that much is private and invisible and not a social force at all (except insofar as anything that an individual holds or does has some sort of bearing on the order around him or her). On the collective level, it is important to note that the practical, ritual, and behavioral correlates receive almost all attention in the New Religions from the East just as they did in those that came from the past (Egypt, and so forth) or the future (reincarnation, other worlds).

The members of Eastern groups shared in the benefits of demarcation that they offered, the support for identity their collective life gave. After the Second Vatican Council, "being a Catholic" told the world less and less about a person. Being a Protestant in most cases projected very little in the way of behavioral expectations. But whoever followed the practices of the International Society for Krishna Consciousness or Vedanta Societies was immediately marked off as being different and doing different things. One knew what to expect.

While Eastern religion had been known to scholars in the West for centuries, in America it was seen as part of the idolatry that Christian missionaries would overcome. Not until after 1893, when Swami Vivekenanda stayed on after the World's Columbian Exposition, to attract attention with his ochre turban and his orange robe, were Americans served notice that religion could move from East to West as well as from West to East. Literature on his version of hatha joga through all the years has concentrated on posture and gesture, on technique and ritual—not on intellectualization or institutionalization or politics.

Through the years an increasing trickle of Hindu and Buddhist groups became visible to readers of the Saturday religion page of Los Angeles newspapers. By 1949 Charles S. Braden could list numerous Asian groups in *These Also Believe*; more and more of them were noticed in successive editions of Frank S. Mead's *Handbook of Denominations in the United States*, where their status as denominations helped rank them as institutionally ordinary. While the *Yearbook of American Churches* (later to include Canada in its title and scope) took notice of their presence, by 1971, at the time of the height of new public awareness of the subject, only the Baha'i Faith (not strictly "Asian"), the Buddhist Churches of America, and the Vedanta Society of New York were classified with the religious groups, though scores of Eastern choices were by then available.[19]

More incredibly, in an update in 1975 of Leo Rosten's *Religions of America* ("A New Guide and Almanac") I find only one reference to the whole cluster. Significantly, it concentrates only on behavior, and that pejoratively in a misclassification of a group. Under "Psychology of Pentecostalism" we read that "the emotionally starved or disturbed (*vide* the weaving, chanting street celebrants of 'Hare Krishna,' reiterated over and over for hours on end) often seem possessed by psychopathological, rather than explicitly religious, aberrations."[20]

The middle-class parents whose children are caught up in a Vedanta-based group would not characteristically ask, "What are the doctrines of the group?" They cared little about the denominational machinery and less about the marginal political implications of what looked to them like drop-out groups. Their questions would be psychosocial in character, as Rosten's answer was. What is their appeal? Do they attract the disturbed? Why do they summon energies of educated and affluent young people, while the poor keep their distance? What spell has been cast? What leads my child to abandon old ways, to leave home, to join a cult, to take such a different spiritual route? What do the rituals, disciplines, diets, and practices all mean? The answers they receive to such questions strangely avoid or transcend intellectual or institutional formulations and stress practice and perception.

While in their effervescent stage most of the Asian groups seemed to be extravagantly different from Western religions, with the passage of time many of them accommodated themselves or were co-opted by the mainstream culture. In his short season as a television celebrity, the Maharishi Mehesh Yogi was portrayed as a kind of Himalayan guru with all the trappings of religious symbolism. When that moment was past and as Transcendental Meditation came to be a more commercial venture, propagated through a university in Iowa and a network of teachers, the nonreligious context and meaning received all the attention. Fairly orthodox Christians took up the technique; their insistence that there was no doctrinal abrasion is the important point. TM, as it came to be called, had to do with a style of consciousness and of living.

If the behaviorally more exceptional Vedanta Societies failed through six decades to attract suburbanites, yoga translated for suburbanites did. A matron might go for yoga to the Young Women's Christian Association, hardly designed originally as an agency commissioned to promulgate other religions. A Presbyterian executive might just as well find yoga techniques taught on Tuesday night at his own church. Neither of them would come across theological clashes between two religions; institutionally the yogis were adaptive to what was present and politically they were passive. The experience was focused on the body, on health, the sense of well-being. But many a practitioner found that his or her instructor moonlighted as a full-fledged Eastern religionist who also saw these practices to be locked into an alternative mode of perceiving reality, one that hardly paralleled the linear-historical and purposive Western religious type.

Wheresoever two or three yoga or Zen students gathered, conversation almost never had to do with intellectual constructs but with liberation from them. These religions dealt not with institutions but with transcendence of them; with alternatives to, not expressions of, political and social concern. The talk would have to do with gestures and posture, garb and bodily awareness.

Most consistent and most demanding of the New Religions, as Americans comprehended them during the 1960s, was Zen Buddhism. Thanks to efforts of intellectuals, "Instant Zen," a near-commercialization of this ancient religion, was made available to thousands, many of whom began to attend temples or retreats. The first signs of a Zen presence in America also appeared around and after 1893, when the Abbot Soyen Shaku of Engaku Monastery at Kamakura, Japan, visited America. Better known around the middle of the twentieth century was the tireless Daisetz Teitaro Suzuki, his disciple, who publicized and taught this form of Buddhism. After the poets and novelists had taken it up in the 1950s, it "caught on" in the midst of the religious ferments of the 1960s. While the movement resisted denominationalization, Zen centers on campuses lined up next to other religious foundations, and there were also centers like the major one at Tassajara, 150 miles south of San Francisco. A determinedly nonintellectual movement, as Westerners measure these things, in the public eye it is also measured for its practices and conduct, temples and postures, masters and "koans," haiku poetry and swordsmanship, attempts to halt the productivity of the "monkey mind," a practical tough-minded relation to life, meal ceremonies and tea rituals, disciples and disciplines, daily routines and life-long ways.

When rejection came from some circles, it was also on behavioral grounds. Theodore Roszak found it vulnerable to "adolescentization."[21] Its anti-intellectualism was, he thought, too jejune; its American forms a perversion of Oriental ways of transcending ordinary consciousness and rationality. But it did serve well as another organizing center for those who found the larger American patterns of behavior too diffuse, too inclusive. It is not for ideas that one goes to Americanized Asian faiths; of dogma there has been plenty in the West, say those open to conversion. They are more at home with organizations that offer and expect syndromes of behavior; for that, it is better to "travel light" intellectually. Thus E. Pinard de la Boullaye, a sociologist of religion, has observed:

> The more the number of beliefs agreed upon by the members of the same social group is reduced, the more is the uniformity of thought and feeling among them restricted. . . . Likewise, the more the number of common doctrines is reduced, the more does social union produce participation in the same liturgical action, or in the same temporal advantages.[22]

While no nonadherent can judge the internal behavior or get inside the ideational context of an adherent, he can as an observer of external behavior notice how few are the beliefs, yet how strong is the uniformity of thought and feeling and how focused in social union is the liturgical action. One knows *exactly* what to expect of Baba-lovers, followers of the (half-Eastern) Reverend Sun Myung Moon, or Hare Krishna chanters—there are no surprises. That is how the members want it; therein is much of the appeal, in an age of identity diffusion and absence of demarcational lines in society and most of its faiths. Or, as Allan W. Eister put it in an impressive study of language in the recent past:

> dislocations in the orientational and communicational institutions of contemporary societies—and especially in the norms and elements of communication of 'meaning'— should be regarded as a major factor in the current surge of interest in cults.[23]

So far we have spoken chiefly of whites, members of the dominant culture, who felt themselves dislocated, so far as "the orientational and communicational institutions of contemporary" society are concerned. They thus turned to occult or Eastern cults. (The non-Asians in America have given relatively little attention to the Asians who have always practiced religions of the Orient; theirs has been a kind of "invisible religion" as far as most people outside the San Francisco Bay area are concerned.) Many more reasons for the feeling of dislocation are evident in the case of American Indians and American blacks. Even for us to speak of their renewed faiths as part of the New Religions illustrates the point. Highly aware of the historical length and depth of these religions and equally aware that the present approach can easily be misunderstood, we should insist upon this point: for mapping religious America, one must look not at the literal truth—whatever that may be—but at the "myths" of the American majority. This is, in a sense, a history of perceptions in contemporary history. And the faces of Indian and black religion in their more militant and tribal forms are unfamiliar to non-Indians and nonblacks.

Vine Deloria, the most eloquent spokesman for recent American Indian Religion, could not be more clear on this point. Scores of pages in his *God Is Red* (1973) are justifiable complaints that the white culture does not know the Indians and their religion. Or they think that this religion, with all its species, belongs only to a past. All the issues discussed in the present work can be seen in magnified form when one reads *God Is Red* or its lesser counterparts.

The American Indian, therefore, has a problem of finding and expressing his identity not so much in reference to his tribal subculture but in every contact with the larger culture. He or she has tradition, but for hundreds of years white society has denied its validity and foreseen its end; this causes stress for young persons in Indian cultures. While the reservation spatially segregates Indians and has made possible the perpetuation of traditional practices, many of the negative features of pluralist life have reached the reservation, and the urbanized Indian is almost overwhelmed by them.

The reader of Deloria will also see how all the levels of access to a religion have to be employed. Lest anyone be condescending about the role of ideas or beliefs in religions that are not transmitted basically through libraries, Deloria's pages should be studied in detail. He is well known for his rejection of Christianity because of its "linear" history and styles of rationality. Therefore, schooled as he has been in Christian theology—he once went to a denominational seminary—he is also careful not to regard as normative the Greek or Germanic modes that seem standard in so much Western theology. But on a different set of terms there *is* a theology. His chapter titles point to its outlines: "Thinking in Time and Space"; "The Problem of Creation"; "The Concept of History"; "The Spatial Problem of History"; "The Origin of Religion"; "Death and Religion"; "Human Personality"; "The Group." Anthropologists often despair of subsuming the highly particularized views of the disparate tribes under too-general categories, and some would fault Deloria for overgeneralization. But his overall point is established: despite centuries of threat to them, the Indians' *creencias* hold together. That is, they have subcultural ideas or beliefs that are held so deeply they do not even know they hold all of them until they are asked. They are not ideas that Indians "have" but ideas that they "are."

These *creencias* are also linked to the *vigencias*, the binding customs of life. The mapper who wants to study the institutionalization of Indian Religion will find field work to last a lifetime. While many Indians are members of Christian churches, their denominational life differs from the norm. On the reservation Christianity was often supported by the state, as a result of President Grant's Indian policy. Unlike most denominationalists, Indians were given little room for initiative in shaping those borrowed or imposed institutions. What is more, they were often left in such isolation or were so successful at maintaining it, that they could sustain tribal institutions that differed from mainstream culture's churches.

In the last few years tribal religions have seen a renewal of interest that astounds many people. The Pueblos of New Mexico and the Navajos of Arizona had managed to retain much of their ceremonial life throughout the period of religious suppression. The Hopi in particular preserved many of their ceremonies with relative purity. The Apaches also had kept a number of their tribal ceremonies. In the Northwest some of the tribes kept their ceremonies by holding them in secret on the isolated reservations lacking sufficient federal resident staff to prohibit them.

The third paradigm for telling the story of American religions is applicable at every stage to the Indian narrative, and will continue to be so. The Bureau of Indian Affairs, as a governmental agency, shows up at each turn of each story, usually as a negative reference point. The great incidents of the decade which brought more visibility to Indians were completely mingled with political affairs. These would include the event in December 1970, when President Richard M. Nixon signed into law a bill that saw the return of the sacred Blue Lake back to the Taos Pueblo Indians. Deloria sees the year 1969 as marking "the beginning of the massive and sustained drive by American Indians to bring their message to the American public." This drive issued in confrontations on a bridge to Canada; at a Gallup, New Mexico, ceremonial; at Alcatraz; in South Dakota; and most of all at the Bureau of Indian Affairs in Washington. The Wounded Knee, South Dakota, incident suggests how potent the political aspects of Indian life and religion are and will no doubt remain for years to come.

These institutional and political expressions grow out of the *creencias*, the beliefs that make up the world view of Indians. But they are most visible as *vigencias*, customs and habits in the elaborate set of rituals, ceremonies, and practices. If the thesis of this book holds up, that we are a "nation of behavers," then in this as in other ways the American Indians are the true Americans. They established the prototypes into which so much other American religion is growing. If in the 1960s and 1970s there was a notable tribalism in American group life, it was learned from the Indian, who was "there" first. Recoveries of nature endowed with spirit, a realization of the ritual character of the human, a search for an identity bonded with a land—all these were anticipated in Indian life. So the very old religions called here the New Religions did provide a new infusion into other religions.

As Deloria outlines Indian beliefs, he must do so in constant reference not to how one theologian responded systematically to another theologian but rather how different tribes enacted similar visions. What codes of conduct, taboos, moral expectations issued from the beliefs about reality held by the tribes and the individuals that made them up? He did not even need separate chapters on behavior; it was through the social behavior and the oral tradition of Indians that he discerned what we are here calling their theology and their belief-systems.[24]

A white Jesuit, accepted more than are most non-Indians on the reservations, also wrote on American Indian Religion, with special reference to its relations to Christianity. Carl F. Starkloff, in *The People of the Center*, devoted one of five chapters to the *creencias*. These were "the mythical and doctrinal dimensions," gathered under the categories of the High God, Divine Intermediaries and Demigods, Creation, Eschatology, and Cosmology. He cannot be accused of having slighted this thought world.

The rest of the book is devoted to the *vigencias*; the proportion seems proper. Thus the second chapter is devoted to "the ritual dimension." Ritual is a sacrament of creation, reinforced by song and dance, rites of play and humor, and related to "the ritual of the life cycle." He then turns to "the ethical and social dimensions" of behavior, there to deal with tribal justice, individual and social development, and myths as morality tales. A fourth expository chapter treats "the experiential dimension" and touches the importance of the senses, Indian prayer, and suffering and religious experience. Reciting or paraphrasing a book's chapter titles is not an exciting form of literature; the purpose here is to show how

interpretations of Indian Religion inevitably stress social behavior in its nexus with few but firmly held beliefs.

The New Religion of American Indians, as perceived by
non-Indians, appeared as part of the episode of upheaval
during which America's religious map was being redrawn in
the late 1960s. Deloria knew that in part the public consciousness derived from changes worked by the black Civil
Rights movement, which came to public attention fifteen
years earlier and reached new Black Power stages around
1960, almost a decade before Deloria's *annus mirabilis*, 1969.
While Deloria saw much white sentimentalization and commercial exploitation, Starkloff could also accurately report:

> There is a new openness to the great values that lie at
> some level of Native American life: the deep religious
> instincts and symbolism, the sense of solidarity with
> creation, the primitive and profound philosophies of life,
> the unique gifts of personal and social integrity.[25]

White and other Americans, in search of their own identity
and tradition, were looking at land and tribe and were finding
the native Americans' religions as a means of gaining access—or were finding that cluster of religions intrinsically
valid. The counterculturalists often made fads of their borrowings from the Indians. Critics of rational institutionalism
and intellectualism in the conventional churches quoted with
favor expressions like that of Chief Joseph: "We may quarrel
with men sometimes about things on this earth, but we never
quarrel about God. We do not want to learn that."[26]

Just as occult and Eastern New Religions in the American
sixties came with elaborate prehistories, so did Indian faiths.
Deloria notes that these were not easily available to a new
generation; "The American Indian Movement became so at-
tached to the tribal religious ceremonies that more experienced Indians began referring to them as the Indian version
of the 'Jesus freaks.' " But, he went on, "few Indians realized
the extent to which the world had changed since the days of

Chief Joseph." No longer could one charge the wagon train. Yet activists tried to do that during the occupation of the Bureau of Indian Affairs. They were ready to die. "It was almost as if the Ghost Dance had returned with its tragic vision of Wounded Knee."[27] In that one paragraph he referred to two high points of that prehistory, the leadership of Chief Joseph (d. 1904) and the ritual outburst of Indian messianism after 1888 and culminating in the massacre of 1890.

Another ongoing Indian traditional religious motif that attracted attention in the late 1960s was that expressed by the Native American church. The counterculture welcomed it because the central ritual involved the chewing of *laphophora williamsi*, a cactus "button" that induced a kind of mystical experience. And scientists or theologians also were interested because they were studying mind-expansion, altered states of consciousness, and the like. Theologically, the church blended a kind of Protestant fundamentalism with traits of Indian faith. Institutionally it displayed full-scale denominational form, claiming more than 50,000 members. Politically it was important as a test of laws dealing with church and state, since the peyote drug was outlawed outside ritual; could it be permitted within it? Most of all, it was studied as an exemplification of a "ritual behavior [that] . . . is principally Indian in character."[28] Too much can be made of this church, which also had roots before the 1960s, but it symbolized the way in which what is often called the "revitalization" of Indian culture, beginning in the 1880s and coming to new crest in the late 1960s, showed up as a religious behavioral Gestalt. In the face of the "dislocations in the orientational and communicational institutions of contemporary society," the Indians found resources in their religion. So did many non-Indians.

The final major species of the genus the New Religions is Black Religion in America. Once again I feel constrained to remind readers that I know that black faiths, African, Afro-

American, American, Christian, or whatever, are very old. But in this history of perceptions and mappings, something happened to bring them to the attention of nonblacks and to help them "alter the consciousness" of many blacks, who appropriated them or used them in new ways. If the public first saw the movement in simply political terms, as a march toward fuller civil rights, gradually it became clear that roots were in something more than the merely tactical.

Historians may be reluctant to speak of "watershed years," but there are some reasons to agree with Clifton F. Brown, who saw 1968 as such a time. "The death of Dr. Martin Luther King and the publication of *The Black Messiah* by Rev. Albert B. Cleage, Jr.—the former representing the end of a dream, the latter heralding a new hope," provided a hinge.

> Young black militants were demanding more direct and forceful means to ameliorate the black man's plight in America. New concepts, often diametrically opposed to King's concepts of Christian love, nonviolence and integration, surfaced in the black community. "We shall overcome" was being replaced as a slogan with such phrases as "Black is beautiful" and "We are not the Black minority but the chosen few." A social movement was turning into a holy cause. With the publication of Cleage's *The Black Messiah*, the "religiocification" of the revolution began in earnest.[29]

This "religiocification" may have only been a momentary part of the black revolution. Hard-headed pragmatic politics and some retreat from militancy followed it. The black community is as secular or as invisibly religious as the white, from many points of view. But it was a sufficiently profound event that it established an awareness of Black Religion on this part of America's religious map. The religiocifying blacks had to invent their black faith, "invent" meaning both to fashion and to find. They found it in Africa, in slave culture,

in the segregated underground, in modern movements that
fused blackness with spirituality.

The prehistory of the new Black Religion stage has subsequently been traced in earnest. The scholars progressively
came to the conclusion that the African roots would never
become easily accessible but that they also would not go
away; conversely, that the black Christian growths were often
different from those of whites, but that they also would not
disappear. The Christian theologians in the Negro communities had to warn against romanticism and revolutionary rejection. Thus J. Deotis Roberts complained that it was "dis-
turbing to see the young repudiate the faith that sustained
their black forefathers and made life possible for them. . . .
A religious experience that has brought such fulfillment, comfort, and strength for our people is surely worth having and
should not be glibly discounted as a mere opiate." Daily,
Roberts said, "we see black youth snap their fingers in de-
rision against one of the richest spiritual traditions known to
man." Such finger-snapping was a threat since "people cannot make it without meaning, especially if they are an
oppressed people seeking liberation." They would have to
live with what W. E. B. Du Bois had described as their
"doubleness." They could not truly go back to the real Africa,
but only to a symbolic one in their religion.[30]

The debate was not beside the point; it centered on the
questions of identity and power that motivated so much of
the religious change and, in turn, the redrawing of the map
of American religion. The full story of the incident of the
sixties and early seventies does not belong and cannot be
told here. For mapping purposes, we must only underscore
once again the behavioral concentration that made possible
the isolation of the movement.

So far as the belief systems, ideas, cognitive aspects are
concerned, the myths and stories were as complex in Black
Muslim, Black Israel, Black Christian, or Black African
faiths as they were in American Indian religion. The fact

that many had been transmitted in a nonliterate culture did not mean that there were no beliefs, no *creencias*, no immediate ways of looking at the world and of telling the stories of the people. But historians of theology would be little moved by the kind or content of these ideas, and would tend to overlook most of the movement. Institutionally, Black Religion adhered to most of the denominational, sectarian, and cultic sociological patterns already established in the wider culture. Politically there was potency, and the story of the impact of Black Religion on the *polis* remains largely untold. But it is the conduct and practice, the ritual enactment and the expression in song, that is most distinctive and revelatory.

The behavior characteristics are central to the ongoing debate about the Africanity of American Black Religion. A classic statement of one side was made as early as 1942 when Melville Herskovits pointed to several presumed characteristics that had survived intercontinental transit. These included spirit possession, dancing, African singing forms, "river-crossings," walks, shallow burials, the passing of small children over a coffin, the inclusion of food and money in coffins, fear of cursing, and improvisation of ridicule songs. The challenges came at once. Were these characteristic of any large body of African-American religious groups? Could they not have developed spontaneously in two continents? Were racist characterizations involved? What anthropological presuppositions were implied in the pro and con statements?[31]

In 1944 Arthur Fauset came out with a full-dress response to those who made too much of racial characteristics and African ties. "Common sense requires us to believe that everything cultural which the Negro brought over with him from Africa could not have been eradicated from his heritage." But if earlier students made too much of the complete eradication of African survivals, "neither can we accept every chance correspondence which might appear to indicate survival."[32] What is significant about Herskovitz's arguments and Fauset's findings in a study of cults is that both of them and their successors find it necessary to debate the issues of cultic life, of gesture, of racial trait and behavioral correlates more than theological content, institutional inventiveness, or political impact, though the latter remain very strong.

Some of the earlier cults had come with full-blown cognitive symbol systems; the Kingdom of Father Divine was one of these. Here were complete microcosms, as two scholars called them,[33] that failed their adherents as they re-entered "the world of reality." But while Father Divine's myth issued in ritual and conduct addressed to every aspect of life, its grand theme had little to do with blackness. The development of that motif came in various movements in black peoplehood. Thus as early as the second decade of the century "Black Jews" were rewriting the history of their past—and observing it with quasi-Jewish ritual. Howard M. Brotz's survey of the movement locates it as one of "status-oriented behavior."[34]

Black Jews, "Moors," "Moslems," "Coptic Egyptians," Black Israel and other attempts to establish an alternative sense of peoplehood for oppressed American blacks came to a climax in the much better-known Black Muslim movement. While it existed as early as 1930 in Detroit, only in the 1960s did it come to attention of enough blacks and whites to make it part of the perception of New Religions. In a forty-item bibliography on the Muslims, only one address by the prophet Elijah Muhammad and one article dating from 1959 antedate the 1960s.[35] First of the remaining 38 items in prominence and almost in time was C. Eric Lincoln's decisive *The Black Muslims in America*, published in 1961.

Lincoln saw the Muslims in the context of Third World strivings; they were "symptomatic of the anxiety and unrest which characterizes the contemporary world situation," in which threats to the continued existence of a group or to the

values without which existence to the group would be mean-
ingless motivate militant response. "Whenever there is an
actual or felt discrepancy in the power relations of discrete
systems or subsystems, a condition of social anxiety will
emerge." The Black Muslims were among "the best organized
and most articulate of the power movements." No one could
accuse Elijah Muhammad of failing to provide beliefs and
myths for his followers. But he succeeded so well in keeping
his people from assimilating into the mainstream culture that
he had to come up with a complete system of conduct and
ritual to reinforce their new world view. It is precisely in
this guise that the Muslims present themselves to the world:
as a Puritanical, morally rigid group, following routinized
and prescriptive ethical patterns that help distance the members from what Lincoln calls "the American creed," and
producing the Fruit of Islam, people who exclude whites
from their rallies.[36]

With the passage of time the Black Muslims began to enter the mainstream, the extreme moment of their disaffiliation having been past. Paradoxically, it was the popularity
of dissident Muslim Malcolm X, who had been assassinated
in a factional conflict that found him a heretic, that helped
give the movement respectability in the non-Black Muslim
world. Soon after the death of Elijah Muhammad in 1975
there was a lessening of antiwhite mythology and behavior,
the prophet himself having signalled a moderation in his last
year; by the summer of that year the press was delighting in
reports of expensive social occasions sponsored by the Black
Muslims at which whites of prominence were present.

The 1960s saw the flowering of many other lesser-known
movements of black peoplehood or religion; these often
were new articulations of "black theology" in Christian circles. Important as they were as interpretations of life, they
reached only the few and were similar in location and potency
to Christian theology produced by whites in the same period.
More noticeable to the population at large were the practices

and behavior of the militant groups or those that stressed identity and black traditions. In another study of the Black Muslims James H. Laue uses a term that applies to the goal and product of so many of these observed groups, whether Indian or black, countercultural or whatever: they shaped a substitute identity which the hostile or uncaring larger society could not supply.

Laue's research was based on a theory of revitalization movements that had been proposed by anthropologist A. F. C. Wallace in 1954. Wallace offers the promising metaphor of a "mazeway," a mental image of self, society, nature, and culture through which values operate in maintaining social order.

> Whenever an individual who is under . . . chronic
> stress receives repeated information which indicates that
> his mazeway does not lead to action which reduces the
> level of stress, he must choose between maintaining
> his present mazeway and tolerating the stress, or chang-
> ing the mazeway in an attempt to reduce the stress. . . .
> It may also be necessary to make changes in the "real"
> system in order to bring mazeway and "reality" into
> congruence. The effort to work a change in mazeway
> and "real" system together so as to permit more effective
> stress reduction is the effort at revitalization; and the
> collaboration of a number of persons in such an effort is
> called a revitalization movement.

The New Religions were vitalization or revitalization movements along these lines. Those who were occultists or who practiced Eastern religions entirely privately, in the sphere of "invisible religion," changed the mazeway and reduced the stress; so did those who quietly joined passive but satisfying cults. The counterculturalists, who, along with the militant Indians and blacks, wanted to change the whole society, went further, hoping to make changes in the 'real' system as well. Wallace saw people moving from discontentment with their original "steady state," through a "period of increased individual stress" and "cultural distortion," to a "period of revitalization" and then to a "new steady state." Later historical glances may confirm the impressions of the mid-seventies that the New Religions have reached such a state. "A new *Gestalt* is in operation, both for the members of the revitalized group and the host and/or neighboring cultures. . . . [T]he movement has been institutionalized."[37]

The neighboring cultures had a new Gestalt. I have spoken not only of the establishing of the New Religions on the landscape and in the description of the landscape but also of their "suffusive" character. Western religionists meditate; "secular man" thinks there *may* be something to astrology; collegians follow the Indians back to nature and tribe; Catholic liturgists adopt what they can from black revitalization religions. The episode may have passed, but the New Religions, even in "steady state," had changed the religious map and opened a new vista and made new options available to the subsequent generation.

Ethnic Religion

Churches, sects, and cults belong to the familiar landscape of contemporary religion; their landmarks represent few problems to mappers. But the attempt to recover a bond between ethnicity or race and religion carries the observer to subterranean levels and seems to have to do with archaeology, with a forgotten past that is being artificially unearthed. Most people are aware that in primitive societies there were tribal religions; they know of the myths of peoplehood used to explain the divine origin of various races or nations. The coming of international world religions like Buddhism, Hinduism, and Islam should have left such primeval faith behind. In any case, the universal design of Christianity ought to negate tribalism; at worst, the aftereffects of tribalism should disappear as the memory of separate immigrations to America recedes in the modern setting.

Despite these assumptions about the passing of ethnic or racial religion, an episode of the 1960s "put it back on the map," or at least brought to view something that many had begun to forget. The incident was a world-wide fresh expression of racial self-consciousness, as part of the new nationalist and anticolonial impulses in what came to be called the Third World. The domestic version of this expression was most visible in the articulation of American black pride and power. Accompanying this was a corollary awakening of interest by American Indians, or a public awareness of their self-images; the same could be said of Chicanos and other minorities. Southern and eastern Europeans in America, sometimes by way of compensation or backlash and at others as part of a simple assertion of their own traditions and identity, came to be known as "ethnics" who had their own voice. And the old American majority, "white Protestants," most of them of Anglo-Saxon descent, were finally seen to be a racial or ethnic expression, much as they had regarded the classic "minorities" to have been.

Little of this American situation could have been or was foreseen in the 1950s, though now and then there were prophecies of war on racial lines; in 1966 Ronald Segal summarized the issues in a book ominously called *The Race War*.[1] Prophetically, William E. Burghardt Du Bois had looked ahead in 1900 and had said, "The problem of the twentieth century is the problem of the colour line—the relation of the darker to the lighter races of men in Asia and Africa, in America and the islands of the sea."[2] Between 1945 and 1960 eight hundred million people in forty countries revolted and won their independence from white colonial powers. "Never before in the whole of human history had so revolutionary a reversal occurred with such rapidity," says Geoffrey Barraclough.[3] In 1960 Adlai Stevenson recognized that "due to the admission of so many new countries, the United States and the western democracies no longer control the United Nations."[4] With that change, a white or Western-based secular ecumenical ideal began to fade. The religious counterpart, which came to crests in 1948 with the founding of the World Council of Churches and from 1962 to 1965 with the convoking of the Second Vatican Council, also was compromised and countered by a reassertion of racial, ethnic, national, and denominational loyalties.

The great revolution of which Barraclough spoke could hardly have occurred without a base in or an engendering of ideology; nor could it have occurred without having reverberations in the United States. Seldom do people assert ideology without accompanying or supporting it with religious or quasi-religious sanctions and ceremonies. Maoism is thus seen as a new secular religion. The American racial movements regularly found religious expressions. As a result sociologists, historians, theologians, and other cartographers of the religious terrain had to go back over the traces and come up with new vocabularies and methods. The language of denomination, church, sect, and cult was not sufficiently broad to cover the ethnic or racial context. In a summary article, "Ethnicity: The Vital Center of Religion in America," Harry S. Stout looked back on the years immediately preceding 1975 and pointed out that

> like church historians, ethnic historians are also noting
> the interrelationship of ethnicity and religion. Most
> notable are the historians of American politics who, in
> pointing to "ethno*cultural*" factors in American political
> behavior, focus primarily on ethno*religious* factors. . . .
> No one has [yet] explained what was the nature of
> the interrelationship between ethnicity and religion in
> America, and, more importantly, why the two were
> so closely linked. Perhaps, as Martin Marty suggests,
> ethnicity is so close to American religion that historians
> have been reluctant to explore its deepest implications.[5]

If the act of mapping "ethnoreligion" is the scholars' response to an episode of the 1960s, it cannot be said that the category itself is new in America. Those who may have been reluctant to use the word "tribal" in connection with literate religions never hesitated to see it central to that of American Indians. While the tribal motif inevitably was qualified or half-forgotten by Africans in America, because of the social jostling brought about by slavery, whoever took pains to look closely could recognize that there were recessive and latent religious explanations of the black peoples' reality. The concept of peoplehood was never foreign to Jewish religion or to anyone who looked at Judaism. While it had thinned out in the experience of Catholics in pluralism, most Americans were aware that some sort of differences persisted between, say, Italian and Irish Catholics. Largely overlooked was the union of Protestant religious themes with the peoplehood of Anglo-Americans in the American majority.

What is more than mildly interesting about the older version of peoplehood which prevailed until around 1960 was that most members of each group took and were even taught to take generally negative attitudes toward the tribalism of every other group; in the 1960s, they came to put a premium on appreciating it. Thus before 1960 the American Indians' religion either went unnoticed, was criticized, or seen as a survival that would pass as they were Christianized. Black Religion was seen by whites as a kind of lower and crude adaptation of their own faith, tinged though it might have been with survivals of African supersitition ("voodoo") or marked by extravagant or exaggerated rituals resulting from blacks' purported racial traits ("rhythm").

Gentiles seldom grasped the horror of the Holocaust, the cosmic negative event that just before mid-century had led Jews to reassert their Jewishness. Nor did all of them understand or agree with the Jewish people's positive assertions in relation to Israel. The latter were regarded as a kind of deterrent to smooth interfaith dialogue, something that would have to be covered over for the sake of harmony. Non-Catholics tended to see Catholicism as a dogmatic and hierarchical homogeneity, its internal variety on ethnic lines lost from view or regarded as passing. Non-Protestants or nonwhites had little difficulty seeing the imperial pretensions and racial pride in the American majority, but that majority thought of both as merely minor legacies. Yet, to use a metaphor or image I have used elsewhere, ethnicity had turned out to be the framework or skeleton of religion in America; around 1960 that skeleton was taken out of the closet.[6]

If old bonds between ethnicity and religion were being forgotten, it should also be said that the new racial consciousness was not universally regarded as having a religious context. (Not every dimension of it did, of course.) It may be that economic determinism had colored the researches of too many scholars, so they were blind to all features except social class in accounting for religion. H. Richard Niebuhr, responsible for so much inquiry about social classes, had actually pointed as well to ethnic diversity. But, as Harold J. Abramson remarked in his article "The Religioethnic Factor and the American Experience,"

> We seem to have forgotten H. Richard Niebuhr (1929, 1957). Or if we have not forgotten him, we have come to ignore his work and too often assumed that ethnicity, as a social source of diversity, is no longer of consequence in religion. When we wish to argue, for a host of ideological and particularistic reasons, that social class is a more enduring and more compelling source of diversity than ethnicity, we make two common mistakes. In the first place, we assume that ethnicity, in the form of national origin, denomination, and/or region, is dead. Thus, we find ourselves dependent on class alone as *the* sole major explanation of structural influence. We lose out in our understanding of the more subtle shadings of the changing American experience.
>
> And secondly, we end up inevitably ignoring the dynamics of change. And here is the greater problem. We too often assume that the American experience means the same thing to all groups. . . . The movements of the 1960's for ethnicity . . . have taught us differently, and the inevitable ethnic assertions of America's blacks, Chicanos, Puerto Ricans, and native Indians, should remind us that the American experience is one that is at least partly ethnicity and partly social class.[7]

Just as there was a bias toward observing social class at the expense of race, so there was a tendency to limit too much the definition of religion to that which can be observed in discrete institutions. Thomas Luckmann has complained

of the narrow focus on "the identification of church and religion" or of the methodological assumption that "religion
may be many things, but it is amenable to scientific analysis
only to the extent that it becomes organized and institutionalized," and of the tendency toward "a rather narrowly con-
ceived sociography of the churches."[8] The recovery or new
visibility of ethnic and racial senses was concurrent with
many efforts by theologians and anthropologists to enlarge
the focus and the range to include phenomena that had
earlier not been regarded as religious.

The new map of American religion, then, leads its users
to retrace both the ways in which religious impulses inspired
movements of people and the ways in which movements of
peoplehood experienced what black leader Albert B. Cleage
called "religiocification."[9] At the outset, two things should
be noted. First, Ethnic Religion is usually part of "plural
belonging." A person may be a Baptist and a black religionist, a celebrator of Polish pride and a Roman Catholic, an
Appalachian white and a Pentecostalist. This ought to go
without saying, but saying it serves as a reminder that there
are not many formal institutions intentionally designed to
bond religion and race. Exceptions are the Black Muslims,
the Native American Church, and, in more ways than many
would like to think, the Ku Klux Klan.

Second, it should be noted that not all those who are re-
asserting racial and ethnic themes in religion intend thereby
to be purely tribal, to distance themselves entirely from the
pluralistic processes. It is true that in extreme forms there
prevails a kind of tribal solipsism, "the view that my insight
is mine alone and cannot be shared by another."[10] Many use
the identity and power they gain through retreat into their
tribes as instruments for reentry into the larger conversation
and process. The revived ethnic sense helps citizens deal in
a way other than denominationally with the *plures*, the par-
ticularities of American life; they may need the Church

catholic or a national Civil Religion as another part of their "plural belonging" in order to help them realize something of the *unum*, the whole of societal existence.

With those advance cautions in mind, it is possible to examine ethnicity and religion more closely. At this point it is important to say that ethnicity is not all of one piece. The episode of ethnic recovery in the 1960s had artificial dimensions, and they are quickly pointed out by those who are cynical about many claims made for it. From the viewpoint of social behavior, at least two styles of affirming peoplehood became apparent. We can call them Ethnicity A and Ethnicity B, to avoid any hint of the pejorative in dealing with either. The behavior patterns of the two will not necessarily always differ markedly, but the style and tone of each has grown out of different grasps of ethnic or racial backgrounds. Ethnicity A was inescapable, automatic, and reflexive. It issued from people who may have experienced "pluralistic ignorance," having been unaware that there were alternatives to their tribe and its ways. Or they may not have been free to borrow from these alternatives. Needless to say, this form of behavior seemed always to have been in the process of dying out, since new immigrant or otherwise unexposed groups were decreasing in number. Ethnicity B was at least partly escapable, intentional, and reflective. The black who had once "passed" now wore an "Afro," and instead of obliterating African traces in worship, now elevated them. The Jew who had had his name Anglicized restored the original name and, perhaps, turned orthodox and observant.

Ethnicity A produced forms of activity that were associated with newly arrived immigrants who looked out on a hostile world or into a mirror, seeing there only fellow ghetto residents and their ways. Occupational gatekeepers might mediate a larger world before the age of media and mobility, but after it began, only with strenuous efforts such as those taken by Lubavitscher Jews in Brooklyn, Hutterites in South Dakota, Doukhobors in Western Canada—through their chosen geographical remoteness or high ghetto walls—could anyone minimize outside influences.

Ethnicity B issued from a more sophisticated generation, comprised of people who had overcome pluralistic ignorance and had known critical exposure to other clans, tribes, groups, or peoples. "You can't go home again." In typical cases they were sons and daughters of immigrants, people who had at college picked up at least basic sociological or psychological instruments for reflecting on the blur and bewilderment produced by American pluralism. They may have experienced some sense of a loss of personal identity, may have smarted as they heard ethnic slurs and misplaced racial humor. They made a virtue of necessity when they could not escape their tribal ties or a virtue of luxury when they could but chose not to. Having recognized past or present oppression against their group, they became style-setters or spokespersons for other people who shared their lineage but neither their freedoms nor their platforms.

A black church in the South or in an urban slum may, into the 1950s, have kept alive forms of worship and styles of singing that grew out of the plantation experience. A middle-class black congregation, having made its passage through blended Protestant worship forms and having purchased hymnals from its denominational headquarters might by the mid-1960s have found that the almost forgotten spirituals and Gospel songs were available and applicable to their new situation. Theirs was a tradition whites did not have, but could only borrow. The urban church would therefore restore long-forgotten and sometimes even repudiated styles, to serve as an affirmation of blackness and an identification with the struggles of suffering ancestors. But a visitor from the southern rural church would hardly recognize what had been borrowed from him, so radically would it have been transformed by those who can only express Ethnicity B.

The Lubavitscher Jews wore distinctive garbs, followed all orthodox dietary laws, shunned intermarriage, and were overtly hostile to strangers. They incarnated some of the styles of the small community or *shtetl* of Eastern Europe, and in their transplantation of the same were immediately recognizable as part of what we are calling Ethnicity A. A secularized or Reform Jewish coed on a university campus in 1967 might have thrown in her lot with the Arabs. Her choice would have been based on conscious identification with what she thought was the Third World, over against an Israel that to her looked to be part of American imperialism. As time passed, she would become unsure of herself and her loyalties. Eventually she might reaffirm Judaism and choose to follow its orthodox forms. Quite likely, she would write a book advocating Ethnicity B.

Or the experience of mixed marriage and conversion has often led to affirmation of Ethnicity B. Thus a Gentile girl loves a Reform Jewish young man on a college campus. After careful exploration of alternatives she converts and they marry. She is determined that their child will grow up conscious of their Judaism. She will take pains to have a family visit to Israel; they will tend to Jewish practice. Soon they challenge the Jewish parents-in-law to do away with the family's "traditional" Christmas tree. The child receives a Jewish name as his father had not. An acquired ethnic sense demands a different kind of nurture than an inherited one.

Old German Lutheran ministers, though in doctrinal agreement with their Norwegian counterparts, were separated from them behaviorally. At a conference the Germans might take their recreation with a softball game after which the losers would buy the winners a case or five of beer. (The theologically strict Germanic "Missouri Synod became the most thoroughly wet denomination in America, or in the world, for that matter," observes historian Richard Jensen.)[11] They were dimly aware that their fellow-believers among Norwegian pietists disapproved of the practice. As years passed the differences between the groups' patterns diminished. The Germanic lore dwindled as pastors' sons named Sidney or Bruce adopted Anglican styles of clerical garb when they entered the ministry. But in the confusion of ecumenical and pluralist America they reread the old Lutheran writings that their fathers had taken for granted but never studied. They gave *their* sons Germanic names. They studied in Europe. They tried to become Germans of the Germans again—though without letting go of any mixed blessings of the pluralist experience. Ethnicity B.

According to the familiar accounts, the movement from Ethnicity A through pluralist experience to Ethnicity B then seems to be only one-way traffic. The pluralist or critical stage is decisive. But one can with a different handle grasp the old symbols, whether of peoplehood or of the religion bonded with it. The philosopher Paul Ricoeur has made helpful comment on this situation in a much-noticed passage. We cannot go gack to a primitive naiveté. "Something has been lost, irremediably lost: immediacy of belief. But if we can no longer live the great symbolisms of the sacred in accordance with the original belief in them, we can, we modern men, aim at a second naiveté in and through criticism."[12] To carry it a step further: we can through criticism begin to live the great symbolisms in a different way. What Ricoeur regards as an intellectual problem for interpreters can be a behavioral issue for those seeking an identity.

Max Weber anticipated the distinction between the people in what we are calling Ethnicity A and Ethnicity B; his distinction should be kept in mind by anyone using this map of American religion:

> Any aspect or cultural trait, no matter how superficial,
> can serve as a starting point for the familiar tendency
> to monopolistic closure. . . . Almost any kind of similarity
> or contrast of physical type and of habits can induce the
> belief that a tribal affinity or disaffinity exists between

groups that attract or repel each other. . . . The belief in tribal kinship, *regardless of whether it has any objective foundation*, can have important consequences especially for the formation of a political community. Those human groups that entertain a subjective belief in their common descent—because of similarities of physical type or of customs or both, or because of memories of colonization and migration—in such a way that this belief is important for the continuation of non-kinship communal relationship, we shall call 'ethnic' groups, *regardless of whether an objective blood relationship exists or not*. . . . Behind all ethnic diversities there is somehow naturally the notion of the 'chosen people,' which is nothing else but a counterpart of status differentiation translated into the plane of horizontal coexistence. The idea of a chosen people derives its popularity from the fact that it can be claimed to an equal degree by any and every member of the mutually despising groups.[13] [Emphases mine.]

In the American context, some sort of "objective foundation," or "objective blood relationship" will often exist, but it will have been weakened or attenuated through generations of mixed marriage, cultural neglect, or the assimilation processes. This observation leads to another, one with portents for the future. Just as it is difficult to predict or project long-range outcomes for the other five zones on the map of American religion, it is not easy to forecast just how long the religion of Ethnicity will remain a potent phenomenon or epiphenomenon in religion. Too few immigrants arrive to keep Ethnicity A vital. The motivations for expressing Ethnicity B may diminish in a period in which the question of personal identity or group power would be experienced as urgent by fewer people. It may be that some styles of group life can be expressed without recourse to the burden or symbols associated with religion at all. There are, after all, what are by almost all current definitions secular blacks, Indians, Chicanos, Jews, Poles, and Anglo-Americans who are quite conscious of their heritages but do not raise their symbols to the level of ultimate concern and support them ceremonially.

Suffice it to say that from the end of the second third to the beginning of the last third of the century countless Americans did find it valuable to associate religious symbols with racial and ethnic assertions. Significantly, it was during these years that the very word "peoplehood" worked its way into *Webster's New International Dictionary*, whatever such lexicographical status that location may imply. "Peoplehood: the quality or state of constituting a people; *also*: awareness of the underlying unity that makes the individual a part of a people." Similarly, in this period, in common usage the word "ethnic" also came to be not only an adjective but also a noun. Both occurred at a time when assimilative processes seemed to be intensifying; as the authors of *The Real Majority* pointed out, "ethnics are dying out in America and becoming a smaller percentage of the total population."[14]

In the case of the less visible minorities, the southern and eastern European ethnics, the decline was from 26 percent of the population representing "foreign stock" in 1940 to an estimated 15 percent in 1970. They were being taught by the Second Vatican Council—for most of them were Roman Catholic—that they belonged to a single "people of God." But at that moment they also wanted to be members of peoples of God, marked not only by a single magisterial theology, a simple loyalty to a Roman institution, an ordinary licit American polity. They wanted separate identity.[15] Behavioral studies of the extent of the quest for identity are necessary. Could it be that the search is exaggerated by particularly rootless and romantic intellectuals, as some critics suggest? While easily documented in the circles of educated blacks, it has been less substantiated in many white groups, and may be in part a psychological projection by the observers. For now, it remains a very strong hypothesis, weakened by some minor data and confirmed by others.

The recovery of the religious roots and ties to ethnicity would not easily have been discovered nor the discoveries systematized or comprehended had there not been in the same period a growth of curiosity about social behavior. In the terms of this book, the three dominant models or paradigms were at best of meagre service to scholars.

What fresh ideas, at least what ideas of the kind that interest intellectual historians, inspired or issued from the movements? It is hard to think of any real innovations or philosophically deep expositions. The change came in a time when experience was favored over interpretation. In the oft-quoted words of psychiatrist R. D. Laing as he reported on the period: "We do not need theories so much as the experience that is the source of the theory."[16]

Vine Deloria applied rather conventional categories from the history of religion and theology to the American Indian experience to produce *God Is Red.*[17] Among the most eloquent systematic approaches to black religious thought were James H. Cone's *Black Theology and Black Power* and *A Black Theology of Liberation.*[18] Both were greeted by friend and foe alike as a kind of translation of European thinker Karl Barth's theology to the experience of American blacks and were read more for their ingenious reflections on that experience than for any fundamental intellectual breakthroughs. Not a single work was presented as a theology appropriate to the Chicano or Puerto Rican experiences and, for that matter, none accompanied the numerous sociological studies or political notices of white ethnic or white Protestant groups. The single prominent exception to the pattern was the set of books typified by Richard Rubenstein's *After Auschwitz*, a radical theology inspired by the Holocaust and the subsequent intellectual and experiential problems for Jews. To dismiss many of these theological efforts in these terms may seem condescending. It should be remembered that Mainline theology was also not very creative in the years 1965–75, and that few claims were being made that the ethnic religious movements were issuing in first-rate intellectual interpretations. Perhaps, to put the venture in another light, people like Vine Deloria were in their writings trying to turn their back on a European model of "doing theology" in America, to find new categories for mediating group experience and interpreting it.

There are, similarly, very few cognitive differences in the religion of Lithuanian, Latvian, and Estonian Roman Catholics in America. But if these three peoples make up a single "Baltic" reality to outsiders, members of the three national groups are highly conscious of differences in their experiences. These differences may show up in wedding ceremonies, dietary preferences, naming, reverencing diverse local saints, and the like. These are people who suffered their own kind of Holocaust, but have not found it possible or necessary to produce a reflection comparable to *After Auschwitz.*

A recovered sense of ethnicity may even work to blur lines of distinctiveness in theology and in institutional life. There are important interpretive distinctions between Orthodox and Reform Jews. They may read the books in their tradition in varied ways. They may even conceive of God in not fully compatible sets of terms. But the experience of the Holocaust in Europe, the birth of Israel, and the movement from the ghetto to the suburb in America have combined to blend them into a less differentiated kind of Judaism. Israel Bond Drives, United Jewish Appeals, and common responses to anti-Semitism or anti-Zionism were more effective bonding agents than were what Christians would call theological differences.

It was on behavioral grounds, as we have seen in discussing differences between Fundamentalists and Evangelicals, that Protestant groups could often best be sorted out from each other. When Father John A. Hardon, a dogmatically informed Roman Catholic conservative scholar, wrote *The Protestant Churches of America*, he dealt with the cognitive features of each as they are classified in formal works of dogmatics or theology. His renderings were quite accurate, but none of them "felt" right to Protestants, who did not measure themselves in these terms.[19] More explanatory of their modes of being were novels that portrayed the life of New England aristocrats or southern rural Protestants.

Something similar might be said of the institutional metaphor. For the most part the ethnic religiosity was housed in existing denominations or societies. The Black Muslims might be seen as innovative, since their organization was not in all details similar to what had been denominations or protective societies; because of its uniqueness, the movement has been studied in some detail.[20] The Native American Church among the American Indians bore some features of the denomination and some specialized features—but it antedated the period about which we are speaking. For the most part, the new racial consciousness was, to use a biblical metaphor, "new wine in old bottles." The sociologist of religion needs few new categories to observe it institutionally; the historian needs no new vocabulary; the casual observer would recognize almost nothing so far as the form and structure of organizations are concerned.

The third model is more availing, since there were political changes, most of them closely related to the social behavior of the participants. For instance, it was during this period that in city after city the sense of a Roman Catholic bloc vote weakened. Not that the Catholic presence was not being taken seriously. But the people were singularly unresponsive to any formal charges or appeals by their hierarchs. Catholic candidates who acted as "one-issue" politicians to represent presumed Catholic positions on abortion regularly lost even in strongly Catholic districts to non-Catholics who soft-pedaled the issue or even took an independent stance. The

Catholic vote in ethnic wards remained important; Michael Novak even contended that it could be determinative in presidential elections.[21] But it had to be appealed to on the grounds of persuasion with little reminiscence of the at least implied coercion that once could be counted on. That shift is of great political importance and relates both to theological change after Vatican II and behavioral change in pluralist America.

Similarly, it can be shown that during this period white Protestants yielded space; that is, if previously oppressed minorities found new status, they had to do so at the expense of someone. Protestants had the most to lose and became less and less a recognizable political force. Numbers of books critical of the Protestant enterprise appeared;[22] they helped show Protestants how to see themselves as a minority among the minorities. This alteration has political consequences. The converse of this recognition is the growth of power, accompanied by religious sanctions, among blacks: they were led, after all, by the Reverend Martin Luther King, the Reverend Jesse Jackson, the prophet Elijah Muhammad, and the like. Each of these had certain, if circumscribed, kinds of political power, and religious symbols enhanced that power and cast an extra aura of authority over it.

The entire new racial and ethnic religious consciousness represented problems for those who had always stressed the *unum* in national life, for those who favored ecumenical, cosmopolitan, international, and interreligious activities. It seemed to be at least in partial conflict with the concurrent tendency toward the development of a Civil Religion (see next chapter). Against the background of American history it also came as part repudiation, part surprise—at least in the light of one major tradition that had sought a degree of homogenization, perhaps on generalized Protestant lines. Since in the beginning of the nineteenth century race did not count for much—Indians and blacks had no voice, Jews were few—and since Catholics were regarded as agents of a

foreign power, the original centripetal energies had all related to the problems of political partisanship and denominational contention. But the unifying vision was clear. Lyman
Beecher, a Protestant cleric, gave voice to it in the 1820s:

> The integrity of the Union demands special exertions to
> produce in the nation a more homogeneous character and
> bind us together with firmer bonds. . . . Schools, and
> academies, and colleges, and habits, and institutions of
> homogeneous influence . . . would produce a sameness of
> views, and feelings, and interests, which would lay
> the foundation of our empire upon a rock. Religion is the
> central attraction which must supply the deficiency of
> political affinity and interest.[23]

By 1829 Princeton's Charles Hodge could claim that Americans were overcoming Europe's problem of disunity by becoming one people, "having one language, one literature,
essentially one religion, and one common goal."[24]

The vision of one people was easier to sustain in the 1820s
than it would be in the 1860s. By then there were two peoples divided on sectional lines. They divided largely over
another issue having to do with two peoples, blacks and
whites. And the whites were dividing on religious-ethnic
grounds as Irish and Continental Catholics came to confuse
the old picture of "sameness" that white Protestants had
cherished. Theologically the North and the South and the
white and the black among Protestants were similar to each
other. Institutionally they were all denominationalists. Politically they took different sides of issues that they all
recognized. Behaviorally they were vastly different, and the
practices of Roman Catholics and, later, of Jews, further
contributed to the pluralism.

In the midst of this diversifying of life the Protestant church
historian Philip Schaff, who often tried to fuse Continental
and British lineages in America, provided a typical prospect
as he looked ahead on the basis of a

process of national amalgamation [that] is now also going on before our eyes in America; but peacefully, under more favorable conditions, and on a far grander scale than ever before in the history of the world. America is *the grave of all European nationalities*; but a *Phoenix grave*, from which they shall rise to new life and new activity.[25]

But even the gentle and expansive Schaff could not entirely transcend ethnocentrism. The scholar went on to say that this new mix would be "in a new and essentially Anglo-Germanic form." Yet in the process he had given voice to an ideal that was to live on during the second half-century, when the pluralism of peoples in America was so dramatically reinforced and perceived while new immigrants of non–Anglo-Germanic stock appeared. The idea that a "process of national amalgamation" would continue became prevalent. Frederick Jackson Turner, the historian who wanted "the peopling of America" to be studied, looked to the frontier. "In the crucible of the frontier the immigrants were Americanized, liberated, and fused into a mixed race, English in neither nationality or characteristics."[26]

Americanized they became; liberated, probably; "fused into a mixed race?" Hardly. And as the frontier filled and the urban setting became the new area for confrontation, the public schools were called upon to be agencies of assimilation. But they were perceived by Jews, Catholics, and Lutherans to be integrators of the values of white Protestants of British lineages.[27] The attempt to preserve religious differences led some to work especially hard to conform to what they regarded as political norms. "Half-suspect, they bow too low," says Catholic historian John Tracy Ellis in reference to the superpatriotic but mistrusted Catholics of the period.[28] Because they looked and sounded and in their own circles they behaved differently—even though they shared on the cognitive level a support of informal American creeds and dogmas—they were most compelled to display the flag and salute it. They had to demonstrate loyalty in the face of military ventures through World War I, to show that the word "American" meant more than the ethnic reference if they were "hyphenated Americans."

By the end of the century a new metaphor had been called forth, the familiar one remembered in the title of Israel Zangwill's play, *The Melting Pot*.[29] This important half-satisfying half-truth was apt and potent enough to last until at least the mid-1950s, when Will Herberg redrew the map of American religion. He suggested that there were three melting pots, Protestant, Catholic, and Jewish; in 1961 Gerhard Lenski added a fourth in *The Religious Factor*: black Protestants.[30] "The process of national amalgamation" had not been smooth, but ethnic, racial, and religious groups seemed all to have been on a course toward the development of the process—until the 1960s.

After that time the old integrating dreams seemed to be dying. What had become of Ralph Waldo Emerson's old hope? Let the immigrants come: "The energy of Irish, Germans, Swedes, Poles, and Cossacks and all the European tribes—and of the Africans and of the Polynesians,—will construct a new race, *a new religion*, a new state, a new literature."[31] In place of that version Americans seemed to be moving toward what we have called tribalism, with reference to religion in an era when to people

> religion appeared . . . a matter purely local; and as there were gods of the hills and gods of the valleys, of the land and of the sea, so each tribe rejoiced in its peculiar deities, looking on the natives of other countries who worshipped other gods as Gentiles, natural foes, unclean beings.

The words were James Lord Bryce's,[32] but they were appropriate to describe what many regarded critically as they listened to the rhetoric and observed the practices of ethnic religionists in the 1960s and 1970s. Historian Rudolph J. Vecoli argued with some cogency that his fellow academicians were often caught off guard by the change in climate, since so many of them were committed to "the prevailing ideology of the academic profession," a "prime article of the American creed," one that had foreseen the triumph over tribalism based on a "profound confidence in the power of the New World to transform human nature."[33]

The Black Muslims of the 1960s did not play the game; they looked like a revision in religion to happily forgotten days of tribalism. Black Israel, a small Negro group, thought that both Black Muslims and Black Christians had the wrong tribal deities, and supplied a third. Each deity called for differing behavioral responses. "Ethnicity in American historiography has remained something of a family scandal, to be kept a dark secret or explained away,"[34] observed Vecoli; now it was coming into the open and historians had to reckon with it.

If the 1960s were a period of new particularism, in which people used what W. B. Yeats called the gloved hand of the nation to grasp the universe, or saw them get their bearings in the universe through their "race," because they were "immersed in it like the drop of water in the passing cloud," to use José Ortega y Gasset's phrase, it was only natural that they would generate religious ideologies to justify the steps they were taking.[35] In a rather representative instance, Thomas H. Clancy took off in *America* magazine from a statement of Daniel Patrick Moynihan, one of the more notable earlier commentators on the failure of assimilationist or "melting pot" theories. Moynihan had written:

> The sense of general community is eroding, and with it the authority of existing relationships while simultaneously, a powerful quest for specific community is emerging in the form of ever more intensive assertions of racial and ethnic identities.

Clancy added first, "Black nationalism caused the white ethnics to remember what they had been taught to forget, their own origins." In that moment, as a Catholic, he set forth a theology of unlikeness:

> The year 1970 is the date when the drive for group rights became more important than the struggle for individual rights. (In the demonstrations and rallies of the future most signs will bear an ethnic adjective). . . . For a long time now we have been exhorted to love all men. We have finally realized that for sinful man this is an unrealistic goal. The saints and heroes among us will still face the challenge in a spirit of unyielding despair. The rest of us will try first to love our own kind. This is the year when 'brother' and 'sister' began to have *a less universal and hence truer meaning.*[36] [Emphasis mine.]

One commentator in one journal does not necessarily make a whole case. But one need not look far to find innumerable parallel expressions of an emerging ethnic ethic.

As with religious, so with ethnic pluralism: it represents both problems and possibilities. One need not agree with the theology of the following first sentence in order to agree with the reporting and the prophesying in the second and the third. John Courtney Murray: "Religious pluralism is against the will of God. But it is the human condition; it is written into the script of history. It will not somehow marvelously cease to trouble the City."[37]

In the years of the new particularism in ethnic and racial religion, some scholars at least began to discern and advocate a counterforce, a "common faith" for the whole, an entity they came to call Civil Religion. For some tribalists, Civil Religion was the church of which they were sects; for others, it was a competitor. In any case, it is difficult to recognize distinctions between the two unless one gives attention to the way the people together practiced the faith, to their social behavior. If Ethnic Religion would have been virtually invisible to one who came to the landscape curious only about theological or institutional novelty, and barely discernible on political grounds, the early stages of the Civil Religion debate were carried on almost entirely in intellectual terms by scholars. Their eyes had described the problem created by the behavior of the separate peoples in America, a nation of nations, a people of peoples.

8   Civil Religion

Civil Religion's advocates make a claim that differs from those of the other five elements or clusters on America's new religious map. They are to be faiths for the part, while it would be a faith for the whole. They are all admittedly and obviously particular, while it professes to be, in many senses, universal and inescapable. Each of them would provide adherents with a sense of identity by helping them find a subcultural tradition and giving them means for sorting out values from the competing signals of a pluralist society. Civil Religion would provide them with a sense of identity by fitting them into an American tradition that is coextensive with the culture or society, in which apparently competing signals could be integrated or from whose viewpoint they could be dismissed.

The cases of Mainline, Evangelical, and Pentecostal-Charismatic religion are only apparently compromised by the fact that the Christian majority in each is part of a religion that aspires to be universal. All serious advocates of each know that historically and sociologically they have had to settle for being particular. When I become a Methodist, a follower of Billy Graham, or a speaker in tongues, I may remain in the human family and the one, holy, catholic Church. But my identity is based on a separate tradition, and I use its distinct mode of looking at reality in order to keep claims of others at a distance.

The New Religions are, for the most part, cultic in appearance. Of course, they would like to grow. Some of them see themselves potentially as cosmic faiths that will one day win all people. But these claims strike all nonmembers as absurd; they stand little or no chance of being substantiated in the future; in practice their "particular class of regularities of behavior" (Bagby) stamps them as subcultural. The fifth cluster, Ethnic Religion, is most exclusivistic of all. With rare exceptions, unless one has been born black, brown, red, yellow, or white and unless one identifies with the tradition of that race or ethnic group, he or she can never belong.

Civil Religion, on the other hand, even in its modest and gentle guises, appears as a religion that would be coextensive with American culture and society. This does not mean that it would be appropriated the same way by all its practitioners. Even its most zealous proponents do not claim that there are not internal varieties within it. But they see it as an institutionalized and available outlook or mode of behavior that "comes with the territory" for all people situated in America. Only the radical dissenter who would with great determination reject the larger society could be seen as exempt from its claims. Perhaps he or she, by the very vehemence of the rejection, could be seen as a prophet from within—just as some Christian theologians have seen the dedicated atheist to be the one who best understands religion and may be the best professor of religion.

Civil Religion, then, in its ideal form would be a religion for those who have no other, who are usually regarded as "secular" or holders of "invisible religion." It would also be a faith for "plural belongers," people who might be Presbyterian, Nazarene, Pentecostal, Zen Buddhist, a believer that "God is Red," and *still* within the circle of claims of Civil Religion. Those who favor it seem to be echoing the words of St. Paul as reported on in Acts 17:22–24:

> Men of Athens, I perceive that in every way you are very religious. For as I passed along, and observed the objects of your worship, I found also an altar with this inscription, 'To an unknown god.' What therefore you worship as unknown, this I proclaim to you.

In other words, Civil Religion is the *real* religion of the American people by the mere fact of their being American people. Critics of Civil Religion often turn this discernment into a charge and accuse members of various churches of having Civil Religion as their *real* religion, to the detriment of vital faith.

I have stated the universalizing claims of Civil Religion in somewhat bald and exaggerated terms, and will permit its advocates to qualify these somewhat later. The purpose in setting it aside from the other five elements on the nation's spiritual landscape has been to point as clearly as possible to the extravagance of this contribution to the religious map during the years of turning from the second to the final third of the twentieth century. It is not possible to take the term for granted, as these paragraphs have done. Just as it is un-necessary to define it (except for the purposes of precision in debate) in academic and scholarly circles where the junc-tures of culture and religion are familiar, it is entirely neces-sary to do so inches away from these elites.

The term "Civil Religion" appears only in books, articles, or reports of theologians, sociologists, historians, and social critics. Once or twice politicians have used it in the public sector, where it has not yet grasped the imagination. The term would inspire only bemusement and puzzlement in the neighborhood tavern, St. Boniface Parish, or a meeting of the American Legion. The absence of awareness on the part of the majority, and what we may safely presume would be considerable rejection of its implications on the part of many, did they know of it, are indicators to students of religious social behavior that in the first ten years of debate the entire issue formally has been in the hands of elites. They are talk-ing about the mass of people. Almost no empirical studies of the peoples' involvements with Civil Religion exist. The discussions have had to do with intellectual-theological, in-stitutional, and political themes and methods of study and almost never with behavioral observation or with diagnoses based on anything but the most superficial visions of how Civil Religionists act or what the meaning of their rituals might be.

If one wished to put a date on Civil Religion's arrival on the scene of the map, it could well be winter 1967. In one sense, to agree to this date is to join in playing a game. Americans had civic faiths from the time of Columbus or the Mayflower; native Americans had tribal equivalents before that. The founding fathers expressly advocated what has since been called "the religion of the Republic." In the middle of the twentieth century there had been numerous recognitions of religions of the American Way of Life. But there is no question that an article in the winter 1967 *Daedalus* established the term and its concepts and contexts for at least the present generation.

Robert N. Bellah, a sociologist or, in some ways, an anthropologist who had an eye for social behavior and a mind for ideas, brought together his notions on the subject in an article now called "classic" in that journal of the American Academy of Arts and Sciences. It is important to note that he first presented the formulation to a small conference of the Academy at Boston in October 1965; the date is significant because his essay reflects the liberal academicians' briefly held positive views of the American process. These were inspired by identifications with the New Frontier and the Great Society of the Kennedy and early Johnson years. By the time the essay appeared, the climate had already changed, but the category remained.

In a passage that sounds more egocentric and less objectively analytic than it is, Bellah in 1973 reviewed his part in locating the category on the religious map:

> In a sense, and not in a trivial sense, civil religion in America existed from the moment the winter 1967 issue of *Daedalus* was printed. Of course many of the examples I gave existed long before 1967 and . . . other observers had analyzed some of the same things under different

terms. By saying civil religion in America came into
existence in the winter of 1967 I do not mean that the
notion was arbitrary, fanciful, or a myth, in the pejorative sense of that word. But I do mean that it was what
Peter Berger would call a social construction of
reality. It was an interpretation, to some extent a new
interpretation, of various pieces of evidence many of
which were themselves first-order interpretations,
first-order social constructions of reality. What I am
trying to say is said very simply by Wallace Stevens when
he wrote, 'We live in the description of a place and not
in the place itself.' The very currency of the notion of
civil religion is the earnest of its reality. *It is now part of
the description of the place in which we live and that
at a certain level is that.* [Emphasis mine.]

Reviewing the earlier essay, Bellah said he had used the
phrase Civil Religion "to describe the religious dimension
of American political life that has characterized our Republic
since its foundation and whose most central tenet is that the
nation is not an ultimate end in itself but stands under transcendent judgment and has value only insofar as it realizes,
partially and fragmentarily at best, a 'higher law.' " In 1967
he had spoken less critically of the nation and had made less
of transcendence when he pointed to the fact that "there
actually exists alongside of and rather clearly differentiated
from the churches an elaborate and well-institutionalized
civil religion in America." Not only did it exist alongside
church religion; it had a "pervasive and dominating influence
within the sphere of church religion" as well. In the face of
critics he maintained that "the American civil religion is not
the worship of the American nation but an understanding of
the American experience in the light of ultimate and universal reality."

Bellah both recognized and then distinguished his views
from those who had spoken up in the years of the prehistory
of Civil Religion. Thus he acknowledged Sidney E. Mead's

designation of "the religion of the Republic," William Lee
Miller's "the religion of the American Way of Life" (which
was close to Will Herberg's designations, as well), and my
"American Shinto" or "America's Fourth Major Faith"
(alongside Protestantism, Catholicism, and Judaism). He
preferred the term used by Jean-Jacques Rousseau in *Social
Contract*; says Bellah, "Yet it was the phrase 'civil religion
in America' that took on a life of its own." He was right, as
any one who peruses subsequent bibliographies will soon
learn.

The reality of Civil Religion, says Bellah, "depends less
on the existence of certain things out there than on a consensus that it is a useful way of talking about things that indubitably are out there." Bellah's polemics ever since 1967
have had to be directed at two groups: those who do not believe there is anything "out there" and a larger group of those
who believe that there is, but that it is largely bad for the
republic or for true religion. He did not want "the erroneous
conclusion" to be drawn that "I think civil religion is always
and everywhere a good thing or that the American civil religion in all its manifestations is a good thing." To prove
this, he who had been enamored of John F. Kennedy's inaugural address as a decisive text in the tradition looked at
Richard M. Nixon's second inaugural address and rued: "If
I had had this document before me seven years ago the tenor
of that piece might have been different."[1]

In an introduction to a collection of essays on the subject,
Russell E. Richey and Donald G. Jones sort out five uses or
interpretations of Civil Religion, all of them valuable for
mapping the details of the terrain.

"First is the notion of civil religion as *folk religion*." Sociologists Will Herberg, Robin Williams, and the pioneering
Lloyd Warner would see it thus, for they see it emerging "out
of the life of the folk." They examine "the actual life, ideas,
values, ceremonies, and loyalties of the people," and come
closest to careful behavioral analysis. Among these, Herberg

has been best known for denouncing Civil Religion, and had done so in his best-selling *Protestant-Catholic-Jew* as early as 1955. Civil Religion, he said,

> is an organic structure of ideas, values, and beliefs that constitutes a faith common to Americans as Americans, and is genuinely operative in their lives; . . . Sociologically, anthropologically, it is *the* American religion, undergirding American national life and overarching American society. . . . And it is a civil religion in the strictest sense of the term, for in it, national life is apotheosized, national values are religionized, national heroes are divinized, national history is experienced as a *Heilsgeschichte*, as a redemptive history.

Secondly, Civil Religion "may be categorized as the *transcendent universal religion of the nation*," as it had been done by Sidney E. Mead, the historian whose work anticipated Bellah's conclusions by several years. For his Civil Religion precisely stands in judgment over Folk Religion; this cosmopolitan "religion of the Republic" is "essentially prophetic."

A third meaning is indicated by the phrase "religious nationalism" and is to be associated with the work of Charles Henderson, critic of Richard M. Nixon's theology, or, though Richey and Jones do not mention him, historian Carlton J. H. Hayes who had included a critique of America in 1960 in his *Nationalism: A Religion.*

Fourth, Civil Religion may mean the "democratic faith" as it had in Gunnar Myrdal's discussion of the American creed, in John Dewey's *Common Faith*, and in the calls for democracy-as-religion issued by J. Paul Williams in the 1950s.

Finally, some see Civil Religion as "Protestant civic piety," as it has been diagnosed by historians Yehoshua Arieli, James Smylie, James Maclear, Winthrop Hudson, and Robert Michaelson.

These five uses are "all closely connected and in some instances overlapping," and together they make up "the social construction of reality," the "description of a place" if "not . . . the place itself," the civil "things that indubitably are out there" under the blanket that Bellah called Civil Religion.[2]

If the Civil Religion episode came to its climax in the years around 1967, it also entered a stage full of problems immediately thereafter. In many senses, it simply gathered up debates of the 1950s, when most of the academics and theologians spoke critically of it, or the celebrations of the early 1960s, when some of them were more favorable. If Bellah first worried about critics who wondered whether there was anything "out there," he soon had to reckon with those who believed that there had been, but that it was already gone. They were not atheistic about the gods of Civil Religion; they simply announced the death of the gods.

Bellah took particular note of Sydney E. Ahlstrom, a preeminent historian of American religion. In his extensive *Religious History of the American People*, Ahlstrom had credited Will Herberg, not Bellah, with popularizing the category of Civil Religion—Herberg used the word "civic" instead of "civil"—and in a footnote seemed to concur with Herberg that "the postwar form of civil religion debased the older tradition which had reverenced the Union as a bearer of transcendent values and summoned citizens to stewardship of a sacred trust." By the late sixties, said Ahlstrom, this patriotic Civil Religion "was subjected to extremely severe criticism."

> The old nationalistic rhetoric was widely repudiated as
> hollow and deceitful. Nor did this civic faith die only
> in youthful hearts, for superannuated legislators were
> at the same time transforming the calendar of national
> holy days into a convenient series of long or lost week-
> ends. . . . It was in connection with governmental
> priorities that sharpest conflict developed. . . . Even

flag-flying became a divisive symbol of the debates on law-and-order versus social justice.

In the same year in which his history appeared, 1972, Ahlstrom also wrote in *Worldview* magazine:

> The country's civil religion reveals its own contradictions. A major survey finds 47 per cent of those interviewed expressing fears of an impending national "breakdown." Congress demeans the patriotic tradition by transforming the national holy-days into a series of long—or lost—weekends. Given the uninspiring lead of their elders, students of all ages use American flags to patch their jeans. One senses a widespread loss of faith in the nation. Flag-waving becomes the special proclivity of militant fundamentalists, racists and the law-and-order crowd. . . . We are threatened, in short, by the snapping of those bonds of loyalty and affection essential to the health of any collective enterprise.

He even went on to ask, "Is it possible that [in the designation of Civil Religion] we have evidence of a familiar fact—namely, that we often study the history of something only after its demise?"[3]

In his response, Bellah was reluctant to agree completely. "I think it would be safer to say that the national God, and I would quickly point out how offensive that very phrase would be to at least one major strand of the civil religion, though sick, is not dead." Both Senator McGovern and President Nixon, he observed, had used the rhetoric of Civil Religion in 1972. "And finally, if one thinks the civil religion is dead, he need only wait until 1976 . . . [for] the bicentennial." . . . "What I am suggesting is that American civil religion is a present fact and one we will likely contend with in the future, and not only in its one-dimensional form but in a whole series of competing and conflicting versions."[4]

Both Ahlstrom and Bellah were correct. In Stevens's terms, "the place" had changed and, with it, the description.

But the description as a category did survive. New things were going on in that "indubitably . . . out there" place, but it is likely that they will continue to be addressed in their manifoldness and transformations under the term Civil Religion. Bellah's predictions for the bicentennial came true in part. Despite the fact that the national mood had not improved since Ahlstrom wrote of the possible demise of Civil Religion, religious observances in 1976 took thorough note of the theme.

The best illustration of this ongoing and probably permanent interest appears in the journal *Forward*, published as a bicentennial project by the Interchurch Center. *Forward* was designed to stress "America's Religious Heritage" as "A Source of National Values for our Third Century." It gathered the energies of Protestants, Catholics, and Jews; sometimes accused of being the voice of the establishment, it at least found that establishment in a self-critical mood. *Forward* could be described as speaking for an elite, but it was this elite's most ambitious effort to carry the debate about its topic into the widest possible sphere.

To that end, the winter 1975 issue was wholly devoted to books recommended as resources for bicentennial reading. These were divided into three categories; the middle one was "Civil Religion in America." It offered eight titles as "Forerunners of the Civil Religion Thesis"; twenty items as the "Civil Religion Debate"; eight historical works as "Basic Reference Texts."[5] Every sign indicates that while Herberg's and Bellah's furnishings may be shifted or removed, their tent will remain; some features may change, but the "place" they have described will remain on the religious map. What is needed now is clear empirical study of the behavior of that citizenry which is devoted "out there" to something called Civil Religion. While Lloyd Warner, Will Herberg, and, to a lesser extent, Robert Bellah were sensitive to this need and curious about the subject, few other debaters from 1955 or 1967 on had been. To the extent that they were neglectful of the religious social behavior in the civic field, they were denying the tradition that they were advocating or calling attention to.

Intellectual historians alone have reckoned with the events by which Civil Religion was seen to become an established force in America. It plays little part in social or political history. A rereading of these pages would confirm that understanding. In outline, the story is as follows: A sociologist in 1955 writes a book critical of civic faith in an era in which intellectuals do not favor the current expressions of such faith. Between 1955 and 1967 a historian writes articles that are increasingly positive about the idea of a religion of the Republic. In 1965 a sociologist reads a paper favoring Civil Religion and in 1967 prints that paper. The time for the idea had come, and other people in academic life responded positively. But by 1972 a historian raised questions about whether Civil Religion had survived the 1960s, and a year later the sociologist himself, after expressing some second thoughts, reaffirmed the idea of its existence.

Except for an occasional reference to presidential inaugural addresses, to the fact that there are such things as civil rituals and that the Congress has passed laws affecting them, and to flag-waving or flag-wearing, the entire episode occurred without much examination of the actual practices of the American people, the reported professors of Civil Religion. Future studies will have to focus on what goes on "indubitably . . . out there."

W. Lloyd Warner had paid attention to public faith and ceremony in 1952 when he wrote *The Structure of American Life*. By 1959, in *The Family of God*, he developed an as yet largely unused framework for study of the ceremonies that then blended religion into national life. As early as 1949, in *Democracy in Jonesville*, he had used Durkheim's concept of "collective representations which express collective realities" to observe patriotic gatherings.

It was Warner who began posing the problem of subcultures in the larger culture, of the life of particular subcommunities in America's larger spiritual community. "Our communities are filled with churches, each claiming great authority and each with a separate sacred symbol system. Many of them are in conflict, and all of them in opposition." Ethnic traditions and fraternal orders, he noted, also devoted themselves to private sacred symbols systems. So the community members had to ask, "do we have sacred symbol systems which permit integration and collective action through their use by everyone in the community?"[6]

In 1951 sociologist Robin Williams picked up this question and at least called attention to the social behavioral issues when he argued that

> every functioning society has to an important degree a
> *common* religion. The possession of a common set of
> ideas, rituals, and symbols can supply an overarching
> sense of unity even in a society riddled with conflicts. . . .
> Men are always likely to be intolerant of opposition to
> their central ultimate values.[7]

Will Herberg and the other critics of the religion of the American Way of Life spent the late fifties paying some attention to what people actually *did* in support of their "*common* religion," and Herberg in particular accepted the evidence of public opinion polls and sociological accounts of religious practice as means of understanding the peoples' history. It was the critics who ordinarily gave most attention to how the public behaved. Carlton J. H. Hayes, for whom Civil Religion was largely "religious nationalism," concentrated on the cultus of national faith in his summary book, published in 1960.

Hayes followed the cultus through the career of a citizen. It begins at birth with "the secular registration of birth" as a surrogate for baptism. Then the state follows the citizen through life,

tutoring him in a national cathechism, teaching him by
pious schooling and precept the beauties of national
holiness, fitting him for life of service . . . to the state,
and commemorating his vital crises by formal registration
. . . not only of his birth but likewise of his marriage,
of the birth of his children, and of his death.

Membership is compulsory; in the modern world, the citizen may move from nation to nation and thus "may change his sect, so to speak, but not his religion." Flag ceremonies, solemn feasts and fasts, hymns and other music, processions and pilgrimages, national holidays and saints' days, temples and shrines, icons, images, and relics are public displays of the sacred. A fully developed mythology, intolerance of unorthodox behavior or belief, and the call for sacrifice mark the pure-form expressions of this religion.[8]

The positive side of civic faith received attention in the writings of J. Paul Williams, a college chaplain who through the 1950s was promoting the idea that Americans should look on the democratic ideal "as the Will of God, or, if they please, the Law of Nature. . . . Democracy must become an object of religious dedication." Since the churches and synagogues canceled each other out, despite their good intentions, the schools should be the new cathedrals where there could be metaphysical sanctions *and* ceremonial reinforcements of the common faith. "This argument ought to be answered if possible, not ignored," said historian Sidney E. Mead, who was then still nervous about a religion he was soon to tout.[9]

Mead's entire contribution to the debate has been in the mode of intellectual, never social, history. He criticized the critics for their attention to the actual practice of the American people, claiming that they were biased by their own theological assumptions. These critics faulted citizens for not living up to the creed of the religion of the Republic but did not pay enough attention to the faults of the faithful in church and synagogue—a charge that is hard to substantiate in the career of Will Herberg and other critics of the practices

in religious organizations. Mead focused not on the failures
of creedalists but on their creeds, arguing with Alfred North
Whitehead that "great ideas enter into reality with evil asso-
ciates and with disgusting alliances. But the greatness remains, nerving the race for its slow ascent." And great ideas
he found in Benjamin Franklin or Thomas Jefferson among
the founders, Ralph Waldo Emerson and Abraham Lincoln
in the national period, and occasionally in subsequent thinkers. Rare indeed were his references to what Whitehead called
"the special forms appropriate to the age in question," to
flags and rituals. Mead called his book on the subject *The
Nation with the Soul of a Church*, basing his title on G. K.
Chesterton's famous but debatable observation that America
was uniquely such a nation because the Declaration of Independence was a creed.[10] Bellah, as a sociologist and anthropologist, at least recognized the behavioral and ritualistic
sides of American Civil Religion and was ready to move
beyond the merely cognitive aspects that preoccupied Mead.
A line from Wallace Stevens ("We believe without belief,
beyond belief") moved Bellah to argue that post-modern
religions might make less of ideas, and he on some occasions
recognized the "special forms appropriate to the age in question." He did little, however, to discover how the ideas of
his heroes, among them John F. Kennedy, were picked up
and practiced in social behavioral spheres.[11]

Ahlstrom was correct: if Civil Religion was valued so
highly in the Republic, why would legislators deprive the
public of that holiday calendar, with its Memorial Days and
Veterans Days and other regular occasions for civic ritual?
Why did the people not protest? Why, when they did protest, was there such a gap between their stated beliefs and
actions? After the Supreme Court in 1962 and 1963 ruled
out public school prayer and devotionalism, the Gallup poll
found 70 percent of the national sample opposing the ruling.
The Survey Research Center of the University of Michigan
sampled a public in 1964 and found that 74 percent ap-

proved school devotions while 63 percent were entirely negative about the Supreme Court; more of those polled spoke critically on this issue than on any other in the 1964 political campaigns, according to that survey.[12] Yet, if the reports of school administrators are to be trusted, there had been Bible reading in only 41.74 percent of the schools before the Court decisions. Much of the opposition to the rulings came from California; but the West could hardly complain that the Supreme Court was taking away what the West had possessed. Only 11.03 percent of the sampled schools in the West had had Bible reading just before 1962. Only 6 percent of Midwestern schools and 2 percent of the Western schools engaged in homeroom devotional exercises, but 70 percent of the people reportedly protested their removal. Here is an illustration of the field day field workers will have when they examine the nexus between belief and behavior, ideation and conduct in the realm of Civil Religion.[13]

However tantalizing and promising the glimpses of public opinion and action in the field of Civil Religion may be, they are only beginning to be followed up. Until they are, thoughtful citizens will have to be content with a debate that misses much grounding in American life because it restricts itself to nothing more than scholars' impressions of practices that go on "indubitably . . . out there" and the same scholars' exegesis of high cultural documents or logical and theological expositions of a national creed. Despite all the limitations in the argument to date, it is already clear that both those who favor and those who oppose Civil Religion, and most of all those who take a dialectical view of it are touching on durable and urgent themes of life in the Republic. They are dealing with its central problem and, one might even say, its mystery: the spiritual dimension of *E pluribus unum*, "out of many, one," the relation of particular parts to the national whole.

If America cannot sustain itself purely secularly or through only private and invisible religion, as most citizens seem to think it can not, where do Americans locate and repose their spiritual visions? What bearing do the denominations have on the whole, if they cancel each other out and disagree on ultimate values? What help can come from renewals of these or from new counterreligions that would begin on a whole new basis, if they also remain subcultural and mutually contradictory? The old moral remnants of the Protestant establishment that had once bonded Americans kept on disintegrating. Would there be any substance to the new pluralism; would it produce valuelessness and anomie or even more disintegrative results? In Paul Ramsey's paraphrase of a biblical question, "How Shall We Sing the Lord's Song in a Pluralistic Land?" Theologian Ramsey joined those who see the pluralistic vacuum being filled with a new *unum*, a new whole, a "subpagan" culture that a vital Civil Religion could creatively address. "The findings are rapidly coming in from this one attempt in human history to erect a civilization upon other than some religious foundation." The result is a loss of human dignity. "Therefore the acknowledgment of God in the public life is itself a matter of supreme earthly importance."[14]

In this context Sidney Mead carried on a polemic against the religions of the many, the sectarian faiths. The religion of the Republic is "not only *not* particularistic; it is designedly anti-particularistic. . . . Under it, one might say, it is religious particularity, Protestant or otherwise, that is heretical and schismatic—even un-American!"[15] But, asked critics, is not Civil Religion also sectarian and particularized? It is itself the faith of only some citizens, at least so far as formal profession is concerned. Therefore it merely adds one more "denomination" to an already crowded religious map. As Richard Dierenfield's survey of school devotionalism begins to hint, it may be as regionalized as were the Southern Bap-

tists, the Utah Latter-day Saints, or the Pennsylvania Dutch
sects. Scholarly elites, as we have shown in detail, are as
divided in the camp of Civil Religion as they are in the
Christian church. There is in both a gap "between pulpit and
pew," between the signals leaders emit and those that followers hear, want to hear, and follow. It is divided along the
lines of class: the Civil Religion of those devoted to John
Dewey in the camp of Unitarianism differs vastly from that
of members of the Veterans of Foreign Wars or the Daughters of the American Revolution. Women complain that it
is as sexist as the particular faiths had been. Black historians
and others consider it racist, and call for "the reform of the
racist religion of the republic."[16] British visitor D. W. Brogan considered it to be a very particularized creation of Protestants or former Protestants.[17] Civil Religion has its right
wing and its left wing. It remains, as does much in Judaism
and Christianity, an eschatological or messianic vision, a
prospect for the future that has begun to be manifest now.
Thus Sidney Mead favorably quoted Ronald Osborn ("possi-
bly there is merit in what appears just now to be a very minor
refrain"):

> What we are beginning to realize is that God in his
> providence has permitted a common type of faith and
> life to emerge from the freedom and the denominational
> variegation of American Christianity. Out of separate
> historical traditions which find it increasingly difficult
> to maintain their relevance we find ourselves meeting
> one another with common convictions, a common
> sense of mission, and common methods of doing our
> work. Many of us would like to join in a large-scale
> union.[18]

Parallel to but hardly less urgent than this debate over
the one and the many, the American universal and the denominational parts, is an argument over the degree to which
the Civil Religion allows for the civil order and, most of all,

the nation, to be transparent to a transcendent order of being. Or does it serve to help people make the state into an
object of worship, and the public process into a religious
ultimate? Will Herberg fears the worst. He thinks that in a
pluralistic society a Civil Religion is inevitable and that it
is inevitably idolatrous, calling forth prophetic denunciation.
No one has more consistently watched the behavior of its
practitioners and more persistently criticized it. Even when
Herberg spoke positively, he was merely winding up for a
particularist judgment:

> I . . . regard America's civil religion as a genuine religion;
> . . . The fact that . . . America's civil religion is . . .
> congruent with the culture is no argument against it; . . .
> Furthermore, America's civil religion . . . strikes me as
> a noble religion, celebrating some very noble civic
> virtues. . . . On its cultural side, I would regard the
> American Way of Life, which is the social face of
> America's civil religion, as probably the best way of life
> yet devised for a mass society. . . . So I certainly would
> not want to disparage America's civil religion in its
> character as religion.
> But, if it is an authentic religion as civil religion,
> America's civil religion is not, and cannot be seen as,
> authentic Christianity or Judaism, or even as a special
> cultural version of either or both. Because they serve a
> jealous God, these biblical faiths cannot allow any claim
> to ultimacy and absoluteness on the part of any thing
> or any idea or any system short of God, even when what
> claims to be the ultimate locus of ideas, ideals, values,
> and allegiance is the very finest of human institutions;
> it is still human, man's own construction, and not God
> himself. To see America's civil religion as somehow
> standing above or beyond the biblical religions of
> Judaism and Christianity, and Islam too, as somehow
> including them and finding a place for them in its over-
> arching unity, is idolatry, however innocently held and

whatever may be the subjective intentions of the believers. But this is theology.[19]

And it is this theology and the "sectarianism" that embodies it which Sidney Mead, on the other side of Herberg's either/or, found so abhorrent. He found such criticism to be overinfluenced by European biblical theology and existentialism. No, "the religion of the Republic is essentially prophetic" and does not amount to "worship of the state or nation." Of course there was danger if "this or any nation assumes the traditional garb of the church" by "becoming heteronomous vis-a-vis other peoples and nations—asserting that they 'must be subject to a law [our law],' strange and superior though it may be to them."[20]

Bellah's position was more congenial to the both/and view. With Herberg and Mead he acknowledged the major deposit of biblical faith in Civil Religion and, latterly, began to worry about the weakness of the churches as well as over the theological crisis in them. But he concentrated almost entirely on the possibility that Civil Religion could serve as the agency for the word of transcendent judgment on society. "Without an awareness that our nation stands under higher judgment, the tradition of the civil religion would be dangerous indeed. Fortunately, the prophetic voices have never been lacking."[21] (In 1972 in a widely circulated book, Lowell Streiker and Gerald Strober, both advocates of the Judeo-Christian tradition, asserted that "*the America* of American civil religion is scarcely less 'transcendent' than is the God of the Judeo-Christian tradition." [Emphasis mine.] Priestly voices have also not been lacking!)[22]

Bellah also sees a larger universalism than that of the national whole to be available, seeking "the incorporation of vital international symbolism into our civil religion, or, perhaps . . . it would result in American civil religion becoming simply one part of a new civil religion of the world." Such a world civil religion, Bellah claims, would be a fulfillment, not a denial, of the American version and has always been a part of its eschatological hope.[23] Studies of civil religious behavior might begin to demonstrate whether or to what degree Americans were putting eschatological dreams of transcendence and universalism into practice in their pieties and actions.

It is not our present purpose to enter into the theological debates; now it is important only to show how related they will have to be to the study of behavior. We have seen that, whereas without social behavioral studies it is not likely that the other five "locations" on America's new religious map would have been so readily discovered and outlined in the 1960s and the 1970s, Civil Religion has emerged without much close attention to how the ideas of the faith are put into practice. Yet it is difficult to picture an area in which more materials are available for study, or a scene that has been more frequently described as being characterized by a religion of practice, *praxis*, action, concreteness, and conduct.

When Lyndon B. Johnson read his inaugural address as president on January 20, 1965, he entered his chapter into the canon of high cultural documents so beloved by Civil Religion's exegetes. Along with so many predecessors, he commented on the American creed, in lines that have become well-known:

> We are a nation of believers. Underneath the clamor of building and the rush of our day's pursuits, we are believers in justice and liberty and union, and in our own Union. We believe that every man must some day be free. And we believe in ourselves.[24]

The listener who heard or the reader who read these lines could do so hardly noticing that this president joined the others in simply taking for granted the fact that we are also a nation of behavers. He knew that we were a busy people, a clamoring, building, rushing, pursuing populace. These features he implicitly relegated to secondary status, seeing them as distractions that had to be overcome if we were to find our true selves. He typically gave no attention to the possibility that clamor, building, rushing, and the day's pursuits might very well be accurate indicators of citizens' deepest beliefs about the realities to which his creed pointed. Once again, Suzanne Langer: social behavior has roots which "lie much deeper than any conscious purpose . . . in that sub-stratum of the mind, the realm of fundamental ideas." It may well be that we should then look for "the American mind" not only in high cultural documents but in social behavior and its effects. Also once again, George Boas: "when an idea is adopted by a group and put into practice, as in a church or a state, its rate of change will be slow" because it is reinforced in so many ways.[25]

Benjamin Franklin and Thomas Jefferson were as concerned with the living as they were with the soul of that nation whose creed, according to G. K. Chesterton, they had "set forth with dogmatic and even theological lucidity."[26] George Washington in his farewell address had feared that the "permanency of your felicity as a People" would be forfeited unless "we" paid due attention to religion, manners, habits, political principles, and memories. He feared "mere speculation" about the nation and its design.[27]

The ideas of the founding parents of the nation "trickled down" to the millions at their most formative stages in the form of chapters in the textbooks that Ruth Miller Elson interpreted so well in her appropriately titled book *Guardians of Tradition*. She found almost no attention to the cognitive matters that had been set forth "with dogmatic and even theological lucidity."

The schoolbooks are guardians of what their authors consider [the] national ideals to be. In defining proper attitudes and behavior for American youth they spell out the ideals seen by their authors as those of the American nationality. . . . All books agree that the American

nation politically expressed is the apostle of liberty, a
liberty personified, apostrophized, sung to, set up in
God-like glory, but rarely defined. To discover what liberty
means in these books is a murky problem. The child
reader could be certain that it is glorious, it is American,
it is to be revered, and it deserves his prime loyalty.
But for the child to find out from these books what this
liberty is would be astonishing.[28]

During the formative periods, virtually every visitor to
America who published his or her observations stressed the
behavioral character of the national religiosity. These voyag-
ing voyeurs were convinced that the United States was a
nation of behavers who acted rather consistently on the basis
of a few unquestioned and usually unexamined beliefs about
social reality. From the people themselves they heard almost
nothing of dogmatic or theological lucidity. "Every sect there
is held as good, every road as correct, and every error as the
insignificant weakness of poor mortals," complained George-
town College President (between 1812 and 1817), the Italian
Jesuit Giovanni Grassi. When asked about their religion,
they usually "do not answer, 'I believe,' but simply, 'I was
brought up in such a persuasion.' "[29]

The most famous of them all, Alexis de Tocqueville, advised: "Go into the churches [he referred to the Protestant
churches, then in the vast majority], you will hear morality
preached, of dogma not a word."[30] Fourth of July orations
and other rhetorical occasions in the civil realm bore the
same marks. In the recent past, D. W. Brogan did carry that
motif into the civil realm. "The political function of the
schools is to teach Americanism, meaning not merely political and patriotic dogma, but the habits necessary to American life. The ritual of flag-worship and oath-taking in an
American school is a religious observance. . . . Thus Americanization by ritual is an important and necessary part of the

function of the American school." And religion was a "matter of conduct, good deeds, of works with only a vague background of faith."[31]

In the churchly sphere, notable leaders regularly lined up with evangelist Billy Sunday, though their language was less flamboyant, when he boasted that he did not "know any more about theology than a jack-rabbit knew about ping-pong."[32] A nation's humor is revealing. The familiar rabbi-priest-minister jokes are almost entirely devoted to the broad outlines of practice and behavior. Supreme Court Justice William O. Douglas could take for granted that his readers recognized the practical character of American piety when he summarized: "The matter was put humorously by the comedian Bob Hope: 'Once I was flying in a plane that was hit by lightning! "Do something religious," a little old lady across the aisle suggested. So I did—I took up a collection.' "[33]

In the political order, as Carey McWilliams pointed out, because "external behavior is always regulated by internal norms," attention has to be paid to ideas or beliefs and their consequences. The two are mutually reinforcing: "Actions and behavior [in turn] affect the thought of men." But it is only the external behavior that is enforced and forcibly exacted. Remarkably, new citizens after they have undergone training for citizenship as immigrants are not even asked to give formal assent to the American creed:

> American politics has eschewed any claim to control more than external behavior; the "oaths" which it has imposed on newcomers and themselves have not been concerned with doctrinal orthodoxy—one is not required to swear by the Declaration or *The Federalist*—but with obedience to law and the rejection of "force, violence, or other unlawful means."[34]

The form of the symbols counts more than the cognitive awareness of the content. D. W. Brogan commented on the high regard in which these symbols are held by the typical citizen, even though "he may have no more knowledge of the historical context than the badly frightened citizen who, rescued from a lynching bee, protested: 'I didn't say I was against the Monroe Doctrine; I love the Monroe Doctrine, I would die for the Monroe Doctrine. I merely said I didn't know what it was.' "[35] The textbooks about which Mrs. Elson writes had evidently done their job well on him.

To suggest that advocates or enemies of Civil Religion or users of the map for charting all the zones of religion in the American present or past should pay attention to social history and group conduct or practice is not to call for non- or anti-intellectualism. It is to work for historical and reportorial accuracy, to express regard for "the peoples' history," to take them as they are or have been, and then to ask what their future might be. If the behavioral paradigm supplements and complements the models of intellectual, institutional, and political history that have already been so developed, it is certain that America will be regarded not only as "a nation of believers" but also as "a nation of behavers." And users of the map will experience more of the possibility of living not only "in the description of a place" but also "in the place itself."

Epilogue
Mapping the
American Future

If this is a plausible fourth map of religious America, some day there will be fifth or sixth maps. If this is a palimpsest or a transparent layer imposed on the spiritual landscape, future historians will be superimposing other layers. If we have pointed to "a nation of behavers," future social necessities will call forth other substantial dimensions of American religion and different metaphors will come into play. If there has indeed been an "identity incident," that can end, to be replaced by other kinds of events and preoccupations.

For now, understanding that a basic secularity and the private styles of invisible religion "undergird and overarch"[1] American styles, the six clusters or zones in this book are intended to account for all forms of social religious attachments and expressions. Just as we could discover no significant phenomena that did not appear in these zones, so there were also good reasons for drawing or observing the lines between them. This map should serve for further explorations as Americans enter the last quarter-century of the second millennium A.D. or C.E. I hope, too, that the concern for social behavior will also be reflected in more studies of more remote pasts.

"For now": those opening words of the previous paragraph are an American historian's alert signal. This is a fluid society, rich in continuities but also subject to some sudden changes and surprises. The line of Sydney Ahlstrom's quoted in respect to Civil Religion should haunt anyone who seeks a final map: "Is it possible that here we have evidence of a familiar fact—namely, that we often study the history of

something only after its demise?"[2] Where on the scale of rise
and demise are the phenomena isolated in this book?

The occasions for the incident that led Americans to be
preoccupied with identity are not disappearing, but they have
been lived with long enough that they might begin to be
addressed in different ways. Many psychologists tell us that
the needs expressed in the search for belonging and social
location are "structured in" to the human condition, but they
need not always seek the same outlet. It is equally possible
that in the immediate future fewer people will see religion as
an effective means of finding their identity or base for any
kind of power. That basic secularity has been partly obscured in America during a decade of religious effervescences.
A rebirth of faith in politics or reason could well lead to a
new critique of or dissatisfaction with the more extravagant
and exotic religious forms.

Mainline Religion has begun to be chastened and to cut
its losses and find some sense of direction. Never likely to be
an unchallenged establishment again, it should survive, be
transformed, and be joined by new groups. Its leaders will
no doubt work to develop at least a few patterns of behavioral
correlates for reaffirmed beliefs. Evangelicalism and Fundamentalism successfully exploited a decade of societal disarray; they have deep roots in American culture and will
prosper, though probably not as they did between 1965 and
1975. The Evangelicals are making more and more compromises with the larger culture, and Fundamentalism seems
to be reaching the outer limits of its potential market.
Whether Pentecostalism and the Charismatic groups are part
of a fad, as their critics claim, or the signs of a normative
new Christianity, as they appear to be in their southern
hemispheric base, is a question that leaves them most up in
the air.

The New Religions now have their cultic place under the
sun and they will continue to influence and suffuse other
religious groups. But even as I write they draw less attention

than they did. Their most effervescent period may well be past. Similarly, Ethnic Religion seems to have crested, once Americans became used to living with aggressive minority movements and the backlash to them. Assimilative pressures are too strong to project that this form of demarcating American religion will prevail. Civil Religion shares with Mainline Religion the problem of satisfying people who seek "identity foreclosure," and lacks the institutional base of the Mainline. Even the American Bicentennial observance did not seem fully to awaken a new religious response that might live up to the dreams of proponents of Civil Religion.

In a quotation in the Introduction to this book, H. Stuart Hughes chartered historians to deal with the contemporary scene, unafraid to make predictions or to be chagrined at being occasionally caught out on a limb. My "likelies" and "possibles" in this epilogue hardly amount to predictions; they are ways of hedging one's bets and locating oneself in the stream of history. But I am trained not to be chagrined at the end of a limb. It is simply a too delightful and advantageous position from which to continue observing this "nation of behavers" and to map their ever-changing ways. In the days of the counterculture, Emmett Grogan charged that "anything anybody can say about America is true."[3] But some things said are more true than others, and it is the historian's task to attempt to say true things when he works at describing the social constructions of reality, when he engages in activities of pointing and mapping.

Notes

1. Mapping Group Identity and Social Location

1. H. Stuart Hughes, *History as Art and as Science: Twin Vistas on the Past* (New York: Harper and Row, 1964), pp. 89–90, 93, 95.

2. Peter L. Berger and Thomas Luckmann, *The Social Construction of Reality* (Garden City, N.Y.: Doubleday, 1966).

3. Frank S. Mead, *Handbook of Denominations in the United States* (Nashville, Tenn.: Abingdon, 1970), also lists the other titles, pp. 235–36.

4. Sidney E. Mead, *The Lively Experiment: The Shaping of Christianity in America* (New York: Harper and Row, 1963), chap. 7. Mead actually referred only to the shape of Protestantism, but his design applies to most American religion.

5. Edwin Scott Gaustad, *Historical Atlas of Religion in America* (New York: Harper and Row, 1962), insert; Douglas W. Johnson, Paul R. Picard, and Bernard Quinn, *Churches and Church Membership in the United States: An Enumeration by Region, State, and County* (Washington, D.C.: Glenmary Research Center, 1974), insert.

6. Will Herberg, *Protestant-Catholic-Jew: An Essay in American Religious Sociology* (Garden City, N.Y., 1955), pp. 88–104.

7. Charles Y. Glock and Rodney Stark, *Religion and Society in Tension* (Chicago: Rand McNally, 1965), chap. 5, pp. 86ff.; Andrew M. Greeley, *The Denominational Society: A Sociological Approach to Religion in America* (Glenview, Ill.: Scott, Foresman, 1972).

8. Michael Hill, *A Sociology of Religion* (New York: Basic Books, 1973), pp. 67–70 includes fifty bibliographical items on this subject, most of them having to do with the American scene.

9. Thomas Luckmann, *The Invisible Religion: The Problem of Religion in Modern Society* (New York: Macmillan, 1967). Chap. 1, pp. 17ff., calls for and announces new theoretical explorations.

10. Mead's second book on the religion of the Republic, *The Nation with the Soul of a Church*, appeared in 1975 (New York:

Harper and Row); Sydney E. Ahlstrom, *A Religious History of the American People* (New Haven, Conn.: Yale University Press, 1972).

11. Ahlstrom, *A Religious History*, pp. 1103–5, gives bibliographical data on all but these three titles: Robert T. Handy, *A Christian America: Protestant Hopes and Historical Reality* (New York: Oxford University Press, 1971); Edwin Scott Gaustad, *Dissent in American Religion* (Chicago: University of Chicago Press, 1973); Franklin Hamlin Littell, *From State Church to Pluralism: A Protestant Interpretation of Religion in American History* (New York: Macmillan, 1971).

12. Quoted by Don S. Browning, *Generative Man: Psychoanalytic Perspectives* (Philadelphia: Westminster, 1973), p. 166, in a fruitful discussion of Erikson; see also Harold R. Isaacs, *Idols of the Tribe: Group Identity and Political Change* (New York: Harper and Row, 1975), pp. 31–32.

13. J. Stillson Judah, *Hare Krishna and the Counterculture* (New York: John Wiley and Sons, 1974), chap. 8, pp. 138ff.

14. Quoted in Isaacs, *Idols of the Tribe*, p. 22.

15. Quoted in Ibid., p. 35.

16. Helen Harris Perlman, *Persona: Social Role and Personality* (Chicago: University of Chicago Press, 1968), p. 177.

17. Isaacs, *Idols of the Tribe*, p. 1.

18. Perlman, *Persona*, pp. 178–79.

19. Isaacs, *Idols of the Tribe*, pp. 19–21, 24, 154, 147–48.

20. Luckmann, *The Invisible Religion*, p. 97.

21. Bruce Mazlish, quoted by Isaacs, *Idols of the Tribe*, p. 28.

22. Martin E. Marty, *The Modern Schism: Three Paths to the Secular* (New York: Harper and Row, 1969), chap. 3, pp. 59ff. See also Martin E. Marty, "Secularization in the American Public Order," in Donald A. Giannella, *Religion and the Public Order, Number Five* (Ithaca, N.Y.: Cornell University Press, 1969), pp. 3ff., and especially the bibliographical footnote on p. 7.

23. Thomas Luckmann, *The Invisible Religion*, pp. 104–5.

2. History and Religious Social Behavior

1. Robert Jay Lifton, *Boundaries: Psychological Man in Revolution* (New York: Random House, 1970), pp. 43–44.

2. See G. J. Renier, *History: Its Purpose and Method* (Boston: Beacon, 1950), pt. 1, chap. 1, pp. 13–32.

3. Leonard W. Doob, "Goebbels' Principles of Propaganda," *Public Opinion Quarterly* 14: 435.

4. See Juan Friede and Benjamin Keen, eds., *Bartolomé de Las Casas in History: Toward an Understanding of the Man and His Work* (DeKalb, Ill.: Northern Illinois University Press, 1971); Peter Gay, *A Loss of Mastery: Puritan Historians in Colonial America* (Berkeley: University of California Press, 1966).

5. They are introduced in Henry Warner Bowden, *Church History in the Age of Science* (Chapel Hill, N.C.: University of North Carolina Press, 1971), chaps. 2 (Schaff) and 3 (Shea); see also Henry Warner Bowden's abridgment of Robert Baird, *Religion in America* (New York: Harper and Row, 1970).

6. On Turner and Beard, see David W. Noble, *Historians against History: The Frontier Thesis and the National Covenant in American Historical Writing since 1830* (Minneapolis: University of Minnesota Press, 1965), chap. 3, pp. 37ff., and chap. 4, pp. 56ff. Gay discusses the character and fate of Bradford's manuscript in *A Loss of Mastery*, pp. 31ff.

7. Ruth Miller Elson, *Guardians of Tradition: American Schoolbooks of the Nineteenth Century* (Lincoln: University of Nebraska Press, 1964). She includes a 71-page bibliography of textbooks, pp. 343ff.

8. 343 U.S. 306, 313 (1952). This saying was *obiter dicta* by William O. Douglas, subsequently quoted by the Court in decisions.

9. As one example, see the essays in Donald E. Smith, ed., *Religion and Political Modernization* (New Haven: Yale University Press, 1974), especially pt. 2, "The Secularization of Polities," for reference to Nepal, Burma, Thailand, Egypt, Israel, and Latin America.

10. In *Unsecular Man: The Persistence of Religion* (New York: Schocken, 1972), pp. 14f., Andrew Greeley, after having minimized secular impacts, responded to Peter Berger's conversational rejoinder to him by saying, "But something must have changed," and then cited some of the changes mentioned in these paragraphs.

11. E. Harris Harbison, *Christianity and History* (Princeton: Princeton University Press, 1964), wrestles with the questions that secularization in the historical discipline has posed for Christian historians; see especially pp. 3–68.

12. Bowden, *Religion in America*, pp. 94, tells the story of significant turns in this period.

13. Robert Allen Skotheim, *American Intellectual Histories and Historians* (Princeton: Princeton University Press, 1966), includes

discussions of Morison, Murdock, Miller, Gabriel, and Boorstin, and provides bibliographies; see esp. pp. 249–50.

14. Kuhn's book first appeared in 1962; a revised edition was published in 1970 (Chicago: University of Chicago Press). David A. Hollinger, "T. S. Kuhn's Theory of Science and Its Implications for History," in *The American Historical Review* 78, no. 2 (April, 1973): 370ff., is a helpful discussion.

15. For elaborations on their thought, see Peter Gay, *A Loss of Mastery*. For an introduction to Perry Miller, see Skotheim, *American Intellectual Histories*, pp. 186ff.

16. Abdel Ross Wentz, *A Basic History of Lutheranism in America* (Philadelphia: Muhlenberg, 1955); John Tracy Ellis, *American Catholicism* (Chicago: University of Chicago Press, 1956, 1969); Mead, *The Lively Experiment*; Ahlstrom, *A Religious History*.

17. This opening passage from his eight-volume *History of the People of the United States* achieves a kind of canonical status as an introduction to social history in a guide for young people, Fon W. Boardman, Jr., *History and Historians* (New York: Henry Z. Walck, 1964), pp. 103–4.

18. Harry Elmer Barnes, *A History of Historical Writing* (New York, 1937), p. 304.

19. David Hackett Fischer, *Historians' Fallacies: Toward a Logic of Historical Thought* (New York: Harper and Row, 1970), pp. 217–18.

20. For the case of fiction, see David Greenhood, *The Writer on His Own* (Albuquerque: University of New Mexico Press, 1971), "Definitions: Their Sterility," pp. 67–72.

21. Gustaf Aulén, *Church, Law and Society* (New York: Scribner's, 1948), p. 91.

22. See the remarks by which Albert Camus separated himself from Christians at a Dominican Monastery in 1948, "The Unbeliever and Christians," in his *Resistance, Rebellion and Death* (New York: Alfred A. Knopf, 1961), pp. 67ff.

23. See Joseph H. Fichter, *Sociology* (Chicago: University of Chicago Press, 1957), pp. 157–59.

24. Kurt Lang and Gladys Engel Lang, *Collective Dynamics* (New York: Thomas Y. Crowell, 1961), includes historical summaries of the term identified in 1922 as "collective behavior" by Robert E. Park and Ernest W. Burgess. The authors point to others who have contributed to the field in sociology: Robert E. Faris, Anselm Strauss, Ralph H. Turner, Lewis Killian, and Herbert Blumer. For extensive bibliographies on social or collective behavior from psychological or

sociological points of view, see Ralph H. Turner and Lewis M. Killian, *Collective Behavior* (Englewood Cliffs, N.J.: Prentice Hall, 1957), and Elliott McGinnies, *Social Behavior: A Functional Analysis* (Boston: Houghton Mifflin, 1970).

25. Henri Desroche, *Jacob and the Angel: An Essay in Sociologies of Religion*, trans. John K. Savacool (Amherst: University of Massachusetts Press, 1973), p. 22. Le Bras' article appeared in Henri Desroche, "Domaines et méthodes de la sociologie religieuse dans l'oeuvre de Gabriel Le Bras," in *Revue d'histoire et philosophie religieuse, No. 2* (Strasbourg, 1954).

26. On civility, see Harold Nicholson, *Good Behaviour: Being a Study of Certain Types of Civility* (London: Constable and Company, Ltd., 1955).

27. Robert F. Berkhofer, Jr., *A Behavioral Approach to Historical Analysis* (New York: Macmillan, 1969). Berkhofer's footnotes are extensive bibliographical references to many subjects under discussion here. He is far more at home with the concept of behaviorism or behavioralism as it is used in the social sciences today, and finds its philosophical connotations more congenial than do I. In general, his work complements and greatly amplifies many of the themes in this chapter and raises issues that cannot begin to be extensively addressed here.

28. Le Bras is quoted in Roger Mehl, *The Sociology of Protestantism* (Philadelphia: Westminster, 1970), p. 108; Elliott McGinnies, *Social Behavior*, p. 1.

29. Richard T. LaPiere, *Collective Behavior* (New York: McGraw-Hll, 1938), p. 3.

30. Fichter, *Sociology*, pp. 157–61.

31. *Comparative Study of Cultures and History: Prolegomena to the Comparative Study of Cultures and History* (Berkeley and Los Angeles: University of California Press, 1963), pp. 77–92, especially p. 88; pp. 104–5. See also Berkhofer, *A Behavioral Approach*, pp. 87–88, 114–16.

32. For bibliographic details of the following, see Ahlstrom, *A Religious History*, pp. 1107 ff. The text refers to these titles: Mark Zborowski and Elizabeth Herzog, *Life Is with People: The Culture of the Shtetl* (1952)—though it deals with Europe; E. Digby Baltzell, *The Protestant Establishment: Aristocracy and Caste in America* (1964), which is primarily sociological; David Bertelson, *The Lazy South* (1967), where references to religion are few; Kai T. Erikson, *Wayward Puritans: A Study in the Sociology of Deviance* (1966), another sociological use of historical materials; Darrett B. Rutman, *American Puritanism: Faith and Practice* (1970); Richard L. Bush-

man, *From Puritan to Yankee: Character and the Social Order in Connecticut, 1690–1765* (1967); Whitney R. Cross, *The Burned-Over District: The Social and Intellectual History of Enthusiastic Religion in Western New York, 1800–1850* (1950), which includes some attention to this topic; Clifford S. Griffin, *Their Brothers' Keepers: Moral Stewardship in the United States, 1800–1865* (1960); Charles A. Johnson, *The Frontier Camp Meeting: Religion's Harvest Time* (1955); David M. Ludlum, *Social Ferment in Vermont, 1791–1850* (1939), with some reference to religion; T. Scott Miyakawa, *Protestants and Pioneers: Individualism and Conformity on the American Frontier* (1964); William R. Taylor, *Cavalier and Yankee: The Old South and American National Character* (1967).

33. See James Hastings Nichols, "American Christianity," in Paul Ramsey, ed., *Religion* (Englewood Cliffs, N.J.: Prentice-Hall, 1965), pp. 195ff.

34. On traces, see G. J. Renier, *History*, pt. 2, chap. 1, "Events and Their Traces," pp. 87ff.

35. Tillich's is the most formidable system produced in modern America; see Paul Tillich, *Systematic Theology*, 3 vols. (Chicago: University of Chicago Press, 1951, 1957, 1963; 1 vol. ed., 1967).

36. On quantification and history see Robert P. Swierenga, ed., *Quantification in American History* (New York: Atheneum, 1970). He defines behavioralists (pp. 44ff.) as those who insist that scientific explanation—the testing of general laws in the study of specific events—is the appropriate model of historical research. Not all users of the quantitative method are behavioralists, but Swierenga identifies Lee Benson, Samuel P. Hays, and others in this camp. Jacques Barzun has penned a lively critique of "Cliometricians" in *Clio and the Doctors: Psycho-History, Quanto-History, and History* (Chicago: University of Chicago Press, ... *Psychoanalysis and History* ...

37. See Bruce Mazlish, ed., ... (Englewood Cliffs, N.J.: Prentice-Hall, 1963); Jay Y. Gonen, *A Psychohistory of Zionism* (New York: Mason/Charter, 1975); Joel Kovel, *White Racism: A Psychohistory* (New York: Pantheon, 1970).

38. Examples of explorations in this field include David Levin, *In Defense of Historical Literature* (New York: Hill and Wang, 1967), and Nelson Manfred Blake, *Novelists' America: Fiction as History, 1910–1940* (Syracuse, N.Y.: Syracuse University Press, 1969).

39. C. Wright Mills, *The Sociological Imagination* (New York: Oxford University Press, 1959), pp. 154, 6, 143–46; Robert A. Nisbet, *The Social Bond: An Introduction to the Study of Society* (New York: Alfred A. Knopf, 1970), pp. 366f., includes a roster of people

who have brought together social history and historical sociology: Max Weber, Robert Merton, Reinhard Bendix, Barrington Moore, Seymour Lipset, Alvin Gouldner, Charles Tilly, and Kai T. Erikson from the sociologists' side; from the historical fraternity there are Fustel de Coulanges, Otto von Gierke, F. W. Maitland, Frederick Jackson Turner, Charles Beard, and Marc Bloch, who "made astute use of what are in fact today's central sociological concepts." None of the historians mentioned have worked with American materials; several of the American sociologists listed have made comments on religion; these include Seymour Lipset and Kai T. Erikson.

40. Berkhofer, *A Behavioral Approach*, pp. 317–20, especially 319.

41. Irving I. Zaretsky and Mark P. Leone, *Religious Movements in Contemporary America* (Princeton: Princeton University Press, 1974).

42. A pioneering programmatic essay on this subject, one that makes no secret of its indebtedness to the work of Mircea Eliade in the history of religion, is Jerald C. Brauer, "Changing Perspectives on Religion in America," in Jerald C. Brauer, ed., *Reinterpretation in American Church History* (Chicago: University of Chicago Press, 1968).

43. A comment from my colleague in the field of history of religion, Joseph M. Kitagawa, led me to conceive of much recent Roman Catholic change along these lines and was a major encouragement for the development of themes associated also with other religious clusters in this book.

44. I refer here to the thought of Robert N. Bellah, who began to develop this theme in "The Historical Background of Unbelief," in Rocco Caporale and Antonio Grumelli, eds., *The Culture of Unbelief* (Berkeley: University of California Press, 1971), pp. 39ff.

45. Suzanne K. Langer, *Philosophy in a New Key* (New York: New American Library, 1952), pp. 41, 39.

46. George Boas, *The History of Ideas* (New York: Scribner's, 1969), p. 88.

47. Karl J. Weintraub, *Visions of Culture* (Chicago: University of Chicago Press, 1966), pp. 261, 263; for Julián Marías, see Harold C. Raley, *José Ortega y Gasset: Philosopher of European Unity* (University, Ala.: University of Alabama Press, 1971), p. 49.

48. Ortega, quoted in Raley, *José Ortega y Gasset*, pp. 50–51; Julián Marías, *Generations: A Historical Method* (University, Ala.: University of Alabama Press, 1967), p. 81.

49. On "peoples' history" from people opposed to the consensus schools, as they called it, see Barton J. Bernstein, ed., *Towards a New Past: Dissenting Essays in American History* (New York: Pantheon,

1968). Jesse Lemisch, "The American Revolution Seen from the Bottom Up," pp. 35ff., illustrates some of the problems discussed in the text. See also Howard Zinn, *The Politics of History* (Boston: Beacon, 1970).

50. Eugene D. Genovese, *Roll, Jordan, Roll: The World the Slaves Made* (New York: Pantheon, 1974).

51. Henry Mayhew, *London Labour and the London Poor* (London, 1851) is a classic in this genre; for a contemporary example, see Studs Terkel, *Working* (New York: Pantheon, 1974).

52. See Robert M. Myers, *Children of Pride: A True Story of Georgia and the Civil War* (New Haven: Yale University Press, 1972).

53. Adolph Harnack, "Über die Sicherheit . . . ," translated in G. Wayne Glick, *The Reality of Christianity* (New York: Harper and Row, 1967), p. 97.

3. Mainline Religion

1. For example, Irving Lewis Allen, "WASP—From Sociological Concept to Epithet," in *Ethnicity* 2, no. 2 (June 1975): 153ff. Allen detects nonpejorative uses of the acronym in social science in the late fifties and a public derogatory use by the mid sixties.

2. Harold Wentworth and Stuart Berg Flexner, *Dictionary of American Slang Based on Historical Principles* (New York: Crowell, 1960), p. 331.

3. Mitford M. Mathews, ed., *A Dictionary of Americanisms on Historical Principles* (Chicago: University of Chicago Press, 1951), p. 1019.

4. Wentworth and Flexner, *Dictionary of American Slang*, p. 331.

5. Herberg, *Protestant-Catholic-Jew*, pp. 43, 272–74, 24–25, 35, 53.

6. Ibid., 137–38.

7. Dean M. Kelley, *Why Conservative Churches Are Growing: A Study in Sociology of Religion* (New York: Harper and Row, 1972), pp. 88–90.

8. Herberg, *Protestant-Catholic-Jew*, p. 213.

9. Nathan Glazer, *American Judaism*, 2d ed. (Chicago: University of Chicago Press, 1972), pp. 151, 155, 169, 170. The whole Epilogue should be consulted.

10. Henry L. Feingold, *Zion in America: The Jewish Experience from Colonial Times to the Present* (New York: Hippocrene, 1974), pp. 299, 307–8, 321.

11. Glazer, *American Judaism*, pp. 178, 184–86, cites the work of Richard Rubenstein and Emil Fackenheim as presenting opposing kinds of reflection on the Holocaust; bibliographical references, ibid., p. 190.

12. For an illustration, see Norman L. Friedman, "Jewish Popular Culture in Contemporary America," in *Judaism, Summer* 1975, pp. 263ff.

13. Herberg, *Protestant-Catholic-Jew*, p. 174.

14. Edward Wakin and Joseph F. Scheuer, *The De-Romanization of the American Catholic Church* (New York: Macmillan, 1966), p. 11.

15. John Cogley, *Catholic America* (New York: Dial, 1973), pp. 168, 144.

16. James Hitchcock, *The Decline and Fall of Radical Catholicism* (Garden City, N.Y.: Doubleday, 1972), pp. 95, 93, 94. Wills was quoted from *Commonweal*, March 27, 1970, p. 60.

17. John Tracy Ellis, *American Catholicism*, 2d. ed. (Chicago: University of Chicago Press, 1969), p. 241.

18. Hitchcock, *Decline and Fall*, p. 122.

19. Ellis, *American Catholicism*, pp. 175–76.

20. David J. O'Brien, *The Renewal of American Catholicism* (New York: Oxford University Press, 1972), p. 10.

21. Ellis, *American Catholicism*, pp. 163–64, 166.

22. Ibid., 181, 179, 194.

23. George Devine, *American Catholicism: Where Do We Go from Here?* (Englewood Cliffs, N.J.: Prentice-Hall, 1975), p. 89.

24. Hitchcock, *Decline and Fall*, p. 111.

25. Ernest Gellner, *Thought and Change* (Chicago: University of Chicago Press, 1964), p. 123.

26. Winthrop S. Hudson, *Religion in America*, 2d ed. (New York: Scribners, 1973), p. 414.

27. This change was chronicled in the editors' Introduction and documented with essays by various authors in Martin E. Marty and Dean G. Peerman, *New Theology, No. 7* (New York: Macmillan, 1970); see especially "The Recovery of Transcendence," the title of the Introduction.

28. Hudson, *Religion in America*, p. 414.

29. Jeffrey K. Hadden, *The Gathering Storm in the Churches* (Garden City, N.Y.: Doubleday, 1969), pp. 3, 9, 211ff.

30. Harold E. Quinley. *The Prophetic Clergy: Social Activism among Protestant Ministers* (New York: Wiley, 1974), pp. 11ff.

31. Glock and Stark, *Religion and Society*, pp. 121, 112.

32. Kelley, *Why Conservative Churches Are Growing*, p. 84.

4. Evangelicalism and Fundamentalism

1. The standard volume for listings and statistics of denominations is Constant H. Jacquet, Jr., *Yearbook of American and Canadian Churches*; reference here is to the 1975 edition (Nashville, Tenn.: Abingdon, 1975).

2. Robert Campbell, *Spectrum of Protestant Beliefs* (Milwaukee, Wis.: Bruce, 1968), p. 8.

3. Hadden includes these data in many tables throughout *The Gathering Storm in the Churches*; see Quinley, *The Prophetic Clergy*, pp. 52ff.

4. Franklin Hamlin Littell, *From State Church to Pluralism: A Protestant Interpretation of Religion in American History* (Garden City, N.Y.: Doubleday, 1962), p. 133.

5. Jerald C. Brauer, "Changing Perspectives on Religion in America," in Jerald C. Brauer, ed., *Reinterpretation in American Church History* (Chicago: University of Chicago Press, 1968), pp. 1ff.

6. For documentation, see Lowell D. Streiker and Gerald S. Strober, *Religion and the New Majority: Billy Graham, Middle America, and the Politics of the 70s* (New York: Association, 1972).

7. Jack Balswick, "The Jesus People Movement: A Sociological Analysis," in Patrick H. McNamara, *Religion American Style* (New York: Harper and Row, 1974), pp. 359ff.

8. Baird, *Religion in America*, pp. 209ff., for "The Non-Evangelical Churches in America," and pp. 257ff., for "The Non-Evangelical Denominations in America."

9. The details of the rise of Fundamentalism are fleshed out in Martin E. Marty, *Righteous Empire: The Protestant Experience in America* (New York: Dial, 1970), 177ff., 210ff. Louis Gasper, *The Fundamentalist Movement* (The Hague: Mouton, 1963), describes the organizational splits between the Fundamentalists and Evangelicals; James DeForest Murch is quoted here, from p. 25.

10. Charles Clayton Morrison, "Fundamentalist Revival," *Christian Century* 74, no. 25 (June 19, 1957): 749–51.

11. William G. McLoughlin, "Is There a Third Force in Christendom?" *Daedalus* 96, no. 1 (winter 1967): 44–45, 48–50, 61.

12. James C. Hefley and Edward E. Plowman, *Washington: Christians in the Corridor of Power* (Wheaton, Ill.: Tyndale, 1975), p. 195.

13. Two of these books have not yet been cited: William S. Cannon, *The Jesus Revolution: New Inspiration for Evangelicals* (Nashville, Tenn.: Broadman, 1971), and Donald G. Bloesch, *The Evangelical Renaissance* (Grand Rapids, Mich.: William B. Eerd-

mans, 1973). For the categories listed here, see Quinley, *The Prophetic Clergy*, pp. 7–12.

14. Kelley, *Why Conservative Churches Are Growing*, pp. 20–21.

15. Erling Jorstad, *The Politics of Doomsday: Fundamentalists of the Far Right* (Nashville, Tenn.: Abingdon, 1970).

16. Cited in note 6.

17. Ernest R. Sandeen, *The Roots of Fundamentalism: British and American Millenarianism, 1800–1930* (Chicago: University of Chicago Press, 1970), pp. xivff.

18. Bloesch, *The Evangelical Renaissance*, p. 41.

19. Richard Quebedeaux, *The Young Evangelicals* (New York: Harper and Row, 1974), p. 19.

20. Carl F. H. Henry, *Evangelical Responsibility in Contemporary Theology* (Grand Rapids, Mich.: William B. Eerdmans, 1957), pp. 45–46.

21. Carl F. H. Henry, *The God Who Shows Himself* (Waco, Tex.: Word, 1966), pp. 59–60.

22. James DeForest Murch, *Cooperation without Compromise* (Grand Rapids, Mich.: William B. Eerdmans, 1956).

23. Charles I. Foster, *An Errand of Mercy: The Evangelical United Front, 1790–1837* (Chapel Hill: University of North Carolina Press, 1960).

24. Thomas E. Baker, *Christ and the Even Balance: A Manual on Fundamentalism* (Millersberg, Pa.: Bible Truth Mission, 1968), pp. 72–74, 76, 85–86.

25. Ockenga is quoted in Daniel B. Stevick, *Beyond Fundamentalism* (Richmond; John Knox, 1964), p. 28; Millard Erickson, *The New Evangelical Theology* (Westwood, N.J.: Revell, (1968), pp. 164–65; Bruce L. Shelley, *Evangelicalism in America* (Grand Rapids, Mich.: William B. Eerdmans, 1967), p. 112.

26. Erickson, *New Evangelical Theology*, p. 178; Ockenga is quoted by Streiker and Strober, *Religion and the New Majority*, p. 112.

27. Wurth is quoted in Henry, *Evangelical Responsibility*, p. 33; the Henry quotations are from pp. 33f., 47.

28. Bloesch, *The Evangelical Renaissance*, p. 24, where Tozer is also quoted.

29. H. Richard Niebuhr, *Christ and Culture* (New York: Harper and Row, 1956) includes these two among five types of relationship.

30. Stevick, *Beyond Fundamentalism*, p. 206; the material not in the indented quotation is Stevick's.

31. Bloesch, *The Evangelical Renaissance*, p. 18.

32. Henry, *Evangelical Responsibility*, pp. 43–44.

33. Kelley, *Why Conservative Churches Are Growing*, p. 84.

5. Pentecostal-Charismatic Religion

1. Vance Packard, *The Status Seekers* (New York: David McKay, 1959), pp. 200–201. For the literature on Pentecostalism, see David W. Faupel, *The American Pentecostal Movement: A Bibliographical Essay* (Wilmore, Ky.: G. L. Fisher Library, 1973). Faupel commends, with some qualifications, the following surveys: John Thomas Nichol, *Pentecostalism* (New York: Harper and Row, 1966); Walter J. Hollenweger, *The Pentecostals: The Charismatic Movement in the Church* (Minneapolis, Minn.: Augsburg, 1972); Nils Bloch-Hoell, *The Pentecostal Movement: Its Origin, Development and Distinctive Character* (New York: Humanities Press, 1964).

2. "The Third Force," *Life*, June 9, 1958, pp. 122–24.

3. Joseph H. Fichter, *The Catholic Cult of the Paraclete* (New York: Sheed and Ward, 1975), pp. 137–38.

4. Ibid., 45–46; Faupel, *The American Pentecostal Movement*, p. 33.

5. Kieran Quinn, "Knox, Me and the Pentecostals," in *National Catholic Reporter*, November 9, 1973, p. 7. See also Tillich, *Systematic Theology*, 1: 112.

6. David Wilkerson, *David Wilkerson Speaks Out* (Minneapolis, Minn.: Bethany Fellowship, 1973), p. 21.

7. Frederick Dale Bruner, *A Theology of the Holy Spirit: The Pentecostal Experience and the New Testament Witness* (Grand Rapids, Mich.: William B. Eerdmans, 1970), p. 59.

8. Edward O'Connor, *The Pentecostal Movement* (Notre Dame, Ind.: Ave Maria Press, 1972), p. 29; quoted in Fichter, *The Catholic Cult of the Paraclete*, p. 4.

9. Vincent M. Walsh, *A Key to Charismatic Renewal in the Catholic Church* (St. Meinrad, Ind.: Abbey Press, 1974), is a catechism representing Catholic Charismatic opinions.

10. Fichter, *The Catholic Cult of the Paraclete*, pp. 20–25.

11. On Troeltsch, see Hill, *A Sociology of Religion*, pp. 47ff. See also the typology of church forms in Roland Robertson, *The Sociological Interpretation of Religion* (New York: Schocken, 1970), pp. 116ff.

12. Fichter, *The Catholic Cult of the Paraclete*, pp. 80ff.

13. Walsh, *A Key to Charismatic Renewal*, pp. 278–79.

14. On snake-handling, see Weston La Barre, *They Shall Take up Serpents: Psychology of the Southern Snake-Handling Cult* (Minneapolis: University of Minnesota Press, 1962).

15. Ahlstrom, *A Religious History*, pp. 819–22, 1059–60, 1086n.; Hudson, *Religion in America*, pp. 345–46, 428–31.

16. William Warren Sweet, *The Story of Religion in America* (New York: Harper and Brothers, 1950), p. 423.

17. *The Commonweal*, November 8, 1968, p. 203.

18. Wayne E. Oates, "A Socio-Psychological Study of Glossolalia," in Frank Stagg, E. Glenn Hinson, and Wayne E. Oates, *Glossolalia: Tongue Speaking in Biblical, Historical, and Psychological Perspective* (Nashville, Tenn.: Abingdon, 1967), p. 77.

19. Bruner, *A Theology of the Holy Spirit*, p. 25.

20. Quoted in Vinson Synan, *The Holiness-Pentecostal Movement in the United States* (Grand Rapids, Mich.: William B. Eerdmans, 1971), p. 102.

21. J. A. Synan, "The Purpose of God in the Pentecostal Movement for This Hour," in *Pentecostal World Conference Messages: Preached at the Fifth Triennial Pentecostal Conference, Toronto, Canada, 1958* (Toronto: Full Gospel Publishing House, 1958), p. 29.

22. D. A. Hayes of Garrett Biblical Institute was quoted by Nichol, *Pentecostalism*, p. xi.

23 Walter Hollenweger, "Spirituality for the World," *Event*, November–December 1973, p. 9, in a remark over Dutch radio.

24. Quoted by Bruner, *A Theology of the Holy Spirit*, p. 23.

25. Walsh, *A Key to Charismatic Renewal*, 280ff.

26. Donald L. Gelpi, S. J., *Pentecostalism: A Theological Viewpoint* (New York: Paulist Press, 1971), pp. 35, 38.

27. Joseph R. Washington, Jr., *Black Sects and Cults* (Garden City, N.Y.: Doubleday, 1973), p. 68.

28. Marcus Bach, *Strange Sects and Curious Cults* (New York: Dodd, Mead, 1961), p. 133; Joseph Washington, *Black Sects and Cults*, p. 118.

29. This set of references comes from casual mentions in *The Pentecostal Holiness Manual, 1969*, p. 12; Vinson Synan, *The Old-Time Power: A History of the Pentecostal Holiness Church* (Franklin Springs, Ga.: Advocate Press, 1973), p. 99; Luther P. Gerlach and Virginia H. Hines, "Five Factors Crucial to the Growth and Spread of a Modern Religious Movement," *Journal for the Scientific Study of Religion* 7, no. 1 (spring 1968): 23–40; Donald G. Bloesch, "The Wind of the Spirit: Thoughts on a Doctrinal Controversy," in *Reformed Journal*; General Conference, *M. E. Church, South*, (Nashville, Tenn.: 1894), pp. 25–26.

30. Walsh, *A Key to Charismatic Renewal*, p. 283.

31. William J. Samarin, *Tongues of Men and Angels* (New York: Macmillan, 1972), pp. 212–16.

32. Skibstedt is quoted by Bruner, *A Theology of the Holy Spirit*, p. 27.

33. Gelpi, *Pentecostalism*, p. 132.

34. Synan, *Holiness-Pentecostal Movement*, pp. 95–96, quotes the *Los Angeles Times*.

35. Don Basham, *A Handbook on Holy Spirit Baptism*, the original source, is reprinted in Erling Jorstad, *The Holy Spirit in Today's Church* (Nashville, Tenn.: Abingdon, 1973), pp. 77–79.

36. Dennis Bennett is quoted in Watson Mills, *Understanding Speaking in Tongues* (Grand Rapids, Mich.: William B. Eerdmans, 1972), p. 14.

37. Walsh, *A Key to Charismatic Renewal*, p. 83.

38. Felicitas D. Goodman, *Speaking in Tongues: A Cross-Cultural Study of Glossolalia* (Chicago: University of Chicago Press, 1972), p. 124.

39. Samarin, *Tongues of Men and Angels*, p. 227–28.

40. Kevin Ranaghan and Dorothy Ranaghan, eds., *As the Spirit Leads Us* (New York: Paulist Press, 1971), pp. 38, 59.

41. In Ranaghan and Ranaghan, *As the Spirit Leads Us*, pp. 61, 70–71, 75–76.

42. Synan, *The Old Time Power*, pp. 50, 58, 61, 72–73, 89–90, 126, 261 include references to conduct.

43. Gary Schwartz, *Sect Ideologies and Social Status* (Chicago: University of Chicago Press, 1970), p. 180.

44. Synan, *The Holiness-Pentecostal Movement*, p. 186.

45. Wilkerson, *David Wilkerson Speaks Out*, pp. 15–16.

46. Samarin, *Tongues of Men and Angels*, pp. 5–6, 10.

47. Steve Durasoff, *Bright Wind of the Spirit: Pentecostalism Today* (Englewood Cliffs, N.J.: Prentice-Hall, 1972), p. 10.

48. Nichol, *Pentecostalism*, p. 79.

6. The New Religions

1. Jacob Needleman, *The New Religions* (Garden City, N.Y.: Doubleday, 1970).

2. Robert S. Ellwood, Jr., *Religious and Spiritual Groups in Modern America* (Englewood Cliffs, N.J.: Prentice-Hall, 1973).

3. Marshall D. Sahlins and Elman R. Service, *Evolution and Culture* (Ann Arbor, Mich.: University of Michigan Press, 1960), p. 83.

4. For a theological comment on this vast literature see the essays in Albert L. Schlitzer, C.S.C., ed., *The Spirit and Power of Christian Secularity* (Notre Dame, Ind.: University of Notre Dame Press, 1969).

5. Quoted in John Taylor, *The Primal Vision* (Philadelphia: Fortress, 1964), p. 26.

6. For examples, see Needleman, *The New Religions*, "Introduction," pp. 1–37; Ellwood, *Religious and Spiritual Groups*, pp. 1–41; 297ff.

7. William Glasser, *The Identity Society* (New York: Harper and Row, 1972), pp. 8, 13, 28.

8. Quoted in Steven Lukes, *Emile Durkheim, His Life and Work: A Historical and Critical Study* (New York: Harper and Row, 1972), p. 422; see Emíle Durkheim, *Sociology and Philosophy* (Glencoe, Illinois: Free Press, 1953), p. 91.

9. Stanley Krippner, "Altered States of Consciousness," in John White, ed., *The Highest State of Consciousness* (Garden City, N.Y.: Doubleday, 1972), pp. 1ff., and especially p. 5.

10. Durkheim, *Sociology and Philosophy*, p. 91.

11. The definition of "demarcation" is taken from *The Oxford English Dictionary*. On spiritualism, see Irving I. Zaretsky, "In the Beginning Was the Word: The Relationship of Language to Social Organization in Spiritualist Churches," in Irving I. Zaretsky and Mark P. Leone, *Religious Movements in Contemporary America* (Princeton: Princeton University Press, 1974), pp. 166ff.

12. On forgetting historical Christianity, see R. W. B. Lewis, *The American Adam: Innocence, Tragedy, and Tradition in the Nineteenth Century* (Chicago: University of Chicago Press, 1955); for the background to the New Religions, see Hal Bridges, *American Mysticism: From William James to Zen* (New York: Harper and Row, 1970).

13. Theodore Roszak, *The Making of a Counter Culture: Reflections on the Technocratic Society and Its Youthful Opposition* (Garden City, N. Y.: Doubleday, 1969), pp. 42–43; Sydney E. Ahlstrom, "Requiem for Patriotic Piety" in *Worldview* (August, 1972), p. 10.

14. Morris R. Cohen, *The Meaning of Human History* (LaSalle, Ill.: Open Court Publishing, 1947), pp. 107, 63–64.

15. Ernest Gellner, *Thought and Change* (Chicago: University of Chicago Press, 1964), p. 123.

16. For illustrations of behavior and practice in all these groups, see Ellwood, *Religious and Spiritual Groups.*

17. Marcello Truzzi, "Definition and Dimensions of the Occult: Towards a Sociological Perspective," in Robert Galbreath, ed., *The Occult: Studies and Evaluations* (Bowling Green, Ohio: Bowling Green University Popular Press, 1972), pp. 635ff. and especially 637.

18. The citations in the next seven paragraphs all derive from quoted material documented in Martin E. Marty, "The Occult Establishment," *Social Research* 37, no. 2 (Summer 1970): 212 ff.

19. Charles S. Braden, *These also Believe: A Study of Modern American Cults and Minority Religious Movements* (New York: Macmillan Company, 1949) Frank Mead, *op. cit.*

20. Leo Rosten, ed., *Religions of America: Ferment and Faith in an Age of Crisis* (New York: Simon and Schuster, 1975), p. 594. On the behavioral characteristics of Asian religionists in America in the next five paragraphs of the text, see Ellwood, *Religious and Spiritual Groups,* and Needleman, *The New Religions.*

21. Roszak, *The Making of a Counter Culture,* p. 35.

22. Quoted by Hervé Carrier, *The Sociology of Religious Belonging* (New York: Herder and Herder, 1965), p. 179.

23. Allan W. Eister, "Culture Crises and New Religious Movements: A Paradigmatic Statement of a Theory of Cults"; see Zaretsky and Leone, *Religious Movements,* pp. 612ff., 622–34.

24. Vine Deloria, Jr., *God Is Red* (New York: Grosset and Dunlap, 1973), pp. 253, 11.

25. Carl F. Starkloff, *The People of the Center: American Indian Religion and Christianity* (New York: Seabury, 1974), p. 13.

26. Quoted in William T. Hagan, *American Indians* (Chicago: University of Chicago Press, 1961), p. 128.

27. Deloria, *God Is Red,* p. 66.

28. See Walter N. Pahnke, "Drugs and Mysticism," in John White, *The Highest State of Consciousness,* pp. 257ff. See also Harold E. Driver, *Indians of North America* (Chicago: University of Chicago Press, 1969), p. 525.

29. Clifton F. Brown, "Black Religion, 1968," in Hart M. Nelsen, Raytha L. Yokley, and Anne K. Nelsen, eds., *The Black Church in America* (New York: Basic Books, 1971), p. 18.

30. J. Deotis Roberts, *A Black Political Theology* (Philadelphia: Westminster, 1974), pp. 59, 54, 53.

31. Melville J. Herskovits, "Africanisms in Religious Life," republished in Nelsen, Yokley, and Nelson, *The Black Church in America,* pp. 44ff.

32. Arthur Fauset, "The Negro and His Religion," republished in Nelson, Yokley, and Nelsen, *The Black Church in America*, pp. 163ff. See pp. 167–68.

33. Hadley Cantril and Mazafer Sherif, "The Kingdom of Father Divine," republished by Nelson, Yokley, and Nelson, *The Black Church in America*, pp. 175ff.

34. Howard M. Brotz, "Negro 'Jews' in the United States," republished in Nelsen, Yokley, and Nelson, *The Black Church in America*, pp. 195ff.

35. Elizabeth W. Miller, *The Negro in America: A Bibliography*, 2d ed., rev. and enl. by Mary L. Fisher (Cambridge, Mass.: Harvard University Press, 1970), p. 292–93.

36. C. Eric Lincoln, "The Black Muslims as a Protest Movement," republished in Nelsen, Yokley, and Nelsen, *The Black Church in America*, pp. 210 ff., especially pp. 210–12, 222.

37. James H. Laue, "A Contemporary Revitalization Movement in American Race Relations: The 'Black Muslims'," republished in Nelsen, Yokley, and Nelsen, *The Black Church in America*, pp. 225ff., especially pp. 232, 227, 228. See A. F. C. Wallace, "Revitalization Movements," *American Anthropologist*, 58 (April, 1956), pp. 264–81.

7. Ethnic Religion

1. Ronald Segal, *The Race War* (New York: Viking, 1966).

2. Quoted in Geoffrey Barraclough, *An Introduction to Contemporary History* (New York: Basic Books, 1964), p. 148.

3. Ibid.

4. Ibid., p. 34.

5. Harry S. Stout, "Ethnicity: The Vital Center of Religion in America," *Ethnicity*, 2, no. 2 (1975): 204ff. See especially p. 205.

6. Martin E. Marty, "Ethnicity: The Skeleton of Religion in America," *Church History*, 41, no. 7 (March 1972): 5–21.

7. Harold J. Abramson, "The Religioethnic Factor and the American Experience: Another Look at the Three-Generations Hypothesis," *Ethnicity*, 2, no. 2 (June 1975): 163ff. and especially 171.

8. Luckmann, *The Invisible Religion*, pp. 22, 26.

9. Quoted in Brown, "Black Religion—1968," p. 18.

10. John Courtney Murray, *We Hold These Truths: Catholic Reflections on the American Proposition* (New York: Sheed and Ward, 1960), p. 129.

11. Richard Jensen, *The Winning of the Midwest: Social and Political Conflict, 1888–1896* (Chicago: University of Chicago Press, 1971), pp. 83–84.

12. Paul Ricoeur, *The Symbolism of Evil* (New York: Harper and Row, 1967), p. 351.

13. Max Weber, "Ethnic Groups," in Talcott Parsons et. al., *Theories of Society*, vol. 1 (Glencoe, Ill.: Free Press, 1961), pp. 305ff.

14. Richard M. Scammon and Ben J. Wattenberg, *The Real Majority* (New York: Coward-McCann, 1970), p. 66

15. An extreme statement of this move is Michael Novak, *The Rise of the Unmeltable Ethnics: The New Political Force of the Seventies* (New York: Macmillan, 1972).

16. Quoted in Roszak, *The Making of a Counter Culture*, p. 49.

17. See chapter 6, note 24.

18. James H. Cone, *Black Theology and Black Power* (New York: Seabury, 1969); idem, *A Black Theology of Liberation* (Philadelphia: Lippincott, 1970). See also Richard L. Rubenstein, *After Auschwitz: Radical Theology and Contemporary Judaism* (Indianapolis: Bobbs-Merrill, 1966).

19. John A. Hardon, S. J., *The Protestant Churches of America* (Westminster, Md.: Newman Press, 1956).

20. C. Eric Lincoln, *The Black Muslims in America* (Boston: Beacon, 1961), is the pioneering effort.

21. Michael Novak, *Choosing Our King: Powerful Symbols in Presidential Politics* (New York: Macmillan, 1974).

22. Two historical accounts that are regularly teamed in this category in bibliographies are Handy, *A Christian America*, and Martin E. Marty, *Righteous Empire*.

23. Lyman Beecher, *Address of the Charitable Society for the Education of Indigent Pious Young Men for the Ministry of the Gospel* (Concord, Mass., 1820), p. 20.

24. Charles Hodge, "Anniversary Address," in *The Home Missionary*, vol. 2 (New York, 1829), p. 18.

25. Philip Schaff, *America: A Sketch of Its Political, Social, and Religious Character* (Cambridge, Mass.: Belknap Press of Harvard University Press, 1961), p. 51. The work first appeared in 1855.

26. Quoted by Rudolph J. Vecoli, "Ethnicity: A Neglected Dimension of American History," in Herbert J. Bass, *The State of American History* (Chicago: Quadrangle, 1970), p. 75.

27. Documentation for this observation appears in Colin Greer, *The Great School Legend: A Revisionist Interpretation of American Public Education* (New York: Basic Books, 1972).

28. Ellis, *American Catholicism*, p. 139.

29. Zangwill's play was produced in 1908; see Herberg, *Protestant-Catholic-Jew*, p. 38.

30. Gerhard Lenski, *The Religious Factor: A Sociological Study of Religion's Impact on Politics, Economics, and Family Life* (Garden City, N. Y.: Doubleday, 1961).

31. Quoted by Stuart P. Sherman in *Essays and Poems of Emerson* (New York, 1921), p. xxxiv.

32. Quoted in Carlton J. H. Hayes, *Nationalism: A Religion* (New York: Macmillan, 1960), p. 21; see the section on "Tribalism," pp. 20ff.

33. Vecoli, "Ethnicity," pp. 74–75.

34. Ibid., p. 80.

35. The Yeats reference is from Robert Bly, ed., *Forty Poems Touching on Recent American History* (Boston: Beacon, 1870), p. 18; for the Ortega allusion see Weintraub, *Visions of Culture*, p. 264.

36. Moynihan and Clancy are quoted from *America*, January 9, 1971, pp. 10–11.

37. Murray, *We Hold These Truths*, p. 28. Gore Vidal in "The Grants," in *The New York Review of Books*, September 18, 1975, p. 12, sees the particularizing trend in the whole society, just as we have seen it in religion. "For both Lincoln and Grant it was *e pluribus unum* no matter what the price in blood or constitutional rights. Now those centripetal forces they helped to release a century ago are running down and a countervailing force is being felt: *ex uno plures.*"

8. Civil Religion

1. Robert N. Bellah, "American Civil Religion in the 1970s," in Russell E. Richey and Donald G. Jones, eds., *American Civil Religion* (New York: Harper and Row, 1974), pp. 255ff. The Wallace Stevens citation finds a parallel in the word of Bill Klem, the baseball umpire, who used to say, according to *Sports Illustrated*, September 22, 1975, p. 9: "They ain't nothing' till I call 'em," referring to the "place" of a ball or strike after he had made his judgment. The Bellah citations are from his essay, pp. 255–57, 259; see also Robert N. Bellah, "Civil Religion in America,' in *Daedalus*, vol. 96, no 1 (winter 1967), especially pp. 1, 12. A ten-page bibliography

titled "Civil Religion in America" appears in *Religious Education,* vol. 70, no. 5 (September–October 1975); Boardman Kathan and Nancy Fuchs-Kreimer compiled and annotated it.

2. Richey and Jones, pp. 15–18. They quote Will Herberg, *Protestant, Catholic, Jew,* p. 90ff.

3. Ahlstrom, *A Religious History,* p. 1084; idem, "Requiem for Patriotic Piety," in *Worldview,* August 1972, p. 10.

4. See the Bellah, "American Civil Religion in the 1970s," p. 264.

5. *Forward,* 1, no. 3 (Winter 1975): 2ff.

6. W. Lloyd Warner, *The Structure of American Life* (Edinburgh, 1952); idem, *The Family of God: A Symbolic Study of Christian Life in America* (New Haven: Yale University Press, 1959); idem, *Democracy in Jonesville: A Study in Quality and Inequality* (New York: Harper and Row, 1949), pp. 289–91.

7. Robin M. Williams, *American Society: A Sociological Interpretation* (New York: Knopf, 1951), pp. 312, 320.

8. Hayes, *Nationalism,* pp. 164ff.

9. J. Paul Williams, *What Americans Believe and How They Worship,* rev. ed. (New York: Harper and Row, 1962), p. 484; Sidney E. Mead, *The Lively Experiment,* p. 71.

10. The reference to Whitehead is from his *Adventures of Ideas* (New York: Mentor Books, 1955), p. 26; Whitehead was quoted by Sidney E. Mead, *The Nation with the Soul of a Church* (New York: Harper and Row, 1975), p. 65; see also pp. 48ff.

11. See Bellah, "Civil Religion in America," for these clear but sparse references to behavior.

12. John H. Laubach, *School Prayers: Congress, the Courts, and the Public* (Washington: Public Affairs Press, 1969), pp. 138–39; see also Kenneth M. Dolbeare and Phillip E. Hammond, *The School Prayer Decisions: From Court Policy to Local Practice* (Chicago: University of Chicago Press, 1971).

13. For reports of these surveys, see Richard B. Dierenfield, *Religion in American Public Schools* (Washington: Public Affairs Press, 1962).

14. Paul Ramsey, "How Shall We Sing the Lord's Song in a Pluralistic Land?" in *Journal of Public Law,* 13, no. 2 (1964): 353ff. and especially pp. 363–64.

15. Sidney E. Mead, *The Nation with the Soul of a Church,* p. 22.

16. See J. Earl Thompson, Jr., "The Reform of the Racist Religion of the Republic," in Elwyn Smith, *The Religion of the Republic* (Philadelphia: Fortress, 1971), pp. 267ff. Thompson himself is not a black but was reflecting the conventional black critique.

17. Denis Brogan, "Commentary," in Donald R. Cutler, ed., *The Religious Situation, 1968* (Boston: Beacon, 1968), pp. 356ff.

18. Sidney E. Mead, *The Nation with the Soul of a Church*, p. 28.

19. Will Herberg, "America's Civil Religion: What It Is and Whence It Comes," in Richey and Jones, *American Civil Religion*, pp. 76ff. and especially pp. 86–87.

20. Mead, *The Nation with the Soul of a Church*, pp. 65, 75.

21. Bellah, "Civil Religion in America," p. 17.

22. Streiker and Strober, *Religion and the New Majority*, p. 179.

23. Bellah, "Civil Religion in America," p. 18.

24. The citation from the inaugural address of Lyndon B. Johnson appears in countless records; a convenient one that shows its "canonical status" is Bruce Bohle, ed., *The Apollo Book of American Quotations* (New York: Dodd, Mead, 1967), p. 57.

25. Langer, *Philosophy in a New Key*; Boas, *History of Ideas* (see chap. 2, no. 45 and 46).

26. Mead, *The Nation with the Soul of a Church*, pp. 48, 59; Mead changed this formula slightly from the earlier version of the essay that I am quoting here from *Church History* 36, no. 3 (September 1967): 1–22.

27. See Paul C. Nagel, *This Sacred Trust: American Nationality, 1798–1898* (New York: Oxford, 1971), pp. 3–4.

28. Elson, *Guardians of Tradition*, p. 285.

29. Giovanni Grassi, *Notizie varie sullo stato presente della republic degli Stati Uniti dell' America* (1819) in Oscar Handlin, ed., *This Was America* (Cambridge, Mass.: Harvard University Press, 1949), pp. 147–48.

30. George W. Pierson, *Tocqueville in America* (Garden City, N. Y.: Doubleday, 1959), p. 99; see the passage on this topic in Seymour Lipset, *The First New Nation: The United States in Historical and Comparative Perspective* (New York: Basic Books, 1963), pp. 151–59.

31. D. W. Brogan, *The American Character* (New York: Vintage Books, 1956), pp. 163–67.

32. William G. McLoughlin, *Billy Sunday Was His Real Name* (Chicago: University of Chicago Press, 1955), p. 123.

33. William O. Douglas, *The Bible and the Schools* (Boston: Little, Brown and Company, 1966), p. 8.

34. Wilson Carey McWilliams, *The Idea of Fraternity in America* (Berkeley: University of California Press, 1973), p. 108.

35. Brogan, *The American Character*, p. 156.

9. Epilogue: Mapping the American Future

1. I owe this delightful image from the world of arches and trusses, foundations and spires, to Will Herberg, who uses it regularly in discussions of civic faith.

2. Ahlstrom was cited on this subject in chap. 8, note 3.

3. Quoted in Art Spiegelman and Bob Schneider, ed., *Whole Grains* (New York: Douglas Links, 1973), p. 52.

Index

Abramson, Harold J., 162
Acts 2, 114
Acts 17:22–24, 181
Ahlstrom, Sydney E., 7, 29, 38, 39, 113, 134, 187–89, 193, 204
Allen, Irving Lewis, 214 n 1
Amalgamation, 175, 176. *See also* Americanization; Assimilation; Homogenization; Melting pot
American Academy of Religion, 25
American Bicentenial, 188, 189, 206
American Council of Christian Churches, 86
American creed, 155, 177, 186, 192, 193, 199, 200, 202
American Indian Religion, 133, 145–50, 160, 161, 170; identity problem, 145, 148; institutional location, 146, 147, 150, 172; political location, 147, 150; prehistory, 149, 150; social behavioral location, 147–50; theological/intellectual location, 146, 148, 150
Americanism, 201
Americanization, 201. *See also* Amalgamation; Assimilation; Homogenization; Melting pot
Anderson, Congressman John, 91, 92

Anthropology, 43
Anti-intellectualism, 13, 48, 101, 109, 143, 203
Arieli, Yehoshua, 186
Assimilation, 169, 175, 177, 206. *See also* Amalgamation; Americanization; Homogenization; Melting pot
Astrology, 128
Aulén, Bishop Gustaf, 33

Baba-lovers, 144
Bagby, Philip, 37, 181
Baha'i Faith, 141
Baird, Robert, 20, 28, 85
Baker, Thomas E., 97
Baptism in the Holy Spirit, 111, 116, 117, 119, 123. *See also* Second blessing
Baptists, 71, 75, 76
Barnes, Harry Elmer, 31
Barraclough, Geoffrey, 159
Barth, Karl, 170
Barzun, Jacques, 212 n 36
Basham, Don, 119
Beard, Charles, 21
Beecher, Lyman, 174
Behavior, 32–39, 41, 45–48, 65, 98; external, 37, 40, 41; internal, 37, 40, 41; social, 33–39; symbolic, 45; nexus with belief,

Behavior (*cont.*)
41, 45–48, 98, 104, 144, 148–
49, 194, 200. See also *Vigen-
cias*
Behaviorism, 35
Belief, 27, 36, 45–48, 65, 98, 110;
nexus with behavior, 41, 45–
48, 98, 104, 144, 148–49, 194,
200. See also *Creencias*
Bellah, Robert N., 183–89, 193,
198, 213 n 44
Belonging, 78, 205. *See also*
Plural belonging
Bennett, Dennis, 107, 110, 119
Berger, Peter, 184
Berkhofer, Robert F., Jr., 35, 43,
211 n. 27
Black Israel, 177
Black Jews, 154
Black Muslims, 154–56, 163, 172,
177
Black   Protestant   Pentecostal
churches, 116
Black Religion, 133, 150–56, 160,
161, 170; Africanity, 152, 153;
identity problem, 152, 156; in-
stitutional location, 153, 172;
political location, 153, 155,
173; prehistory, 150–52, 154;
social behavioral location, 153–
55; theological/intellectual lo-
cation, 152–55, 170
Black revolution, 151
Bloesch, Donald, 95, 102, 103
Boas, George, 45, 200
Bob Jones University, 101
Boone, Pat, 113
Boorstin, Daniel J., 24
Braden, Charles S., 140
Bradford, William, 20, 21, 27
Brauer, Jerald C., 7, 84, 213 n 42

Brogan, D. W., 196, 201, 202
Brotz, Howard M., 154
Brown, Clifton F., 151
Bruce, Lenny, 63
Bruner, Frederick Dale, 110, 111,
114, 118
Bryce, James, 176
Buddhism, 143. *See also* Zen
Buddhism
Buddhist Churches of America,
141
Bureau of Indian Affairs, 147,
150

Campbell, Robert, 81, 82
Camus, Albert, 210 n 22
Canada, 3, 4
Cash, Johnny, 113
Catholic charismatics, 108, 109,
111, 115, 116, 122
Catholicism. *See* Roman Catholi-
cism
Cavnar, James, 121
Charismatic: definition, 107, 108;
hard/soft, 123, 125; newer
movements, 111, 113, 115, 121;
renewal, 112. *See also* Pente-
costal-Charismatic Religion
Cherry, Conrad, 7
Chesterton, G. K., 193, 200
Chicago Declaration of Social
Concern (1973), 100
Christian Century, The, 87, 89
Christianity Today, 86, 99
Church of Jesus Christ of Latter-
day Saints, 71
Churches of Christ, 71
Civil Religion, 16, 173, 178–204,
206; definition, 182–86; iden-
tity problem, 180; institutional

location, 195, 196, 198; political location, 181, 182, 184, 191–94, 202; prehistory, 183–90; social behavioral location, 190–94, 197, 199–203; theological/intellectual location, 190, 192, 193, 197–99
Clancy, Thomas H., 177, 178
Cleage, Albert B., Jr., 151, 163
Clebsch, William A., 7
Clergyman's crisis of identity, 74, 75
Cliometricians, 41, 212 n 36
Cogley, John, 65
Cohen, Morris, 135
Cone, James H., 170
Confessionals, 81, 82
Congregationalism, 70
Constructions of reality, 50. *See also* Social construction of reality
Corinthians, 114, 120
Counterculture, 134–37, 156
Creencias, 46–48, 65, 98, 111, 146–48, 153. *See also* Belief
Culture, 37. *See also* Mainstream culture; Subculture

Daedalus, 89, 183
Daughters of the American Revolution, 196
Death of God, The, 89
Deloria, Vine, 145–49, 170, 171
Denominationalism, 5, 73, 76, 105, 195
Desroche, Henri, 35
Devine, George, 70
Dewey, John, 186, 196
Dierenfield, Richard, 195

Disciples of Christ, 71, 75
Divine Father, 116, 154
Douglas, Justice William O., 202, 209 n. 8
Doukhobors, 164
DuBois, William E. Burghardt, 152, 159
duPlessis, David, 115
Durasoff, Steve, 124
Durkheim, Emile, 131, 132, 190

Eastern Religions, 139–44; identity problem, 140, 144; institutional location, 139–42; political location, 142; prehistory, 140–43; social behavioral location, 140, 141, 144; theological/intellectual location, 142–44. *See also* Zen Buddhism
Ecumenism, 73, 74, 96–98
Edwards, Jonathan, 20, 27
Eister, Allan W., 144
Ellis, John Tracy, 29, 66–70, 72, 175
Ellwood, Robert S., Jr., 126
Elson, Ruth Miller, 21, 200, 203
Emerson, Ralph Waldo, 176
Episcopalianism, 70, 74, 75, 106
Erickson, Millard, 98, 99
Erikson, Erik, 8, 9, 18, 41
Errand of mercy, 97
Ethnic ethic, 178
Ethnic Religion, 16, 158–79, 181, 206; identity problem, 159, 163,, 165, 167–69, 177; institutional location, 163, 172, 174; political location, 172–75; prehistory, 158–61, 169, 173–75; social behavioral location, 164–67, 174–79; theological/

Ethic (*cont.*)
    intellectual location, 170–72,
    174, 178. *See also* American
    Indian Religion; Black Reli-
    gion; Judaism
Ethnicity, 160–71, 177; "Ethnic-
    ity A," 164, 166–68; "Ethnicity
    B," 164–68
Evangelical, defined, 81, 88
Evangelical Alliance (1846), 97
Evangelical-Fundamentalist nex-
    us, 80, 104
Evangelicalism, 16, 80–105, 180,
    205; identity problem, 105; in-
    stitutional location, 16, 80–82,
    85, 86, 94; political location,
    83, 89, 94; prehistory, 84–88;
    social behavioral location, 83,
    86, 95–105; theological/intel-
    lectual location, 82, 83, 87, 88,
    91, 93, 100, 101, 104
Exclusivist-Ecumenical Gradient,
    57–58

Faupel, David W., 109, 218 n 1
Fauset, Arthur, 153, 154
Federal Council of Churches, 85
Feingold, Henry L., 62
Fichter, Joseph, 108, 109, 111,
    112
Fifth Pentecostal World Confer-
    ence at Toronto (1958), 115
Fischer, David Hackett, 31, 32
Ford, Gerald R., 91
Ford, Leighton, 100
Forward, 189
Franklin, Benjamin, 200
Freud, Sigmund, 41
Fromm, Erich, 9
Full Gospel Businessmen's Fel-
    lowship International, 107

Fundamentalism, 80–106, 205; in-
    stitutional location, 16, 80–82,
    85, 86, 94; political location,
    85, 89, 94; prehistory, 84–88,
    216 n 9; social behavioral lo-
    cation, 83, 95–104; intellectual
    location, 82, 83, 87, 88, 93,
    100, 101, 104. *See also* Evan-
    gelical-Fundamentalist nexus
Fundamentals, The, 85

Gabriel, Ralph Henry, 24
Gaspar, Louis, 216 n 9
*Gathering Storm in the Churches,
    The*, 74, 92. *See also* Hadden,
    Jeffrey
Gaustad, Edwin Scott, 7
Gellner, Ernest, 71, 135
Gelpi, Fr. Donald, S.J., 115, 119
Genovese, Eugene, 49
Glasser, William, 130, 131
Glazer, Nathan, 59–62, 64, 66,
    72
Glock, Charles Y., 76, 82
Glossolalia, 117–20
Goebbels, Josef, 20, 30
Goldwater, Barry, 89, 91
Goodman, Felicitas, 120
Graham, Billy, 83, 84, 86–89
Grassi, Giovanni, 201
Greeley, Andrew, 209 n. 10
Grogan, Emmett, 206

Hadden, Jeffrey, 74, 75, 82
Handy, Robert T., 7
Hansen's Law, 54
Harbison, E. Harris, 209 n. 11
Hardon, Fr. John A., 172
Hare Krishna, 129, 141, 144
Harnack, Adolf, 51

Hayes, Carlton J. H., 186, 191
Hefley, James C., 91
Henderson, Charles, 186
Henry, Carl F. H., 86, 95, 96, 99, 101, 103, 104
Herberg, Will, 6, 54–59, 64, 69, 78, 127, 176, 185–87, 189, 191, 192, 197, 198, 228 n 1
Herskovits, Melville, 153, 154
Historians, 19–33, 38–44, 47–51; conflict, 48, 49; consensus, 48; institutional, 29
History: cultural, 37; literary, 41; peoples', 31, 48–51, 203; of religion, 22–25, 30, 43, 44; social, 30–32, 37–39, 48; intellectual/theological, 27
Hitchcock, James, 65–67, 70
Hodge, Charles, 174
Hollenweger, Walter, 115
Hollinger, David, 26
Holocaust, 61, 63, 161, 170, 171, 215 n 11
Homogenization, 173, 174. *See also* Amalgamation; Americanization; Assimilation; Melting pot
Honest to God, 89
Hope, Bob, 202
Hudson, Winthrop, 7, 72–74, 113, 186
Hughes, H. Stuart, 1, 2, 206
Humanae Vitae, 69
Hump of transition, 71
Hutterites, 164

Ideation, 36, 40, 41
Identity: crisis, 8–13, 36, 55; diffusion, 8, 10, 16, 18, 144; foreclosure, 8, 16, 206; group, 3, 10, 12; incident, 8, 13, 204, 205; social, 78; Society, 130, 133. *See also* Social location
Indian messianism, 150
Indian Religion. *See* American Indian Religion
Instant Zen, 143
International Society for Krishna Consciousness, 140
Isaacs, Harold R., 10–12
Israel, 60–63, 161, 171

Jackson, Rev. Jesse, 173
Jefferson, Thomas, 200
Jensen, Richard, 166
Jesus movements, 84
Johnson, Lyndon B., 199
Jones, Donald G., 185, 186
Jorstad, Erling, 94
Joseph, Chief, 149, 150
Judaism, 59–63, 160, 161, 170; 171; Conservative, 61; Orthodox, 61, 62, 171; Reform, 61, 171; identity, 59–62; institutional location, 63; political location, 63; prehistory, 60, 61; social behavioral location, 63; theological/intellectual location, 62, 63. *See also* Holocaust; Israel; Lubavitscher Jews; Six Day War
Jung, Carl J., 41

Kelley, Dean M., 57–59, 76–78, 93, 104
Kennedy, John F., 185
Key 73, 62, 96
King, Dr. Martin Luther, Jr., 151, 173
Kitagawa, Joseph M., 213 n 43
Klem, Bill, 225 n 1

Knox, Ronald A., 110
Krippner, Stanley, 131
Kuhlmann, Kathryn, 109
Kuhn, Thomas S., 26
Ku Klux Klan, 163
Küng, Hans, 47

Laing, R. D., 170
Langer, Suzanne K., 45, 200
LaPiere, Richard T., 36, 37
Las Casas, Bartolomé de, 20
Laue, James H., 156
Lausanne '74, 97
Le Bras, Gabriel, 35, 36
Leek, Sybil, 138
Lenski, Gerhard, 176
Leone, Mark P., 136
Lewin, Kurt, 9
Lewis, C. S., 101
Liberalism, 98
Liberals, 86, 92, 96
Lifton, Robert Jay, 18
Lincoln, C. Eric, 154, 155, 224 n 20
Littell, Franklin H., 7, 83, 84
Lubavitscher Jews, 164, 165
Luckmann, Thomas, 13, 15, 34, 139, 162
Lutheranism, 71, 88, 107; in the Missouri Synod, 46, 166

McDonnell, Fr. Kilian, 113
McGinnies, Elliot, 36
McGovern, George, 188
McIntire, Carl, 94
Maclear, James, 186
McLoughlin, William G., 89–93, 104
McLuhan, Marshall, 130
McMaster, John Bach, 31, 38, 48
McPherson, Aimee Semple, 109

McWilliams, Wilson Carey, 202
Maharishi Mahesh Yogi, 142
Mainline Pentecostal-Charismatic Religion, 109, 121
Mainline Religion, 16, 52–79, 81, 82, 90, 92, 96, 100, 101, 103, 106, 107, 111, 115, 180, 205, 206; definition, 53; identity problem, 55–57, 59, 78–79; prehistory, 53–59. See also Judaism; Protestantism; Religion, American-Way-of-Life; Roman Catholicism
Mainstream culture, 136, 142
Malcolm X, 155
Manifestness, 117
Maoism, 131, 159
Maps of American Religion, 1–17; theological/intellectual, 4; institutional, 4–5; political, 5–7; social behavioral, 1, 2, 12–16, 163. See also Paradigms
Marías, Julián, 46, 47
Marty, Martin, 7, 160, 185, 208 n 22, 215 n 27, 216 n 9, 222 n 18, 223 n 6
Mass media, 21, 129
Mather, Cotton, 20, 23, 27
May, Henry, 24
Mayhew, Henry, 49
Mazeway, 156
Mead, Frank S., 140
Mead, Sidney E., 5, 6, 29, 184, 186, 192, 193, 195, 196, 198, 227 n 26
Meaning, 36, 78
Meditation movements, 128
Melting pot, 12, 176, 177. See also Amalgamation; Americanization; Assimilation; Homogenization; Triple melting pot
Melting Pot, The, 176
Memory, corporate, 19

Methodism, 71, 74, 75, 107
Michaelson, Robert, 186
Miller, Perry, 24, 27
Miller, William Lee, 185
Mills, C. Wright, 42
Modernists, 85–87
Moments of effervescence, 131, 132
Montgomery, John Warwick, 82
Moon, Rev. Sun Myung, 10, 144
Morison, Samuel Eliot, 24
Morrison, Charles Clayton, 87, 88, 93, 95
Mouw, Richard J., 100
Moynihan, Daniel Patrick, 177
Muhammad, Elijah, 154, 155, 173
Murphy, Gardner, 136
Murray, John Courtney, 178
Murton, H. J. D., 137
Myrdal, Gunnar, 186

Naiveté, primitive/second, 167
Narrative, 43, 50
National Association of Evangelicals, 81, 86, 92, 94, 96
Nation of behavers, A, 147, 199, 201, 203, 204, 206
Nation of believers, A, 199, 203
Native American Church, 150, 163, 172
Needleman, Jacob, 126
Neo-Orthodoxy, 72, 73, 98
New England Transcendentalists, 133, 134
New Evangelicalism, 86–88, 91–92, 94, 95, 97–99
Newman, John Henry, 69
New Religions, 16, 17, 84, 126–57, 180, 205; definition, 126; identity problem, 130, 133, 140, 145, 148, 149, 152, 156; insti-

tutional location, 129, 132, 135, 139, 142, 146, 150, 153, 157; political location, 142, 147, 150, 153; prehistory, 127–29, 133–35, 149–52; social behavioral location, 135–39, 147, 150, 153, 154; theological/intellectual location, 135, 142, 146, 150, 152–55. *See also* American Indian Religion; Black Religion; Eastern Religions; Occult Explosion
Nichol, John T., 125
Nichols, James Hastings, 39
Niebuhr, H. Richard, 72, 103, 162
Niebuhr, Reinhold, 72
Nisbet, Robert A., 212 n 39
Nixon, Richard M., 185, 188
Novak, Michael, 65, 173, 224 n 15

Oates, Wayne, 113
O'Brien, David J., 68
Occult Explosion, 130, 132, 134–39; institutional location, 138, 139; political location, 138; social behavioral location, 135–39; theological/intellectual location, 135, 136, 138
Ockenga, Harold, 86, 98, 99, 100
O'Connor, Edward, 111
Ortega y Gasset, José, 46, 47, 177
Osborn, Ronald, 196
Ozman, Agnes, 114

Packard, Vance, 106, 107, 124
Palmer, Ray, 138
Paradigms, 26–33, 38, 39, 51; institutional, 28, 29, 32, 51; political, 29, 30, 32, 51; social

Paradigms (*cont.*)
  behavioral, 30, 32, 38, 39, 203;
  theological/intellectual, 27–29,
  32, 51. *See also* Maps of American Religion
Parham, Charles Fox, 117
Particularism, 177, 178, 180, 181,
  195, 196, 225 n 37. *See also*
  Pluralism; Sectarianism; Tribalism
Paul VI (Pope), 69
Paul, Saint, 122, 181
Pentecostal: definition, 107, 108;
  Establishment, 124; old-line,
  111, 115, 121; new, 115, 118;
  secret, 114, 118
Pentecostal-Charismatic Religion,
  106–125, 180, 205; identity
  problem, 108, 122, 123; institutional location, 16, 108, 109,
  111, 112, 115, 125; political
  location, 112, 113, 115; prehistory, 107–109, 111, 114, 115;
  theological/intellectual   location, 109–111, 115; social behavioral location, 109, 113–
  125
Peoplehood, 154, 160, 161, 163,
  164, 167, 169
Perlman, Helen Harris, 9, 11
Pierard, Richard V., 100
Pinard de la Boullaye, E., 144
Pius XII (Pope), 68
Plowman, Edward E., 91
Plural belonging, 16, 163, 164,
  181
Pluralism, 5, 29, 165, 167, 174,
  175, 178, 195. *See also* Particularism; Sectarianism; Tribalism
Plures, 163
Polis, 6, 7, 30, 100, 153
Pope, Liston, 106

Practices, 35, 36, 39, 40. *See also*
  Behavior; *Vigencias*
Premillennialism, 99
Presbyterian Confession of 1967,
  46
Presbyterianism, 70, 74, 106, 107
Private sphere, 15
Protean man, 130, 133
Protestant-Catholic-Jew, 6, 54,
  186. *See also* Herberg, Will
Protestantism, 70–78, 80, 85, 92,
  96, 97, 108, 122; identity prob-
  lem, 71–76, 78; institutional
  location, 73; political location,
  73–75, 173; prehistory, 70–72;
  social behavioral location, 74–
  76; theological/intellectual lo-
  cation, 72, 73, 76
Protestant Pentecostalism, 112,
  115, 116, 122
Psychohistorical dislocation, 18
Psychohistory, 41

Quantitative methods, 41, 212 n
  36
Quebedeaux, Richard, 95, 100
Quiet revolution, 25, 126
Quinley, Harold E., 75, 82, 93
Quinn, Kieran, 110

Ramsey, Paul, 195
Ranaghan, Kevin, 121
Real Majority, The, 169
Reductionism, 13
Religiocification, 14, 151, 163
Religion: functions of, 12, 13;
  transformation in, 32; American-Way-of-Life, 6, 58, 64,
  183, 185, 191; Evangelical culture, 102; invisible, 14–16, 34,
  55, 139, 156, 181, 195, 204; of
  the republic, 6, 29, 183, 185,

186, 192, 195, 198; secular, 14, 159. *See also* Civil Religion; Ethnic Religion; Evangelicalism; Fundamentalism; Mainline Religion; New Religions; Pentecostal-Charismatic Religion

Religious, 33–34

Retribalization, 10, 12. *See also* Tribalism

Revitalization movements, 156

Revivals in American Religion, 25, 44, 54, 56, 73, 75, 78, 84, 87, 88, 108, 111, 114

Richey, Russell E., 185, 186

Ricoeur, Paul, 167

Roberts, J. Deotis, 152

Roberts, Oral, 109

Roman Catholicism, 63–70, 76, 97, 107, 108, 122, 160, 169, 171; "ghetto culture," 65, 66; identity problem, 63–67, 70; institutional location, 63; political location, 63, 64, 172, 173; prehistory, 63–66; social behavioral location, 64–70, 171; theological/intellectual location, 63, 67, 169

Romans 12:2, 83

Rosicrucian Digest, The, 137

Rosten, Leo, 141

Roszak, Theodore, 134, 143

Rousseau, Jean-Jacques, 14, 185

Rubenstein, Richard, 170

Rudhyar, Dane, 137

Sacred Cosmos, 6, 15

Sahlins, Marshall, 127

Samarin, William J., 118–20, 124

Sandeen, Ernest, 95

Schaff, Philip, 20, 23, 28, 174, 175

Scheuer, Joseph F., 64

Schwartz, Gary, 122

Second blessing, 117–19, 123. *See also* Baptism in the Holy Spirit

Second Great Awakening, 84

Second Vatican Council, 64–69, 140, 159, 169, 173

Sectarianism, 111, 195, 196, 198. *See also* Particularism; Pluralism; Tribalism

Sects, 57, 77, 78, 90, 106

Secular City, The, 89

Secularity, 14, 16, 181, 204, 205

Secularization, 23, 127, 209 n 11

Segal, Ronald, 159

Self-identification, 55, 56

Separation of church and state, 23

Seymour, W. J., 114

Shakarian, Demos, 107

Shaku, Soyen, 143

Shaping by story, 21

Shea, John Gilmary, 20, 23, 28

Shelley, Bruce, 98

Six Day War (1967), 59–63, 68

Skibstedt, Werner, 119

Skinner, B. F., 35

Skotheim, Robert Allen, 24, 27

Smith, Elwyn A., 7

Smylie, James, 186

Snake-handling, 113, 219 n 14

Social construction of reality, 3, 184, 187, 206

Social location, 3, 56, 78, 205. *See also* Identity

Society for Pentecostal Studies, 110

Sociology, 42–43

Soka gakkai, 131

Southern Baptist Convention's Christian Life Commission, 100

Southern Baptists, 71, 76

Speaking in tongues. *See* Glossolalia

Spiritualism, 133, 134, 136

Stark, Rodney, 76, 82

Starkloff, Carl F., 148, 149

Stevens, Wallace, 3, 184, 188, 193

Stevenson, Adlai, 159

Stevick, Daniel, 103

Stout, Harry S., 160

Streiker, Lowell D., 94, 198

Strober, Gerald S., 94, 198

Subculture, 37, 191

Suburbanization, 69

Sunday, Billy, 202

Suzuki, Daisetz Teitaro, 143

Sweet, William Warren, 113

Swierenga, Robert P., 212 n 36

Synan, J. A., 115

Terkel, Studs, 214 n 51

Textbooks, 21, 200, 203

Theosophists, 134

Third Force, 89–91

Third Force Christendom, 106–7, 113, 115

Third World, 115, 154, 158

Thompson, J. Earl, Jr., 226 n 16

Tillich, Paul, 40, 72, 110, 212 n 35

Tocqueville, Alexis de, 201

Toynbee, Arnold, 43

Tozer, A. W., 102

Traces, 39, 40, 42, 49, 50, 212 n 34

Transcendence, 73, 197–99, 215 n 27

Transcendental Meditation (TM), 142

Tribalism, 11, 147, 148, 158, 160, 161, 176, 177. *See also* Particularism; Pluralism; Sectarianism

Triple melting pot, 54, 176

Troeltsch, Ernst, 111

Turner, Frederick Jackson, 21, 175

Tuveson, Ernest Lee, 7

Unification Church, 10

Union Theological Seminary, 106

Unitarianism, 196

Universalism, 180, 182, 198, 199

Unum, 164, 173, 195

Van Dusen, Henry Pitney, 89, 106, 107

Vecoli, Rudolph J., 177

Vedanta Societies, 140–42

Veterans of Foreign Wars, 196

Vidal, Gore, 225 n 37

Vigencias, 46–48, 65, 98, 146–48. *See also* Behavior; Practices

Vivekenanda, Swami, 140

Voluntaryism, 20, 51

Wakin, Edward, 64

Wallace, A. F. C., 156

Walsh, Vincent M., 111, 112, 115, 117, 118, 120

Warner, W. Lloyd, 185, 189–91

Washington, George, 21, 200

Washington, Joseph, 116

WASP, 11, 52

Watson, John, 35

Weber, Max, 167, 168

Weems, Mason Locke, 21

Weintraub, Karl J., 46

Wentz, Abdel Ross, 29

Whitehead, Alfred North, 193
Whitman, Walt, 112
*Why Conservative Churches Are
   Growing*, 57, 76, 93. *See also*
   Kelly, Dean M.
Wilkerson, David, 110, 124
Williams, J. Paul, 186, 192
Williams, Robin, 185, 191
Wills, Gary, 65
Winter, Gibson, 73, 74
Wirt, Sherwood Eliott, 100
World Council of Churches, 159
World's Columbian Exposition
   (1893), 140
World's Parliament of Religions
   in Chicago (1893), 134

Wurth, G. B., 101

Yankee Hindooism, 133
Yeats, W. B., 177
Yoga, 142

Zangwill, Israel, 176
Zaretsky, Irving I., 136
Zen Buddhism, 134, 142, 143; institutional location, 142, 143;
   political location, 142; prehistory, 143; social behavioral location, 143; theological/intel-
   lectual location, 142, 143